My Time in Hawaii

MY TIME IN
HAWAII

A POLYNESIAN MEMOIR

Victoria Nelson

St. Martin's Press
New York

Design by Susan Hood

Library of Congress Cataloging-in-Publication Data
Nelson, Victoria.
    My time in Hawaii / Victoria Nelson.
      p.   cm.
    ISBN 0-312-03690-6
    1. Nelson, Victoria, 1945–   —Homes and haunts—Hawaii.
    2. Hawaii—Description and travel.   3. Hawaii—Social life and
    customs. I. Title.
    DU623.2.N45   1989
    996.9—dc20   89-27052

First Edition
10 9 8 7 6 5 4 3 2 1

To Ken and John

Contents

CONTENTS

Contents

Acknowledgments

The words for "water" come from Mary Kawena Pukui and Samuel H. Elbert, *Hawaiian Dictionary;* translations of "The Royal Hawaiian Hotel," by Mary Pula'a Robins, "Kane'ohe," by Abby Kong and Johnny Noble, and "Hilo Hanakahi" (traditional) are by Samuel H. Elbert and Noelani Mahoe, *Na Mele o Hawai'i Nei;* both books published by the University of Hawaii Press. Translations of the *Kumulipo* are from Martha Warren Beckwith's annotated edition, *The Kumulipo: A Hawaiian Creation Chant,* originally published by the University of Chicago Press; reprinted by the University of Hawaii Press. Extracts from the journals of Captain James Cook come from the Dover edition, edited by A. Grenfell Price. Quotations from Nathaniel Emerson's *The Unwritten Literature of Hawaii* come from the Charles P. Tuttle reprint of the original monograph. The Mark Twain quotations come variously from *Mark Twain's Letters from Hawaii,* edited by A. Grove Day (University of Hawaii Press) and the University of California editions of *Roughing It* and the *Unexpurgated Notebooks.* The account of the purchase of Niihau is taken from Robert Wenkham's *Kauai and the Park Country of Hawaii* (Sierra Club, 1967). Translation of the *hula pa ipu* copyright Kenneth Davids. Lew Welch's "The Song Mt. Tamalpais Sings," from RING OF BONE © 1973 by permission of Grey Fox Press.

ACKNOWLEDGMENTS

Portions of this book appeared originally in *Hawaii Review* and *East West*. The author gratefully acknowledges the assistance of the Marin Arts Council in writing it.

The whole tale of my life is better to me than any poem.
—Robert Louis Stevenson

O kane ia Wai'ololi, a ka wahine ia Wai'olola . . .
O he'e au loloa ka po
O piha, o pihapiha

(Man for the narrow stream, woman for the broad stream . . .
The long night slips along
Fruitful, very fruitful)
—the *Kumulipo,* a Hawaiian creation chant

UNDERTOW

1

Back in the Water

A memory snapshot, out of my time: January 4, 1969, my first day in Hawaii, before I'd been told I was too late, had missed out on everything. From the outdoor walkway of the decrepit old airport near Pearl Harbor, I had my first glimpse of that distinctive patchwork of mountains, valleys, city, cloud shadow, and rainbows spread out under the spiry tips of the Koolaus: Oahu. Dizzy from the long plane trip, I felt buoyed at once, eased by the mild late afternoon air flushed with moisture from bulging rain clouds about to let go again, and knew on the spot this island was no "rock," as I'd been warned. On the contrary, it gave the impression of richness, complexity, an opening up to a new world of widened perspective, enhanced senses.

Ken's old car churned over the Pali highway to the Windward side of the island, where the Koolau range, worn down by the direct impact of the trade winds, was steeper, the patterns of sun and shadow on the precipitous green cliffs grimmer and more exaggerated, where a fairytale ocean lay patterned like the land with cloud shadow and fat healthy stands of banana clogged the roadside—straight on down to funky Kaneohe and the tiny converted World War II hospital my friends had rented.

That night it rained, it poured, the air and the ground burst with water, the house oozed dampness, the Pali highway flooded out and closed down right after we got over, and at first it was like being a child in Florida again, the same plants and humid smells, but those mountains, all the different kinds of people— and it was so wonderfully *seedy*, when I had been expecting something slick and packaged like Miami. No, Hawaii was not Florida, it was far more mysterious and far more beautiful, that much was clear right away.

Next day, kite flying in the Buddhist cemetery, brisk trades whipping the paper samurai toward the attractive and interesting mass of Island clouds always clustered overhead, the formidable green folds of the Windward Koolau palis rearing behind us, bare toes skipping over the metal grave markers depressed in the grass, touching down in bright orange dirt (the ferrous oxide of the volcanic soil noticeably richer on this Windward, rainy side; incredibly, Gauguin had not exaggerated his colors), kite bobbing, the dead underfoot, all light and airy in this strange new natural world so trustingly spread out before me, I felt an unfamiliar sensation: happy.

Who was I? A twenty-three-year-old with a graduate degree. What was I? (As the alchemist said, do not ask *who* but rather *what* a man is.) A bundle of raw affects and impulses unbounded by skin on the outside or shaped by any sort of bone or cartilage on the inside: a kind of sea creature, really. Why did such a jellyfish float to the middle of the Pacific? I had no reason. I had come to visit my friends, who had had no reason either. Like them, I knew why I was there a heartbeat or so after arriving.

Where had I come from? Drab city slum inhabited by short squat people damaged in mind and body, bone-cold winds rustling the trash in sleazy gutters, hard sidewalks waiting for snow, yellow grass, barricaded storefronts, a sad, sour thinness of air laden with smells of garbage, diesel fuel, empty bottles reeking of whiskey, port. In myself and in all those around me, soul compressed to merest kernels no longer visible to the naked eye: Lechmere Square, Cambridge, Mass.

What did I find in Hawaii? *Wai* and *kai*—that is, fresh water and salt water.

I found many ways of being wet: *howai, kakale, kalekale, kele wai, ho'okakale, ukalekale, okalekale, hokale, kele, kelekele, halahalawai, kewai, holowai, wawai, ohulu, palake.* I found cool water *(wai hu'ihu'i)*, sprinkling water *(wai kapipi)*, tingling water *(wai konikoni)*, misty water *(wai noenoe)*, the brackish water where stream mouths hit the ocean, quite correctly called *wai kai.*

I found the mountain pool *(kio kawa)* and stream *(kahawai)*. I found the waterfall, *wailele*, and the upside-down waterfall, *wai puhia* (these are common; the wind blows them back up).

Most of all I found the ocean, *moana*, in all its shapes: the calm, quiet sea *(kai malie, kai malino, kai malolo, kai ho'olulu, kai pu, kai wahine, kai kalamania, kaiolohia)*, the strong sea *(kai ko'o, kai kane, kai nui, kai nu'u, 'okaikai)*, the rough or raging sea *(kai pupule, kai pu'eone, kai akua)*, the deep sea *(kai hononu, kai 'au, kai ho'e'e, kai lu he'e)*, the place where sea and land meet *('ae kai)*, the sea almost surrounded by land *(kai haloko)*, the eight seas around the Hawaiian islands *(na kai 'ewalu)*. Swimming underwater in the salt sea, *kai pa'akai*, I found the miracle of the offshore freshwater springs, unexpected eye-sweetening uprushings from the sea floor.

And with all these kinds of *wai* and *kai* I found as many variations on the color Blue: turquoise, cobalt, indigo, azure, cerulean, powder blue, sapphire, ultramarine, navy shading to lavender, gentian, mulberry, violet, purple. I found it in the sky, the ocean, the streams, set off by the colors Black (lava rock), White (windblown surf spray, *kai ehu*), and Green (trees, vines, plants of all kinds).

All who come to the Islands are encouraged, by those who came before, to think that their time is the next best time; at some earlier point came *the* time, when Hawaii was perfect, before everything changed, before all the people came, as the chorus runs, "before it all got spoiled"—before Statehood, before World War II, before Annexation, before Captain Cook. Even in 1889 Robert Louis Stevenson was bemoaning "vile Honolulu." But there was also a time before Hawaiians—the Polynesian seafarers—lived in Hawaii, before the "native" trees and grasses, seeded from pollen carried by wind and rain, invaded the Islands, before the chain of volcanic mountains breached the surface of the ocean and made contact with the mid-Pacific air. For fifteen hundred years new arrivals have been made to feel that they got to Hawaii a little too late.

The logic of this sentiment was not clear to me until my time was over. Now I know that my time was *the* time, before it all got spoiled; the latecomer is the ghost who tries to come back. Still, Wordsworth's *Prelude,* a work I dozed over then, in my time, hooks me now with its seductive image of remembering: A man in a boat can see the reeds, fish, rocks in the lake under him but is not able to distinguish the "things which there abide/In their true dwelling" from clouds, sun, mountains, his own face reflected on the water's surface. The memory lake, the *wai* where the past leads its glowing second life, allows no separations—here my time *is* now, always. "Yes"—Melville nods—"as every one knows, meditation and water are wedded for ever." I'm back in the water, and it's not too late.

Zori

My Berkeley classmates Ken Davids and John Derrick had made the bold move of becoming instructors at the University of Hawaii. In terms of outer-world logic, a two-week visit thus stretched to five years in this way: a person who, at twenty-three, is so shy it makes her physically ill to get up and give a speech in front of her fellow graduate students is hired by the U.H. English Department on a Friday to start teaching on the following Monday. After a weekend agonizing beyond all description, she walks into the class, stands at the front *(does not take a seat!),* and with trembling voice requests those assembled to take out their pink registration cards. Twenty pairs of hands comply and the known universe flip-flops. A feeling of power surges through her. There is no looking back now. No matter how stupid she is, how inadequate, how inarticulate, they *have* to do what she says: the young professor.

I found a small studio apartment under the eaves of an old Korean house on Punchbowl: $77 a month, screen windows (no glass), tin roof. On this roof the rain thundered every night; dropping mangos hit like cannonballs.

Kaneohe, where I spent the first month of 1969, was wet, windy, rural, but I liked Honolulu, too, that large funky half-Asian city, with its uprush of noise early every morning: birds, traffic, neighbors coughing as they shuffled in their rubber slippers around the sides of their decrepit houses.

Shuffle, slap. Feet, footwear were a focal point of Island experience. They were the wall the outsider hit first.

As I walked the streets of Honolulu, my eye was caught immediately by the numbers of single zoris with broken thongs lying on the sidewalk or in the bushes. I found their presence vaguely disturbing until I realized there was no such thing as a zori repair store. Zoris were the Dixie cups of the shoe world; in a place where 90 percent of the footwear cost no more than a couple of dollars, dead soldiers were left where they fell.

We forget that the concept of the zori did not enter our Mainland sensibility until rubber thongs were brought back from Japan and Hawaii by soldiers and surfers in the mid-1950s. Before that, this supremely sensible footwear was regarded as an object of extreme exoticism. A woman friend who first came to the Islands during World War II recalled the feeling of fright she experienced the first time she saw a big toe unnaturally separated from its neighbor by a piece of straw or rubber. In her mind this was a demonic division triggering images of that level of Dante's Inferno where the feet of the damned began cleaving into hooves. Another friend got his Midwest college roommate to mail-order him a pair in 1958, then hesitated to put them on because he felt, he said, a sudden anxiety about the sexual sensation the thong might cause him.

As a teenager in Southern California I knew zoris as "shower slippers," the basic rubber-molded kind, white on the bottom with a colored thong and a paper-thin sole. They cost 39 cents a pair at Woolworth's and were the humblest things you could put on your feet. Hawaii was different. In Hawaii there were more kinds of zoris than names of God. By unspoken agreement ethnic groups tended to gravitate toward one style or another, from the lauhala, or straw-bottom, black-velvet thonged "Jap slaps" (favored by middle-class Japanese kids, worn to class at U.H. with slacks and a reverse-print aloha shirt never tucked in), to the haole surfer kind made of layers of black rubber with a racing stripe down the side and parachute-material thong, to cork-soled plastic-thonged steamboats made in Taiwan or Brazil, to the Hollywood forties-style wedgie with bejeweled thong favored by Dragon Lady types. The latter you could get at China House, the zori emporium at Ala Moana Shopping Center that catered to Local, not outsider, tastes. And after high technology was brought to bear on zori crafting came everything from the Italian model with the perforated sole that drained water (perfect for rainy Hawaii) to the breakthrough *thongless* rubber soles with a special adhesive that stuck to the bottoms of your feet, a concept almost too much for the mind to accept.

My first full day in Honolulu I spent walking in my Joan Baez leather sandals (soon to turn green and fall apart), and my feet were a disaster. But as soon as I got my first pair of straw-and-velvet slaps a new ordeal by pain began as I wore in my "zori callus" between the big toe and its neighbor. This process took months and several pairs of zoris to alternate the wear pattern so that with each new pair you avoided the blister the previous pair inflicted until it healed, by which time a new blister had formed, so you switched again, and so on.

The reverse of this process was experienced by one Japanese landlady of mine and her family when they took a long-anticipated trip to Disneyland in California, all wearing brand-new Mainland-style shoes bought especially for the occasion. They came back limping like Crimean veterans.

Most everyone in Hawaii followed the Japanese custom of removing footwear before entering the house, a process the zori facilitated by not obliging you to bend over to undo ties or buckles. The Japanese themselves were so fanatical about this custom that when trains were introduced to Japan, it is said, the dignitaries participating in the inaugural ride dutifully left their zoris on the station platform before climbing in the cars. In the evening you saw these piles of zoris outside houses and Buddhist temples all over Honolulu. Drunken partygoers stood hunched on front porches dizzily surveying the pile, the dilemma always how to identify the distinctive dirt marks and wear patterns of your very own velvet thongs among twenty-one other identical pairs. Single women kept a pair of size-13 zoris prominently displayed on their doorsteps to discourage prowlers.

Hawaii knew two types of feet: "haole feet," exemplified by my own (the word *haole*, originally meaning "foreigner," now the universal term for Mainland American white people), and "luau

9

feet," referring to the lower appendages of a large Hawaiian male who had never worn real shoes for more than a few hours in his entire life and whose footprints consequently resembled meteor craters. Even Melville remarked of the Marquesans in *Typee* that "the most remarkable peculiarity about them was the appearance of their feet; the toes, like the radiating lines of the mariner's compass, pointed to every quarter of the horizon." For the owners of such feet, that strange feature known as the "arch" (still found in some extreme cases of haole feet) was no more than an evolutionary atavism, like the appendix.

Along with these two foot types came the widest range of sizes in any such geographically restricted environment in the world: from the −1AAAA of the non-American–born Asian foot (all the second-generation Hawaiian-born offspring of Asian parents were taller and had bigger feet, no doubt the result of a different diet) to the archetypal 17DDDD Polynesian foot. There were the bound feet of my Chinese neighbor's ancient grandmother, whom he had to carry piggyback down the front stairs, and there were my cousin Lorca's size-9 feet, only slightly large for a haole female but made the object of ridicule in her Japanese class when the teacher daintily clunked across the room, her feet swimming in Lorca's clogs, to illustrate the comparative form: Her feet are *bigger* than my feet. My feet are *smaller* than her feet. And so on.

My own feet finally got broken in to their zoris but, like haole feet the world around, never to the point of promiscuous bare contact with the elements, never to the point where I could walk without breaking stride over the spiky little balls that littered the ground under the ironwood trees at the Kaimana Beach Hotel in Waikiki. And never ever, surely, to the point of fastening safety pins to my dirt-calloused soles, as a Korean woman told me she had done in her Wahiawa plantation childhood, so that she might tap dance on the kitchen linoleum, *clickety clack! clickety clack!* just like little Shirley Temple. To the young professor some Island experiences would stay a permanently closed book.

3

The Nuuanu Street Goodwill

A young Hari Krishna disciple rented a room next door to me in the old house on Punchbowl. Several days a week he worked in a print shop in Kailua on the Windward side of the island and rode his heavy old-fashioned tandem bicycle with fat tires and pedal brakes *over the Pali highway and back* to get there, truly a superhuman feat.

One day as I was walking to school the Hari Krishna pulled up beside me. With a nod of his head he indicated the rear seat of the bicycle. I got on behind him, but before I could put my feet in place he was already pedaling furiously, outsize calves bobbing over his ankles like a pair of bowling balls. My pedals, linked to his, churned like eggbeaters. I dared not stick my feet into that blur of motion but let them hang discreetly on each side instead. Pigtail and saffron garments flapping in my face, chanting and pedaling like a madman, he delivered us to Maile Way in ten minutes flat, and I don't *think* he noticed he was doing it all by himself; at least he had the grace not to say anything, though I would have explained, absolutely, if the subject had come up.

Until I got my own beautiful white bicycle, I walked everywhere from my house on Punchbowl.

In the Islands there were only two directions: toward the mountains *(mauka)* and toward the ocean *(makai)*. Honolulu

11

had the added refinement of Diamond Head (southeast) and Ewa (northwest). The four nodes on my personal Honolulu compass were the Nuuanu Street Goodwill store (Ewa), Punchbowl crater (counts as *mauka* even though home base was its lower slopes), the University of Hawaii's Manoa campus (Diamond Head, *mauka*), and Queen's Surf (Diamond Head, *makai*).

The Nuuanu Street Goodwill came first, a one-stop shopping center out of which I equipped the ramshackle Punchbowl apartment. After the grinding urban poverty of Boston and environs, a salary of $300 a month from the university made me feel positively well off. But there was no point just throwing money away—hence the secondhand store.

The first object to catch my eye in the front window of the Nuuanu Street Goodwill, situated between a bar and the Lai Fong Store, was a full suit of samurai armor priced at $100— probably the most expensive item they ever carried, since just about everything else went for under a dollar. The armor set the tone for the whole store: flotsam and jetsam of half a dozen Asian and Pacific cultures washed up on bare wooden shelves, with a little orange price tag stapled on.

In that breathless pause before the tidal wave of Mainland hippies and hip struck the Islands, I knew the satisfaction of being there first. Besides me and a handful of other young haoles (who eyed each other suspiciously, and with good reason: we wanted the same stuff), the Nuuanu Street store's patrons were exclusively older working-class Local folk and newly arrived Pacific Islanders. The changing room for trying on clothes was a modest open-top box—a converted toilet stall, I believe—set squarely in the middle of the store, like a telephone booth. Once, while undressed inside, I noticed two gargantuan zori-slippered feet facing mine on the other side of the stall. I looked up. An enormous Samoan in wraparound aloha print lava-lava and blue suit jacket (ergo, a Mormon) peered down over the top, scowling with delight.

The Nuuanu Street Goodwill yielded dishes and glasses, an array of teapots without lids—it took some time for a dreamy character like me to work out the connection between the absence of lids and their presence in the Goodwill store—lauhala or grass mats, assorted koa wood bowls, and platters. There were muumuus—though like most Mainlanders I was taller than the average Local girl and the bottom hem tended to hit me mid-shin—a purple-and-silver metal Dragon Lady dress with frog fasteners, an Indonesian brocade coat, a tattered Tahitian hula skirt with cowrie belt (a real find: these items went for $80 or $90 new), piles and piles of aloha print cloth for curtains and wall hangings, brass candlesticks, a Matson-print silkscreen scarf that became my talisman, joss sticks, opium pipes, a wrought-iron Chinese dragon candlestick, Filipino papaya-fiber men's shirts. In its pancultural role as home crafts graveyard, the Goodwill also featured air-brush Hawaiiana watercolors by a prolific unsung artist named Uehara, whose career got a considerable second wind as the 25-cent works of the "Goodwill artist" began reappearing on the walls of young haoles' apartments all over Oahu.

Back and forth I trudged from downtown to Punchbowl carrying my treasures in wrinkled brown paper sacks. Downtown Honolulu in the late sixties had an abandoned, ghost-town feeling; its former heyday had been during World War II, when all commerce was geared to servicemen and enterprising fellows like one of my Japanese landlords, a correct, Buddha-quoting businessman, who had made their fortunes in pinball machines and other areas too colorful to mention. The renaissance of downtown as a gussied-up financial district, Mainland style, lay fifteen years in the future. In my time it was lei stands, boarded-up gambling spots, old abandoned brick buildings, cheap bars.

Rundown areas in the Islands, rural or urban, somehow didn't depress me in the same way their counterparts on the Mainland did. Likewise, even the "nicest" places had something refreshingly down at heel about them. I saw the strain, but not that bitter hopelessness and rage that oozes from the urban sprawl of the American Northeast. In a Hawaii not yet overpopulated and polarized you could be poor and still have a life for yourself, dignity, beauty, family—this message, at any rate, is what I imagined I saw reflected in the faces around me.

On my way home from the Goodwill I discovered the flowers of the older parts of the Punchbowl and Makiki districts. I loved all the gaudy blossoms of Hawaii, especially the ones that weren't politically correct. So what if they were "nonnative," like most of the people, so what if the Hawaiians of the very old days depended on bird feathers, not blossoms, for color—must everything imported be bad? I loved the African tulip trees with their blazing orange topknots, the pink Virginia creepers trailing off tin roofs, the passion-flower vines and morning-glories that carpeted fences and even treetops, the shiny phallic anthuriums that must have seemed much more exotic before the invention of plastic, which they so disconcertingly resembled. Among the anthuriums I was especially fond of the green ones streaked with pink: leaves that had heroically tried, and failed, to turn themselves into flowers.

I was partial to the blowsy hibiscus. Most hibiscuses I saw had red, pink, or orange petals with a large light-colored area in the center, out of which jutted a long pink stamen crawling with ants. I preferred the plumper, thick-petaled yellow variety with a circle of purest white in the center. When I came across one, I always stopped and looked deep into that mysterious white center, an act of inspection that never failed to excite my deepest pleasure.

I felt the same sense of awe when I first saw the closed bud of the plumeria, a twisted candystripe whose yellow and pink edges handsomely set off more of that sumptuous satin white. Plumeria buds, a treeful of them shaking in the wind—purely the sight of them carried a dense, complicated message not translatable into words or other organs of sense or any medium at all but simply itself.

A bush of the lemon-yellow hibiscuses grew in a front yard at the top of the little rise on Punchbowl that lay on the route between my house and the Goodwill. Each day, the lifespan of one blossom, I looked down the insides of the new flowers. Once as I was leaning over the bush the sound of a harp came from the second story. Someone from the symphony lived there, I knew. On paper, a fine moment; in reality, background music was unnecessary. A kind of silence lay at the center of the yellow hibiscuses, an inviolate stillness these liquid notes could only overlay, never penetrate.

I loved my stuff from the Goodwill. What I saw in department stores like Liberty House and McInerny's down in the Ala Moana Shopping Center seemed grotesque by comparison—ugly, expensive, soulless, *new.* Ashes to my 79-cent diamonds. When I took my day's haul out of the bag and laid it all out on the bed, the fabric and chipped old dishes gave off the same numinous, unreal glow as the fish I was soon to discover underwater off Queen's Surf. Diving into the cultural Sargasso Sea of the Nuuanu Street Goodwill, I surfaced triumphantly each time with a bright piece of cloth, a monkeypod bowl between my teeth. Materialized out of an unguessable past, these exotic objects were now mine, part of me. Finding them, possessing them made for an experience of almost mystical fulfillment. The old shirts and dishes marked the beginning of my symbiosis with Hawaii, a merged relationship of such intensity that to call it a love affair makes it sound ordinary, and it was not.

4

Queen's Surf

After the Nuuanu Goodwill the second most important node on my Island compass was not my place of employment, the university, but Waikiki, the beach, where, in a manner both desultory and conscientious, I marked the piles of papers I assigned my students (passing them back in class with a shower of sand and suntan oil). Kapahulu Avenue, skirting the end of the moatlike Ala Wai Canal that separated tourists from the citizens of Honolulu, was the back door to Waikiki.

Sights along Kapahulu Avenue:

1. Alex Drive-In, home of the lethal *ono-ono* (meaning "very delicious") peanut butter milkshake, in consistency a kind of sweet, haolefied version of the Hawaiian root-starch staple, poi, and one of the heaviest liquids known to man.

2. Leonard's Bakery, where they made the Portuguese sweet bread, or pao doce, and malasadas, the heavenly fried doughnuts. The bakery's little red-and-white striped trailers went around to all the high school carnivals on Oahu selling hot malasadas. Leonard's also had every kind of birthday and wedding cake imaginable, including, I remember, one with olive-green icing and miniature soldiers in jungle fatigues: a Welcome Home from Vietnam cake for Local boys who got back in one piece. Leonard's, however, was not open twenty-four hours like the Kaneohe

16

Bakery or King's or other doughnut places in the Islands. (On the precept "By what commercial establishment they keep open longest shall ye know them," the Island bakeries of these pre-7-Eleven days stood in stark contrast to, say, the Southern California all-night liquor store and gas station.)

3. Anna's Lounge: a Korean bar, which in the old days meant that a glamorous Korean woman of a certain age, whom the bar was always named after, acted as frontperson for a silent partner. These places routinely supplied "hostesses" and bar girls who sat with the customers for the price of an expensive drink. No place for someone like me alone, but I did go once with Buzz Poverman, another young professor and writer. We played pool with Anna herself (who, complete with forties hairdo, looked exactly as you might imagine she would) and a drunken Hawaiian *paniolo* from Maui. I say drunken, but this cowboy had been deliberately anesthetizing himself with a half-gallon juice jug of mud-brown awa—the pan-Pacific intoxicant, made from the root of the awa vine that numbs the central nervous system (known as *kava* in Fiji, where it forms the basis of an elaborate social ritual)—so that he could pull a front tooth that needed extracting. He opened his mouth wide, displaying the bloody hole, then took Buzz, who had a fascination with such things, into the men's room, where he showed him the six-inch scar on his thigh where he had been gored by an angry bull.

Korean bars were to take a notorious turn later in the seventies, when they began featuring exotic dancers who played the flute and performed other tricks with a highly trained portion of their anatomy. (One performer wrote "Happy Birthday," in a broad, firm "hand," on a piece of paper supplied by my friend Steve.) Anna's was your old-style classic Korean bar, catering like most of them to the most romantically thwarted individuals on the face of the earth, that is, lonely old Filipino bachelors from the plantations.

4. The Love's Bread day-old bakery. I wasn't *that* cheap.

5. Skipping a few blocks, the Honolulu Zoo at the end of the Ala Wai Canal, right across from the beach. When my friend Judy broke the sex discrimination barrier and became the first woman zookeeper hired, her Local male coworkers took her out to an empty cage the first day and instructed her to run hoses down

the rat holes, club the rats to death as they ran out, then feed them to the python, which she did.

When I first came to Hawaii the state legislature was debating whether or not to have second representatives of the various species of lonely solo snakes then residing in the Honolulu Zoo. Because there had been tremendous, and justified, paranoia that someday snakes would be imported to the Islands and reproduce with the same dramatic results as other species, a substantial amount of legislative energy was now invested in discussing how you told a female snake from a male snake, etc. I forget what they finally decided, but rumors persisted about various new animals getting established in the Islands: the dead boa constrictor found on the slopes of Mauna Kea, rattlesnakes run over on the Kauai highways, even the granddaddy of all stories, the gorilla (supposedly escaped from the circus) who lived in the upper valleys on the Honolulu side of the Koolaus.

It was no legend, but absolute truth, that Nuuanu Valley had a family of iguanas, escaped pets that were occasionally sighted by residents who lived near the head of the valley. The big lizards, shy creatures who got their pictures in the paper now and then, reproduced only modestly and did not migrate on to other locations. Later, a few wallabies made similar inroads in Kalihi Valley.

6. Back to Kapahulu. Past the zoo, bordered by the little allotment vegetable gardens that people came down to tend, the P.K. (Princess Kaiulani Hotel) looming on the right, the Waikiki Shell outdoor auditorium on the left, the lifeguard station and the huge rental surfboards dead ahead, a strip of turquoise ocean flashed: Waikiki. And here comes one of those images like a childhood memory—I'm not sure if I dreamed it, if somebody told me about it and like a sprouting seed it gradually took hold in my imagination, or if in fact it was something I witnessed in the real world. Symptomatic, maybe, of this time in my life, when the inner and outer worlds had merged so completely I didn't know which was which, whether I was above the water or below it.

This, at any rate, my mind's eye records: a packed Waikiki beach, bodies glistening with oil in the midday sun, but also crowds standing transfixed, watching something about thirty feet offshore. You look and suddenly you're in a Dali painting: a queen-sized white rubber sheet levitates on the surface of the water, pausing a moment to hover and dip, then moves on. You see the edge of another sheet directly underneath, both sheets skitter and flap, and suddenly in a mad burst they shoot close to shore, veer away, then bolt directly out to sea. Bouncing over the small surf break, for a split second they expose eyes, diamond-shaped bodies, long barbed tails, and you realize that all of you, Japanese tourists and Kansas tourists, Locals and haoles, have been watching a mating of giant manta rays.

Toward the end of Kalakaua Avenue, away from the glut of hotels in the shadow of Diamond Head, was a special little corner of Waikiki, the funky beach bar and restaurant called Queen's Surf. In prehistoric days, of course, this was a taboo surfing spot, reserved for the *ali'i,* or nobility, and off limits to commoners. But the Queen's Surf I'm thinking of, once the site of the Holmes mansion, was the grass-shack prototype of every tropical bar you ever saw in a Hollywood movie, where Franklin Delano Roosevelt himself, it was said, had once drunk a mai tai, where even as late as my day you could walk down the beach, peek over the scratchy dry lauhala-mat screens, and watch Tavana's Tahitian Revue for free.

Razed during a political feud of the early seventies, Queen's Surf survives today as a few coconut trees, the old luau pit, and a bare concrete pavilion where the kids skateboard. No ghosts of the World War II submariners who hung out there when it was called Nemo's, no ghosts of their girls in evening gowns, orchid corsages, and Rita Hayworth "Smoothie" pumps (a whole warehouse full of the latter, a treasure trove from the past, was unearthed in my day), no ghosts of the postwar beachboys, Duke Kahanamoku and the great Hawaiian surf athletes with their enormous sixteen-foot koa wood boards. The Duke had died a few months before I came to the Islands and there had been a big funeral with a fleet of outriggers off Waikiki launching his ashes Polynesian-Viking style into the ocean—as everyone was well aware, the symbolic funeral of yet another era in Hawaiian cultural history, the forties and fifties beachboy scene of old Waikiki.

Old Waikiki. A few times before my time, with the Matson

liners pulling in at the Aloha Tower, boys diving for coins, tea dancing at the Royal Hawaiian. That sadly dated sonnet by Rupert Brooke, "Waikiki," like a glib murmur:

> Warm perfumes like a breath from vine and tree
> Drift down the darkness. Plangent, hidden from eyes,
> Somewhere an ukulele thrills and cries
> And stabs with pain the night's brown savagery.

Of course he got the Hawaiian atmosphere all wrong. It's hard to imagine, for example, a ukulele that "thrills and cries/And stabs with pain the night's brown savagery"; these are sound effects from a different native movie. The second part wasn't so bad if you didn't mind the blatant echoes of "The Eve of St. Agnes":

> And I recall, lose, grasp, forget again,
>   And still remember, a tale I have heard, or known,
> An empty tale, of idleness and pain,
>   Of two that loved—or did not love—and one
> Whose perplexed heart did evil, foolishly,
> A long while since, and by some other sea.

What this sonnet unwittingly and precisely captured, in fact, was that Peter Pan spirit, the ethereal but secretly rather nasty *raffiné* sentimentality of every young haole romantic who ever beached up in the Islands before R.B.'s time or after. Useless to criticize for soppiness, being an all-too-accurate heart X-ray of many who were drawn to the Islands, whether we would have put it quite that way or not.

A later overlay on Old Waikiki: the Waikiki Jungle, that ragtag collection of tin-roof bungalows housing Hawaiians, then pioneering young surfers from California, finally hippies, where, in my time, you could still hear roosters crowing in the back yards of Kuhio Avenue. Near the International Marketplace some unknown magician from Hawaiian Telephone had installed a gaudy neon-lit half-shell pay phone that glowed all colors of the rainbow at night: what sector of the universe, I wondered, could you reach with that fantastic instrument? And out of every corner of

Waikiki, as of all urban Oahu, crept the invincible, all-redeeming *wai* and *kai* funkiness—the mildew, peeling paint, household lizards, and cockroaches that no amount of big money, Californian or Japanese, could ever quite stamp out.

But always, Waikiki for me meant Queen's Surf. The constant rustle of palms in the trade wind, pink battlements of the Royal Hawaiian to my right, Assyrian-style Natatorium and the Outrigger Canoe Club to my left; on weekends the smell of teriyaki chicken wafting from a thousand hibachis at Local family cookouts across the street in Kapiolani Park. The Koolau mountains, patched green and black from cloud shadows, blocking the rainstorms that were letting loose on their Windward side. Overhead, a watercolor Island sky, volatile, full of complicated events (sun, rainbow, blue patches over Diamond Head, dark-purple rain clouds over Ewa); out to sea, the slow procession offshore of container barges on their way to Pearl Harbor. Roils of surf full of ground-up shells advancing, retreating on the steep slope of sand.

And, custom-made for romantics with trouble keeping their feet on the ground, a scant ten feet off Queen's Surf lay the Underworld. Reviving the childhood fantasy of donning a magic pair of glasses and entering another world, I dove masked and finned, like an arrow shot from a bow, into the shallow waters of Queen's Surf. In my time the bumpy labyrinth of coral reef off Waikiki was alive, the water was clean and clear right up to the beach. Fish and eels passed you like commuters along little corridors of coral that led into each other, twisted and deadened before finally opening up to the wider ocean floor.

At first I treated the Queen's Surf reef like another Goodwill store: I collected. Not living things but an old wine bottle, its glass turned milky turquoise, all overgrown with pink algae and barnacles; next, a shard of nineteenth-century ship's china, a real find in Hawaii, where little escaped the pounding surf. As the first flush of collecting lost its charm, gradually I began to feel like a character out of an E. T. A. Hoffmann tale. That is, like a human guest in an allegorical kingdom of dream creatures—parrotfish, needlefish, eels, live coral—that were unbearably vivid, fourth dimensional, realer than real. While others hooked fish, the fish hooked me. A sardonic art film short from my time showed a surf fisherman on the beach pausing in the day's sport to take a big bite from his sandwich. Suddenly a wicked barbed point sprouts from his cheek, attached to a line coming from the ocean. Kicking and screaming, the fisherman is reeled into the sea where, after a brief struggle, the waves close over him: end of movie. I knew just how he felt. First at Queen's Surf and then at Hanauma Bay, I was being pulled in the very same way—pulled, pulled, pulled underwater.

5

Incident at Hanauma Bay

Hanauma, or Crushed, Bay, the famous Oahu snorkeling spot, is an extinct crater broken into and filled up by ocean. I find it these many years later schematically rendered on the back of an old notebook, the map John Derrick drew to guide me there: a long pencil line indicates the road (Kalanianiole Highway), a box for the Standard station at the Hawaii Kai shopping center (last bus stop), then a shape like a wine glass on its side, the notation "H. Bay" and an "X" marking the best entry point to the reef.

What it translated to in real life was this. You trudged up the highway bounded by Koko Head on the left and another big bulge on the right. For the long view, you walked up the right-hand ridge, whose spine was so distinct it came to a point directly under your feet (*it came to a point!*—the eerie sensation of walking in a fairy tale of your own creation). From here you looked down into a perfect womb-shaped tropical bay, where a wedding-cake fringe of surf broke delicately on a crescent beach lined with coconut palms. The coral reef—a mossy brown and green labyrinth dotted with blue pools, standing out as bright and clear as if no water intervened at all—came right up to the sand. At the bay's mouth the turquoise of the holes and channels turned into the cobalt of open ocean. Triangular skeins of foam stretched thinly over the surface as much as thirty yards out to sea, wound and unwound by the powerful undertow on the outer edge of the reef.

Up here on the lip you could see how Hanauma was one of a cluster of three craters. The first was the perfect semicircle of porous black volcanic cliffs, salt-streaked fifty feet above the level of the surf, that formed the bay itself. You could make out the outline of the second crater subtly rimming a recessed marshy forest on the other side of this pointy headland, known as Koko Head. The third was rugged, imposing Koko Crater itself, rearing up across the highway over the suburb of Hawaii Kai. Like every other standing crater on Oahu, Koko Crater was riddled with World War II bunkers and pillboxes. A narrow-gauge railroad track ran straight up its side like a metal zipper.

You walked down the side of the ridge away from Hanauma Bay to inspect the second, hidden crater. In this sunken bowl sunlight tangled with a haze of white wildflowers growing between the kiawe trees. A mongoose skittered away under brown spiderleg fern fronds. Bits of white coral lay scattered among patches of crabgrass gone to seed. On one side a lava flow, a giant prehistoric causeway, fell to the open, churning sea; on the other long steep green folds swept down to the bay.

And if you were lucky you might have seen the other natural miracle I witnessed as I stood in the middle of this complicated geological denouement: a school of humpback whales cavorting directly offshore. Spouting fountains of spray, slapping the water with their tails, those ancient sickle shapes black on one side and white on the other, waving their long flippers like banners, the enormous creatures were playing. Then, just as suddenly, they were gone.

After this long-distance preview you walked down the steep little road to the beach, still uncrowded in this early time, then into the water and there you were, home again in the gray-green world, alongside such impossible creatures you felt you had made them up, dreamed them, though no dream was ever this bright or strange: a pink-nosed fish with an iridescent white body and a hard lemon tail. A fish with skunk markings, others that also seemed to parody animals. A tiny eel poking its mewing mouth out of a hole in the coral. A translucent needlefish. A Moorish Idol, yellow and black with a spectacular dorsal streamer.

24

Wrasses batiked pink and turquoise. A gaudy green-and-blue parrotfish with the formidable coral-chewing beak I would grow so familiar with on archaeological digs: its orange earth-stained jaws stood out in the midden like the prize in the Crackerjack box.

And so, bravely, you passed through the causeways and a series of blue pools, then clambered awkwardly over shallow coral at the far edge of the reef into the deep water and rolling ocean waves, home of the huge groupers and other deep-water fish that were larger, statelier, and less colorful than the denizens of the reef. The open ocean was a more formidable, serious world than the protected reef; it was not a place to linger. And so, getting back through the surf that battered the edge of the coral, you could easily get battered yourself with never-healing coral cuts as the surge raked your body over the rim of the reef and redeposited you into its quiet pools and corridors—where, if you happened to be me, you would find this first immersion in the mysteries of a coral reef working a curious transformation on your psyche. As you emerged from the waters of Hanauma you discovered a boundary no longer existed between inner and outer, between you and the creatures in the bay or even the bay itself, you and the elegant green and orange palm fronds hanging over the beach, you and the stray drifting albatross overhead, you and the natural world altogether: a loss of soul, a kind of drowning, had occurred.

Drowning—a primordial fear on all sea islands, of course. In Hawaii it ranked right up there with being eaten by sharks or pounded to bits on lava rock by a fifty-foot storm wave. Aside from the usual quota of *opihi* pickers, the victims always seemed to be forever one half, or both, of a pair of lovers accidentally swept off cliffs by the flick of a freak wave. It didn't happen that often, but when it did, you remembered. A haole couple in a small plane went down between islands and found themselves frantically treading water along with their pet dog. First the dog slipped beneath the surface, then the wife; only the man was saved. On the second, ill-fated journey of the *Hokulea,* the modern replica of the ancient Polynesian voyaging canoes, the boat capsized off Molokai only hours after we had waved it off at the Ala Wai harbor; as the rest of the crew clung to the inverted keel,

Eddie Aikau of Oahu paddled off on his surfboard in search of help and was never seen again. The research ship *Holo Holo* disappeared with all hands en route from Oahu to the Big Island; later, radar soundings located the ghostly outlines of the sunken hull somewhere in the Alenuihaha Channel.

What was it like, I wondered, what would it *really* be like, bobbing all alone in the middle of the ocean? My own fascination with drowning had its roots in the past: a primal memory of the year 1951, of being six years old and floating alongside my mother, father, and brother in the middle of an inlet of the Choptahatchee Bay. We wore life preservers, bulky, cork-filled canvas vests with rusty metal buckles. It was a sunny Florida Panhandle afternoon. Three feet below the surface of the water the keel of our capsized sailboat—the converted lifeboat of the *Comrade,* our old schooner—hung ghostly and suspended.

We were bobbing in the water, yes, but it was no real occasion for panic; none of us was, or admitted to being, scared. The polluted bay was full of the motorboats my father hated, towing waterskiers. Eventually one roared over in our direction, and though I believe my father would have preferred staying where we were we underwent the humiliation of being rescued by power boat. But still I was twisted inside by a trivial terror, a formless anxiety worse than fear. Several pillows had been in the boat with us. One, a yellow plastic cushion with pictures of nautical knots, proved a jaunty indestructible survivor that went into the motorboat along with its owners and endured a score of moves over the next ten or fifteen years. The other, an ordinary cotton pillow, very much a house pillow, white with rust-colored scenes of American colonial life printed on it, was not to be saved. With a wrenching feeling of loss I watched this pillow skim away on the tide, waterlogged, settling lower and lower in the water. No one thought to halt the gradual descent of the pathetic land object into Choptahatchee Bay.

Only once before in my short life had I seen anything so vulnerable and doomed. When we had first moved onto the *Comrade,* a once-stately, run-down Bahamian schooner built in 1905 that my father had bought in Miami for $2,000, it was docked in the old St. Petersburg yacht basin next to a park full, as I remember, of banyan trees and imitation Greek statues with fig leaves

26

covering their private parts. From September through January the flotsam of hurricanes floated into the harbor from the Gulf of Mexico. Tangled among the old painted boards, portions of roofing, and other bits of buoyant junk, I had once spotted—with the searing grief and horror of the four-year-old spirit—some unknown little girl's bedraggled drowned doll.

I hadn't been keen at first on living on the boat, for the following reason: I was afraid to walk across the dock to get to it because that meant I would fall through the spaces of empty air between the boards. What kept you from falling through the cracks in the docks? What kind of magic could stop that from happening? More to the point, what kind of magic kept you from plunging straight to the bottom of the ocean? Crossing the Gulf of Mexico from St. Petersburg to our destination in northern Florida—a deserted docking near an old shipways in a tiny Panhandle town—I was not yet blasé about the prospect of bobbing on the water, or rather, I had not yet transferred my fears to beloved pillows. That unforgettable first moment under full sail, when the enormous schooner heeled directly on its side into the churning ocean, panicked me. Until this maiden voyage, my brother and I had always known exactly how deep the water was in the crucial loci of our little watery universe: at the dock (where the *Comrade*'s keel, we proudly announced, drew eight feet), in the middle of the harbor, and "up to our chests" (as far as we were allowed to go in at the beach). Now that we were out of sight of land, surrounded by nothing but heaving whitecaps—steeply tipped over *into* them, in fact—my father announced, "The water is fifteen fathoms deep here."

Fifteen fathoms? I, his devoted pupil, knew that meant ninety feet! What was to keep us from slipping straight down? How unspeakable, to fall to the bottom of the Gulf!

I grew up. The waterlogged memories endured. A teenager on the other side of the continent with years of land life behind me, I regarded a new ocean from my safe position on terra firma: to the music of a scratched recording of Debussy's *La Mer,* I imagined myself the sole survivor of an airplane crash, floating in my life preserver across the vast Pacific, blue-green vaults shot through with luminous lights, sea creatures cavorting Disneylike at my side—miraculous rescue, to great public acclaim, of the suntanned, shriveled heroine, timed to coincide with the end of the record.

In college I was to read a book that played this chord of fantasy in a different key: William Golding's *Pincher Martin*. The main character, thrown off a merchant marine vessel during World War II, floats alone in the ocean until he is miraculously cast ashore on a little island in the North Atlantic. Or so he thinks. In reality the man, Martin, has drowned instantly on hitting the water. His tenacious ego, in its driving will to hold on at any cost, defines time and temporarily collapses its limits by imagining a conveniently sited island down to the last unbearably real physical detail. This elaborate self-deception begins with a single lie: that Martin kicked off his seaboots to swim to this island. But of course he hasn't, because he is already physically dead. The persistent intrusion of the suppressed truth—in the homely image of the seaboots—ultimately pulls down the entire fortress of fantasy he has erected against his own dissolution.

In Hawaii I wrote down my teenage imaginary adventure as a story and reversed the ending. My heroine I now saw as a kind of Pincher Martin who was drowned, not saved, and from my new perspective this outcome seemed highly favorable. As the Hawaiians of the very old days knew far better than I did, behind every act in the physical world lies a second, third, and fourth level of meaning. Drowning is no exception. We young Mainland haoles wanted to drown our egos in Hawaii, to escape inside the Island universe that seemed so much richer and livelier than our own.

After my profane baptism at Hanauma I would spend the next five years looking up at the world through a blurry liquid lens, relating to Nature as if it were human and to humans scarcely at all. Alas, then, is she drowned? Drowned, happily drowned. My life in the water had begun, again.

Drowned

And what sort of water was my new element, the salty Island seas? It was dynamic water, water in motion, lifting, falling, going up, coming back. About the Hawaiians' proficiency in the medium Captain James Cook noted in the journal of his third voyage:

> They are an open, candid, active people and the most expert swimmers we had met with; in which they are taught from their very birth: It was very common for women with infants at the breast to come off in Canoes to look at the Ships, and when the surf was so high that they could not land them in the Canoe they used to leap over board with the child in their arms and make their way a shore through a surf that looked dreadfull.

A surf that looked dreadfull. There were plenty of places on Oahu like that. My own proficiency did not progress much beyond simple, mindless immersion as often as possible and the not very stringent demands of snorkeling. But I was a happy voyeur of the more adept, from one famous surfing spot to the next. "Breaks," there were thousands of them; something like 1,700 have been recorded and there are surely many more. All the Island surf breaks, body and board, had their traditional names; the Waikiki litany included Queens, Canoes, Publics, Castles, and Tonggs, to list only a few. The beaches also broke down very precisely according to degree of difficulty, by sport: from baby beaches like Kailua and Waimanalo to intermediate-level bodysurfing beaches (Makapuu), to the really challenging Pounders, Sandy Beach, Sunset, and Waimea. At aptly named Point Panic, located at the mouth of Kewalo Basin, the waves broke directly on the rocky seawall, where the garbage outflow also attracted sharks.

The preferred sport of Locals in those prewindsurfing days was bodysurfing. My surfer friend Kanaina and the other Hawaiians liked using *paipo* or belly boards that you could make yourself, cheaply—a civilized alternative to that tiresome Mainland obsession with expensive state-of-the-art gear, trademark of the high-tech California haoles they fought bitterly for every surf break in the Islands. In winter the Sunset Beach Fire Department, composed mainly of Hawaiian water athletes, achieved heroic rescues on surfboards of drunken GIs who had tried to bodysurf the skyscraper North Shore waves. Yet even this gigantic surf made an oddly muted sound as it fell to pieces on the beach, softer and lighter to my ear than the dull metallic roar of the massive Pacific breakers that beat relentlessly against the western end of the North American continent.

My favorite water spot, *wai* or *kai,* was Waimanalo, a small Hawaiian community just around the bend from Makapuu. The beach strip was occupied by haoles; the cross streets were Hawaiian Homestead lands. John Derrick and Mary rented one of these cross-street houses; two of the other young professors, Steve Shrader and Buzz Poverman, lived on the beach in the top two floors of the enormous sea captain's house known as the Castle. The massive Castle was flanked by the Red Barn on one side and the Nameless House, a three-story white frame house of great elegance and beauty, on the other. Legend had it that the captain's luau on December 7, 1941, had been strafed by Japanese fighters on their way back from bombing Bellows army base as the terrified family hid in the Castle's basement.

Encircled by a broad amphitheater of palis—huge etched, eroded cliffs, the Windward rear of the Koolau range—

Waimanalo floated in a dreamlike suspension from the world and time. Coarsely ground coral gave the beach sand a pinkish tinge; sea grape vines grew down to the edge. Offshore the old volcanic crater Manana, or Rabbit Island, rose up like a clenched fist. Here in the path of the trade winds everything stayed in constant motion, noisily lifting and falling: the dry, crackling palms, the sighing casuarina forest that bordered the beach, crashing combers, boiling foam and spray. It was a place of dramatic vistas, too: in the late afternoon, when the sun sank behind the Koolaus, the ocean went dark while Rabbit Island stayed bright and spotlit for hours—then its color fell abruptly to matte brown, easing into night.

Waimanalo was the perfect bodysurfing beach. The surf was always gentle; there was never an undertow. From twenty feet away the ocean looked turquoise; once you were in the blood-warm water, it turned a rich green. Outside the belt of sandy water where little waves broke on the shore, you stood waiting. Eyes open, ducking under unsuitable breakers, you could watch the breakneck progress of their shadows across the bottom, the swirls of ghostly sand kicked up by your own feet. Occasionally the ocean was saltier, or warmer in unpredictable patches, or had ruffled ponds or mysterious nickel-sized islands of yellow foam floating on the surface, or was laced with the streaky blue threads of the Portuguese men-o'-war.

A more bizarre freshwater sport, fluming, was conducted in the mountains. A mad game, this—I only had the nerve to try it once. Like bodysurfing in big waves, fluming was too anxiety-provoking for me to feel comfortable doing even though the *idea* was irresistible. (Until the moment of writing this down, I had always visualized "flume" as "phlume," like "phlegm," somehow—proof, if needed, that the spoken word was mightier than the written in Hawaii.)

You went deep into the mountains—on Oahu, behind Kaaawa or in other places that stayed well-guarded secrets—following the mule trails bordering the old gravity-run irrigation systems that had been installed in the Islands, at great expense and labor, around the turn of the century. Passing through tunnels blasted in solid rock, the water in these concrete-lined ditches ran at a very slight incline down to the sugarcane fields in the flatlands.

Selecting a suitable flume that someone had test-run before, you climbed into the clear, deceptively still water (about thigh high with a current you could barely feel while you were moving against it). You marched upstream into the bowels of the mountain, sloshing and slipping in darkness—the sides and bottom of the flume were so mossy it was hard to keep your footing—until the tunnel opening was no more than a pinpoint of light behind you. Here you stopped, lay down in the water Hawaiian style (that is, fully clothed)—I watched a girl flume in a voluminous pink-and-yellow flowered Holiday Mart muumuu that spread out in the water like a bright tablecloth—and let the current carry you out of the mountain. The pull that seemed so slight was soon revealed to be powerful, and your body, gathering momentum, raced breakneck down the flume as the circle of light at the end grew larger, larger.

The tricky part came just at the climax, the very instant of rapture as you shot out of the tunnel into bright Oahu daylight: You had to stand up *at once* or you would be carried straight into the bowels of another mountain, where the water spilled down an open fifty-foot chute into a lower flume. Standing up was not an easy thing to do on the slick algae-covered bottom of the ditch. You slipped and staggered to the side, trying mightily to haul yourself over the edge to grass and safety—and wasn't it hard detaching yourself from the flume ditch once, like a creature native and indued unto that element, you were well settled in the flow!

7

Pathetic Fallacy

All violent feelings have the same effect. They produce in us a falseness in all our impressions of external things, which I would generally characterize as the "pathetic fallacy."

—John Ruskin, *Modern Painters*

In material culture terms, I had arrived in Hawaii at the poignant end of an era: the last year or two the fishing fleets used glass weights in their nets. Along with seed pods from a single small mangrove forest miles up the coast, cloudy green balls of assorted sizes washed up on the beach at Waimanalo like Easter eggs. Even more obsolete fishing technology had left its mark here, too. In the very old days these waters had seen an abundance of turtles. Off the state beach park down the way you could spot the shadow of dark lava rocks underwater, remains of a prehistoric turtle pen. All up and down the Windward coast, in every protected cove, you came upon the ruins of this lost, complicated aquaculture.

Scene: a fine Waimanalo afternoon, mild trade wind chopping the ocean, continents of clouds forming and reforming in the sky, off to one side Makapuu ridge bulging dark and green, dotted with prehistoric burial caves. Beach empty except for me and one Local fisherman who has been reeling in something for over an hour. Finally a shape emerges in the waves at the end of his line: the sleek head of something that is not a fish. A seal? Very few of these, only the rare monk seals, were still found in the warm Hawaiian waters. No, it's a turtle, a big one, three feet long, maybe a hundred pounds.

33

I watch, fascinated, as the fisherman hauls him out; I have never seen a turtle caught before. To my horror, the beached creature begins to utter soft babylike cries of misery. Tears roll out of the eyes down the wrinkled, leathery skin. No question where this turtle is headed: the stewpot, not the aquarium. I had always prided myself on not minding the spectacle of animals killed for food—a meat eater, after all, should not be hypocritical—but even so this is all a little too much and I flee the coup de grace, deeply grateful not to have been obliged to witness this scene in the pathetic fallacy state.

What is the pathetic fallacy state? It is, first of all, the experience I had at Hanauma Bay, that moment when all barriers have dropped between the inside and the outside, when the landscape against all logic seems to mirror back every private mood and emotion. The possibility of such an archaic identity of Subject and Object has not been allowed in our culture, as reality or metaphor, for some centuries now. Nonetheless, during my time in Hawaii a whole generation of young haoles gleefully jumped—with pharmaceutical assistance—into that animistic world of frowning leaves and talking chairs and happy mountains which the Victorian John Ruskin, while decrying in art as a cold-blooded tactic of second-rate poets, graciously excused in life as a morbid state bordering, in its most exalted form, on inspiration.

Ruskin, a fragile spirit, had that knack of denouncing what secretly fascinated and drew him; his own devoured child's ego, lacking boundaries, was unable to withstand, and periodically gave way to, the drowning and merging experience. The lesson for my friends and me was clear: if you are the sort who must merge with the environment, then merge with splendor. If you must use Nature as a psychic looking glass, choose a setting of unearthly beauty and maybe it will give you back more than your reflection.

One of the great spots in the world for the pathetic fallacy experience was my very own Waimanalo: the wonderful shallow water and manageable waves, Rabbit Island offshore, the old houses behind the rows of ironwoods, the long, deserted beach, the huge craggy Makapuu ridge rising up directly south (and often melting for me, embarrassingly like a rock album cover, into the banal word "ACID"). And it was a Fellini beach, full of

characters: horses and riders, Hawaiians and haoles in all shapes
and sizes, people you would turn around twice, and a third time,
to look at, three-legged dogs, a woman walking her bird, other
sports of Nature.

Waimanalo was uniquely suited for adventures into the fourth
dimension and, occasionally, back to the second dimension as
well—for the beach had a disconcerting habit, to an observer in
this state, of suddenly tilting on an invisible axis and stretching
into a thousand miles of flat white surface, a cartoon human or
two crawling antlike up or down it, the ocean Cubist slabs of blue
and green. I accepted this vision as real and physically possible
in the same way that, snorkeling in a similar condition at
Hanauma, I accepted the strange image of my own full-length
reflection perfectly mirrored on either inner side of my black
rubber mask.

One day a group of us found ourselves playing in the ocean for
six hours, unable to leave the *aqua vitae* even as our skins puckered. We *were* sea creatures, after all—90 percent of our body
weight being water, as someone managed to point out—so how
could we abandon our true medium? Coming at last to the painful but evolutionarily correct decision, we slowly proceeded to
make the exodus to land. At the last minute, though, one member of our group decided to assert his prerogative to regress and
crawled, an unready amphibian, back into the water.

In some way we understood that God, in either a serious slip-
up or a major act of grace (these are often indistinguishable), had
rescued us from a small, sour fate. We young people who had
spent our youth indoors reading books found ourselves, still very
young, in the surf at Waimanalo discovering our bodies and spirits. For us the pathetic fallacy adventure meant a reprieve from
the unnatural sacrifice we had made and a chance to live fully the
adolescence we had lost. Coming upon those Hawaiian children
playing in the ironwood grove, a split-second sidelong glance
instantly dissolved the barrier between adult and child and our
own wonder was mirrored in their impish glee at the secret we
had involuntarily exchanged. Looking deep into our hearts with
their X-ray eyes, they had found—soulmates, real *children*, in
grown-up bodies!

Suddenly I discovered there were whole new unsuspected

epic dramas to be enacted, riddles to be solved, a great expansion of life's possibilities. During our adventures the benign womb of Hawaii gave birth to character-shaping myths to contain the formless organism that was me. The landscape was bursting with stories, all of them my own. First and foremost was Sheena of the Jungle, a swell part complete with leopard-skin costume, except for the occasional disturbing echoes of King Kong and the more ferocious beasts lurking back in the underbrush. There was the Paradise Child, even happier, but containing its own serious traps. There were pirate adventures, miraculous rescues, complicated discoveries and abandonments.

"The foam is not cruel," John Ruskin declaimed. "Neither does it crawl." But he had never been to Hawaii. Lying half out of the surf, face down in the sand, engrossed in the full drama of species adaptation at the molecular level, I can testify, *contra* Ruskin, that a few times the foam did turn cruel, even if I never saw it crawl. In my notebook an incoherent, beautifully inscribed entry about a "bad and beautiful fairy tale" is accompanied by a sketch of the dead pufferfish on the beach that sent me on this downward spiral. It was like the time some friends conducted a whole trip in horrified examination of a dead cow they found in a field. Too stunned to take in its sum identity—was this material-plane emanation animal, vegetable, or mineral?—they spent hours inspecting the corpse in minute and disgusting detail, entirely unable to come to a satisfactory conclusion.

On the whole, pathetic fallacy adventures seemed to go better in the water. On my first get-acquainted outing with Kanaina and Brian, the two young surfers, one Hawaiian and one haole, I had met while hitchhiking, we trespassed on military land near Schofield Barracks and drove past Duc Long Village, the mock Vietnamese hamlet the soldiers played war games in—already here the sinister atmosphere of an eerie martial Disneyland, as unreal to us draft-exempt children as the whole war would prove to be—to our destination, the three small reservoirs with their training bridges. Each had strung across it a rope bridge of smaller width and increasing difficulty: three strand, two strand, and one strand.

As we cavorted on the one-strand rope, which hung a good twenty-five feet above the reservoir, I had the certainty of falling

I later had at Moa Ula falls on Molokai, and fall I did. I fell, fell, fell, first through air and then water, all the way down until—as it seems now, in Wordsworthian memory—my foot touched the bottom of the reservoir, which was also, in best pathetic fallacy manner, the bottom of my soul. This act of contact triggered the Orange Sunshine. I looked up at the twenty-odd feet of water over me and my head blossomed fireworks. I felt myself rising with exquisite slowness through an amoeba-rich viscous green fluid the consistency of soup. It was like being born, only the process took more than a lifetime, it took ten lifetimes, to reach the source of light a million miles overhead and surface finally, with the force of an explosion, in a frenzy of gasping and choking.

From that auspicious start it went on—and on. As Kanaina and I stared into each other's eyes, we unraveled our genealogies in their colors. If my brown eyes came from England, so did his startlingly blue eyes, whose gold flecks, I speculated, were Hawaiian spirits fighting to get out. We had to interrupt this interesting chain of thought to hide in the bushes from the MPs—not the most relaxing activity in the pathetic fallacy state. In fact, the number and intensity of complicated negative mental ruminations this episode produced in our minds finally made it imperative to leave the area, which we proceeded to do in an extremely haphazard manner, it being no easy matter to drive a wavy ribbon of a road resembling the infinity symbol, dodging machines operated by hard-shelled insects straight out of Hell.

In some manner, after one needlessly complicated stop at a mom-and-dad store for blue vanilla shave ice, we arrived on the North Shore. It was summer, the ocean was flat up here, but the ferocious current still sucked hungrily at the beach. One minute I was playing in the surf; the next, the currents of my being harmoniously merged with those of the water, I seemed to be quite a long way from shore. And so, when Kanaina appeared out of nowhere to retrieve me, I took it as no more than normal and natural, given my new home and new condition: to drift out in the undertow and, just as effortlessly, to be brought back.

WORLD OF LOCAL

8

Local

From where I was, so to speak—far out in, and occasionally under, the Pacific Ocean—I could still make out voices, raucous Local voices, floating across the water. Like magpie-sirens the all-too-earthy human population of Hawaii kept luring this dazed amphibian back to shore. This was good. The waters of Hawaii were working their chemical change on my young spirit, but I needed the people to keep me grounded. The Islands, it turned out, offered not just mystic communion with Nature but a whole new movie called Local, with crowd scenes and a huge cast of character actors, hundreds of thousands of them, the former owners and users of the objects I was bringing home from the Goodwill.

There was a kaleidoscope of faces, "Local" and foreign, to sort out: Americans of Hawaiian, Chinese (a.k.a. "Paké"), Japanese, Korean, Filipino (a.k.a. "Manong," derogatory, as "moke" for Hawaiian), Portuguese, and Samoan extraction as well as assorted Micronesians (from Guam, Palau, Ponape, and other U.S. Trust Territories) and Southeast Asians, mostly Thai and Vietnamese—not to mention American Mainland haoles in a range of subspecies: Gold Coast/*kamaaina* (wealthy and/or longtime resident), tourist, military, hippie, boat bum/surfer. Among the non-Americans, the most prominent and visible were Japanese (tourists or investors), along with a smattering of Tahitians, Tongans, and Cook Islanders (usually from dance troupes at the Waikiki hotels) and retired Canadians (always the most relentlessly tanned sunbathers in Waikiki).

What, in this hodgepodge, constituted "Local"? The term was not synonymous with Hawaiian, though what was called Hawaiian was often not strictly Polynesian but Local. The Polynesian navigators, the first to settle the Islands in the period from A.D. 100 to 500, earned for themselves the name "Hawaiian." After Captain James Cook opened up the Islands to European adventurers in 1778, waves of newcomers followed, from the English and American sailors who married into the devastated Hawaiian population of the early nineteenth century, to the succession of Asian, Filipino, and Portuguese fieldhands imported in the late nineteenth and early twentieth centuries by the pineapple and sugarcane plantations, to the U.S. military during World War II. All these genes swirled around in the benign Island melting pot to produce a distinct new Hawaiian-Asian-American alloy known as Local, the most powerful crucible of cultural assimilation ever seen in the United States.

A Local, then, was a person born and raised in the Islands who looked a certain way, dressed a certain way, talked a certain way, and (most important) was not of predominantly "Caucasian" extraction; he/she could be Hawaiian, Samoan, Filipino, Korean, Chinese, Japanese, Portuguese, or any combination thereof. What that made you beyond Local was not always clear, as a self-described Portuguese interviewed by my friend Jim Mac-Donald for his thesis in anthropology once explained:

I had a heck of a time every time the census came into the school. They'd say, "Check one," and when you have three or four nationalities—which one you gonna check? So I ask the teacher, "What do I put?" They would say, "Are you part Hawaiian?" You say, "Yes." They say, "Check that one." They never ask how much Portuguese you are or Chinese or Caucasian. As a result I have cards listing me as everything. In the military the question is, "Have you got any Mongolian ancestry?" I had to put yes, 'cause I'm one-eighth Chinese. I said, what the heck. On my driver's license I got Caucasian.

Local

A Mainlander could live in the Islands thirty years and consider himself a *kamaaina* (longtime resident); even after fifty years, however, he was not a Local. And even though a haole kid who had spent all his life on, say, the island of Lanai might have been entitled to bear the coveted if socially ambiguous label "Local haole" (only if he had a real, not pretend, pidgin accent—that is, he couldn't talk any other way—and his parents weren't too well off and didn't give themselves airs), he would still never receive the naked in-group accolade "Local." Membership in this fiercely exclusive club was fixed by an inscrutable combination of genes and environment, and you were born to it, not made.

The concept "Local" stretched to the natural world as well. This comedy called Hawaii featured a nonhuman cast of plant and animal interlopers that had entrenched themselves in the Islands in much the same manner as their human counterparts. Like the first humans, the first plants in Hawaii migrated from other parts of the world, their seeds carried by birds or washed up in the ocean. The Polynesians brought their own domesticated plants and animals with them in their outriggers: pigs, dogs, chickens, taro, coconut. Doves, mynah birds, Brazilian cardinals, cats, lantana, blackberry, and Panini cactus sneaked in on the coattails of later human arrivals. So did mosquitoes, cockroaches, and geckos.

The language of Local—human Local—was pidgin, a lingo I had formerly associated with Somerset Maugham stories where Malay boys say "Hurry up quickee alongside boss man," that sort of thing. I heard a lot *about* pidgin when I first came to the Islands, but in the wealth of voices surrounding me I picked up nothing like the Maugham dialogue. I did not associate pidgin with the fact that everyone in the Islands spoke (to my ears) rhythmical, accented English. I thought they all had been born speaking Chinese, Hawaiian, Japanese, Tagalog, Samoan, or whatever and that English was merely their second language. Finally I realized that, among the vast majority, English was the *only* language spoken, and this was just the way people spoke it, a special way, like in the Bronx or South Carolina.

An old, old Korean woman, the mother of my landlady, lived in the front of my house in Punchbowl and patrolled the block in her bathrobe at four in the afternoon like all the other *tutus,* the old ladies, did before retiring for the day. Tiny, gap-toothed, liver-spotted, frail as the afternoon breeze that caressed her nylon nightie, she liked me and often spoke to me, spoke extensively, across the yard. But I could never understand a word she said.

When I told my friends at the university, they laughed and said, "Oh, that's *pidgin*. Listen hard. You'll get the hang of it." So whenever she stopped to speak, I listened. I listened hard. What came out of her mouth still sounded like nothing on earth. This pidgin is really something, I thought.

One evening I went with some friends to a Run-Run Shaw production of a Chinese opera at the Imperial Theater downtown. Although Koreans have suffered the same reversal of stereotype in modern Japan and Japan-dominated Hawaii as the Poles in mainland America, in classical Chinese theater they are always the seers, the poets, the philosophers. The light dawned as I watched the wise men in their little hats and wispy beards chanting and pontificating on the screen. It was not so much from any special intonation of language—they were singing in Chinese, after all—as sheer subliminal association: at that moment I knew the old lady was not talking pidgin to me. She was talking Korean.

After that revelation everything changed and I was even able to make out bits of alien debris in the flow of her native tongue, the few scraps of English the old lady had picked up since coming to the Islands in 1917, and yes, they were a lot more like Maugham than anything I was to hear in the Islands before or after: "me savvy," "you young, strong" (this while giving my arm a good-natured slap, as you would a healthy mare), and so on.

Pidgin in Hawaii ran the gamut from impenetrable plantation argot to the faint, pleasing lilt gracing an educated Islander's voice. To the trained ear, there were different kinds of pidgin— Paké (Chinese) pidgin, Filipino pidgin, Hawaiian pidgin, and so on—all of these specialized lingos, after the democratization brought to the Islands after World War II and the decline of the plantations, gradually breaking down in the great melting pot of "Local" into one distinctive English idiom supplemented by a core group of Hawaiian words used by everyone in the Islands, pidgin speakers or not: *da kine* ("the kind," an untranslatable

Local

generic expression designating something like "you know what"), *pilikia* (trouble), *akamai* (clever or sharp), *kuleana* (your own turf or territory), *lolo* (crazy, as in *pakalolo*, crazy grass, or marijuana), *huhu* (angry), *pau hana* (end of the workday and, by extension, retirement), *kapu* (taboo or off-limits), and on and on.

My mostly Local students at the university were self-conscious about pidgin because of the long tangle of racial-class-colonial labels the lack of Mainland English pinned on them. The other young instructors and I, in the throes of sixties egalitarianism, may have gone too far in the opposite direction by encouraging them to take pride in what they had. Couldn't the time spent proselytizing have been better employed teaching a second way of writing, like double-entry bookkeeping? In the long run it was they, not we—haole Mainlanders effortlessly possessing the desired way of talking as our birthright—who had to go out and climb the ladder of a tight-knit, still-hierarchical Island society.

Language, race, and class were inextricably linked in the Hawaii of my time. When an employer said he wanted somebody who spoke "good English," somebody who could make the tourists feel comfortable, that often meant somebody with white skin from the Mainland. The young surfers and hippies fresh off the Western or Continental flights from L.A. could land waiter/waitress jobs in Waikiki a lot faster than a Local kid born and raised on Oahu could. And how ingenuously surprised the former were—if it even registered on them at all—to learn that this created resentment!

Earthy, funny, succinct, never inarticulate, pidgin was above all an expression of solidarity against the incursion of haoles in the broadest sense of the term, that is, outsiders, the non-Island born of all races. Pidgin was also, within the group, a powerful weapon of ridicule against giving yourself airs, pretending you were anything more than the funky, vain fuckup you knew in your heart you were—wot, boddah you? Excellent antidote for phoniness, but devastating like all group yardsticks when used against the sensitive kid who wants something different but hasn't the words to say what.

I soon discovered that Local people had many sharply developed social and perceptual skills of the old-fashioned kind long since atrophied on the Mainland. For one thing, they were far keener observers of the very old and very young than the average Mainlander.

The woman at the Moiliili lei shop advised me, in buying a lei for my grandmother, to choose one made of flowers that didn't smell, like Vanda orchids. Why? Because, she explained, old people's noses are more sensitive to scents. I was grateful for the information; it would never have occurred to me that a fragrant lei might sicken my grandmother.

In my time favorite hippie money-saving scams with children that could be perpetrated on the Mainland—flying older children on a young child's fare, girls passing the same baby around to get on welfare—didn't work in Hawaii because (1) Local flight attendants could guess the child's age within a few months, and (2) Local social workers could always spot the same baby, even though of another race, after intervals of weeks or months.

Quick take: I'm standing at the trailhead at Haena Point, Kauai, trying to go *ka upu*—"the thumb," that is, hitch a ride—after a few days' camping up the Napali coast. It is 1973 and probably the last year any sane young woman would have wanted to consider *ka upu*, even in the Outer Islands. An orange Toyota pulls over. The driver, a Local guy in his thirties, looks reliable. As I get in the passenger side, I notice a great pile of beer and soda cans, Whopper cartons, in the back seat and feel a twinge of alarm.

No problem, though, this is a Hawaiian Telephone linesman who has had a serious altercation with his wife about thirty-six hours ago and since he is living on an island about thirty miles in diameter, instead of driving to Tahoe or Las Vegas for a big blowout he is burning up the Kuhio Highway from one end to the other, Polihale to Haena, working off his temper. All the way he is killing time in two ways: picking up hitchhikers and listening to the radio. And what has he been listening to? To his amazement he discovers I am completely ignorant of the astounding events of the last three days. Swallowed up in the beauties of Hanakapiai Valley, I have missed the "Saturday Night Massacre" and its cataclysmic two-day aftermath. For it is October 1973, Watergate time, and things are happening very fast.

Overjoyed, in his Local way, at lucking onto a captive audience who has *not heard one word of the story*, my driver proceeds to narrate the disgraceful sequence of events. How Nixon fired the special prosecutor. How Richardson resigned. How the Senate reacted. This is an angry man. He is just as angry at his government as he is at his wife, and the thirty-six hours of nonstop driving and listening have honed his down-to-earth Local pragmatism into a fine cutting edge of manic cynicism. And so my knowledge of these crucial moments in American history remains permanently colored by the nameless linesman's brilliantly clear, no-nonsense exposition of the facts, a measureless improvement over Walter Cronkite's—just as, many years later, when I asked an old Hawaiian man at Queen's Surf what he thought of Ferdinand Marcos, who had just moved to Honolulu, his quick response came, refreshing as a glass of water: "Ah, da crook!" You couldn't fool Local, not on the big stuff.

9

Subject/Object

Whether others there considered us the real thing or not, we outsiders in the Islands learned in time to partake of the distinctive Local sensibility: friendly, humorous, sensible, generous, down-to-earth, and (depending on your point of view) either good-naturedly innocent or the narrow-minded embodiment of that housewife sensibility so perfectly described by the Paké oracle the *I Ching* as "contemplation through the crack in the door."

This worldview found natural expression in certain biases, legitimate and otherwise. Liking was a strong Local quality. So was disliking. A well-known Local interrogative, "You like beef?"— not an invitation to dinner, it translates: Would you care to engage in a fight with me?—was often directed at haoles. Why were haoles not liked? One example out of hundreds: It's Wednesday at the Hasegawa General Store, Hana, Maui, delivery day for the fabulous Kitch'n Cooked potato chips from the small Maui company that so far has steadfastly refused to sell its recipe to Mainland interests (though a host of imitators were soon to flood the market). The deliveryman deposits fifteen red plastic bags in the bin. As I reach for one, someone else's hand snakes past me. This hand, sporting mocha-pink nails, belongs to a middle-aged blonde in sunglasses and designer sportswear, unmistakably haole, subspecies Gold Coast. In a single lightning motion, just like a Bloomingdale's sale, she has scooped up all fifteen bags into her carrybasket and is heading, tight-lipped, for the cash register. With the delayed reaction time of a dream I pull my own hand back. A Hawaiian man in a T-shirt and I exchange involuntary glances. Presents for her friends back home, how thoughtful.

Underneath the surface irritation produced in the Local heart by haole acts of callow aggression, social stiffness, stinginess, and lack of class or *savoir faire* generally lay a perhaps less consciously acknowledged rage at the two centuries of economic and cultural dominance, the constant intrusion, by young and old Mainlanders alike, on cherished Island institutions.

Locals of my time saved up their main dislike, however, for tourists—haole and, increasingly, Japanese. In Hawaii as elsewhere, this resentment rose out of the philosophical dilemma of Subject/Object. The essence of being a tourist is that another land and its residents are made to become the extras in your movie: you, naturally, are the star. Somebody else, his daily life, plays Object to your Subject—Subject, of course, being the one who gets to call the shots. Occasionally a disembodied hand reaches out of the picturesque backdrop to make a rude sign or pluck Subject's wallet out of his pocket, or a minor annoyance such as sunburn or jellyfish sting is inflicted on Subject's person. For the most part, though, the painted scenery stays put, the passive, heavily bribed vessel of Subject's wishes and fantasies.

We haoles in Hawaii had the jump on our Mainland counterparts by getting a good preview of what it was like to live in somebody else's Third World. With the substantial investment of Tokyo money in Waikiki during the seventies, signs in Japanese sprouted on every streetcorner and restaurant window; hotels installed *furos* in their bathrooms. The Japanese were coming to Hawaii in droves. And they wanted to view the colorful natives, a category that haole Americans were naively astounded to discover included themselves.

When two Japanese male tourists approached me one afternoon at Queen's Surf, waving and pointing at their camera, I thought they wanted their picture taken in the archetypal manner of the previous generation of polite solitary blue-suited businessmen who, after solemnly presenting their card, beckoned you over to photograph them in front of Iolani Palace, the Aloha Tower, etc. More waving and miming as I reached for their camera. It developed that each wanted his picture taken *with* me, not by me. When I shook my head, the smaller of the two gave an ugly scowl and, much as you would order a wayward spaniel, jabbed a finger at the blanket beside him. The other man, embarrassed by his friend's action, gestured in frantic apology as I walked away.

There also seemed to be a good deal of condescension on the part of these tourists toward the Japanese-Americans of Hawaii, in their eyes not only languageless and cultureless but also, as descendants of peasants from the Hiroshima prefecture and the island of Okinawa, rather the equivalent of Depression-era Okies. It was easy to tell the two groups apart. Hawaiian Japanese had darker skin—they got suntans like everybody else—and were noticeably taller and straighter-legged than their counterparts from the Old Country, no doubt a consequence of the same Western diet that gave them better eyes along with worse teeth and hearts. They wore shorts, zoris, and T-shirts like everybody else. Japanese Japanese were shorter, incredibly pale, and usually decked out in the latest sophisticated European fashions, which looked as wrong in Hawaii as Hawaiian clothes look anywhere else.

My time saw the debut of the pedicab in Waikiki. A New Age version of the rickshaw, it was always driven, or pedaled, by a muscular young blond haole, male or female, wearing shorts, aloha shirt, and puka shell necklace—*the* Waikiki entry job for every surfer from California. And who were the haole coolies' sole clients for a short, expensive ride around Kapiolani Park? Young Japanese newlyweds who seemed blissfully unaware (or were they possibly highly aware?) that the spectacle they presented was the powerful reversal of a centuries-old stereotype.

We Locals and haoles were busy improving our tans at Queen's Surf one afternoon when a group of adult Japanese tourists marched onto the beach. There, scattered among our prone bodies, they were led by their guide through a round of brisk calisthetics before being permitted to rush en masse into the water, where, impossibly—could this be another memory-dream?—some of the women stood waist-deep in the blue Pacific cradling elaborately dressed dolls, rocking them and crooning little songs. It is always possible this was an asylum of lunatics on vacation, but Hawaii is a place where it is impressed on you as nowhere else that, the Family of Man notwithstanding, cultures do exhibit striking differences.

These denizens of other worlds drifted across the beaches of Waikiki just as they would through city bars or cafés. And like the latter, each beach had its own clearly defined membership and set of regulars: tourist (Waikiki proper); Local (Ala Moana); university and professional class, Local and haole (Kaimana); male gay (the left side of Queen's Surf, of course). Occasionally you spotted powerfully built Japanese men covered from head to toe with a mural of tattoos, often wearing only a sumo wrestler–style loincloth. I spotted one of these fellows lounging at Ala Moana beach in the company of a young haole prostitute whose makeup, melting and running in the sun, was as gaudy as his skin. Such men were *yakuza*, the lower-level Japanese gangsters. As all Hawaii knew from the movies at the Nippon Theater, *yakuza* were supposed to be missing the top joint of their little finger in commemoration of the first man they had killed. The boys who gaped, from a discreet distance, at the tattooed man on Ala Moana beach never dared get close enough to verify this custom—nor find out what a Hawaiian sunburn did to those magnificently reptilian landscapes. In Local eyes tourists of any race were pathetic. Only a few, like the *yakuza*, commanded the respect that is born of fear.

A shared (if mostly politely veiled) disdain for outsiders did not mean Locals of all ethnic groups loved each other, no, indeed. Witness those high school football games, where Island racial and class rivalry was allowed to reach its clandestine but violent peak: Roosevelt (middle class and/or dumb haole) versus Punahou (rich and/or smart haole) versus Kamehameha (middle class and rich Hawaiian) versus Kalihi (poor Hawaiian and Filipino) versus St. Louis (Catholic, ergo Portagee) versus McKinley (Japanese) versus Kahuku (Samoan), versus Radford (military haole and black), etc. In these games the young gladiators enacted ritual murder on each other to the screaming approval of their elders.

It is always startling for a haole, who tends to see Asians as somehow mystically united, to be drawn suddenly into the force field of an ancient grudge. Waiting in line in front of me one day at the downtown post office were a group of Chinese Chinese (obviously not Local because they were talking Chinese, not English). When my turn came at the window, the Japanese postal clerk grimaced conspiratorially: "So *loud,* those Pakés." They did seem noisy, but was this an intrinsic quality of the language or only projected racial dislike? Years later, I took a straw vote among an international group of students in my Munich language school: What nationality has the loudest voice? The answer, unanimously tied among three groups (that is, all respondents listed all three groups): Chinese, Americans, Africans. But still I wondered: Was it *true,* or was it just because they didn't like us anyway?

My own assimilation process meant that even though I was an outsider myself, inevitably I came to look at other outsiders through Local eyes. It is, for example, a long-established tradition for visitors from Europe to describe their reactions of bemused horror on first setting foot in, say, Southern California, a cultural vacuum devoid—save for restaurants, shops, and a few vulgarly endowed art museums—of all marks of Western civilization. For those who venture farther into the American Pacific, the crassness of Waikiki naturally follows a close second. But consider, sophisticated Subjects, how the Object sees you.

One day I visited a friend of mine, caretaker of the Oahu beach house of some wealthy Central European's, who had hit it big selling microchips to the U.S. aerospace industry. In the owners' absence he offered me a peek into the main house. We walked up a rather fussily manicured path, unusual for Hawaii, to the Hungarians' large ornate door. And did we smoke a joint beforehand, which might possibly have contributed to my extreme reaction? All I know is that a few seconds after entering the living room I began to feel a growing sense of dis-ease that mounted rapidly to suffocating panic, as if all the oxygen had suddenly been sucked out of the air.

Gasping, I burst out onto a "terrace"—no lanai, this—furnished with those ghastly iron curlecue-patterned chairs that weigh several tons apiece and whose chalky whitewash comes off on your clothes, chairs the likes of which I hadn't seen since the shuffleboard courts of that other lost time in St. Petersburg, Florida.

Looking back into the house from my position of relative safety, I tried to figure out what had come over me. Gradually the truth surfaced. This stiff, expensive imitation nineteenth-century furniture, the awful paintings of Swiss landscapes, the cut-crystal bowl set on a doily in the precise center of the table all created an interior environment not just diametrically but *outrageously* opposed to the natural spectacle only yards away of crashing surf, white beach, wild-fronded palms.

I felt myself in the sudden grip of an uncharacteristic xenophobia. What business did this grotesque waxworks have in my Hawaii, which had happily absorbed a dozen other cultures with no more than a gentle belch but was clearly spitting out as indigestible these highly polished artifacts of the Middle European bourgeoisie?

From the Island perspective this house was an abomination. A shopping mall was a cathedral by comparison. The very attempt to graft that uncompromisingly Old World interior onto a Pacific Island setting laid bare the former's rigidity and smugness, its claustrophobic exclusion of grace, freshness, and everything new. I felt I had stumbled onto a pod of alien life-forms. My friend was caretaking for Martians. Demon-emanations from Europe. It was a simple test. Their haole nest made my skin crawl.

10

Random Encounters

Rebaptized by *wai* and *kai* a citizen of this new Local world, I was keen to learn all its little ways, find out everything about everybody. The daily standoffs provided much chop suey for thought. As the anthropologist Stephen Boggs once pointed out, "No individual is allowed to remain ethnically unaffiliated in Hawaii." Where no clear racial majority existed, you had your little part to play like everybody else. It made for a raucous ensemble theater featuring everyone and his cousin putting their two cents in, especially when all five or so self-described "master races" got out on the highway in the horrendous Oahu traffic. Your self-perception, your whole identity, subtly changed when you realized nobody was the star and all, including you, were cameo players in a set piece of amusing ethnic types. For Mainland haoles it meant belonging for the first time—and in your own U.S.A.—to a minority that, in the rapidly shifting post-statehood Island economy, was no longer by any means clearly top dog. An illuminating and much-needed mental corrective, this.

A prime interethnic encounter, this time in the bar with the strangest name I ever came across, even in Hawaii, "Ross' Spare Room Hall of Fame": At the pool table in the back room the slim, tough-faced waitress with the lighter pockmarked skin of many *hapa,* or half Hawaiians, was pitted against a big swarthy man, not exactly Hawaiian himself, wearing a shirt the color of blood. The man was cracking jokes, laughing, making noise. A shy blonde hovered in his wake. The waitress had nothing to say. Swift and deft and vicious, she sent balls hurtling across the table. She was beating the stuffing out of this guy, Manuel, and really enjoying it. A collector's-choice collision of stereotypes, this: *tita* (her, tough Hawaiian *wahine*) versus *Portagee* (him).

What is a Portagee?

In a later time and life, watching the famous Sausalito Fourth of July parade and its weird mixture of conventional and crazy, Boy Scouts marching hard on the heels of COYOTE, the prostitutes' union, I was treated suddenly to a vision from the past in the form of a platoon of pale, puffy-faced little black-haired girls in white organdy. It was the confirmation class from the town's Holy Ghost Society (I had often walked past their I.D.E.S.S.T. hall on Caledonia Street). Someone standing nearby was doing the same doubletake. A Japanese family who by a dozen cultural cues of dress and accent identified themselves as Local-from-Hawaii, not from Tokyo or Tulsa, had also spotted the little girls. Over the heads of the crowd a wondering Island voice floated: "Eh, da Portagee!"

Like California with its enclaves of Portuguese and Italian fishermen, Hawaii had its own Portuguese immigrants, the largest Western European group to settle there. But in Hawaii the Portuguese were not considered haoles in the way someone of, say, Italian descent raised on the Mainland would be. This strange glitch in racial and ethnic pigeonholing was based on complex class and historical circumstances. Like the Chinese, Japanese, and Filipinos, a large number of Azores Islanders were imported to Hawaii at the turn of the century to work in the sugarcane and pineapple fields. (Reminiscing about Island life during the 1920s, an old woman Jim MacDonald interviewed for his thesis on the Portuguese in Hawaii told him wistfully: "Ah— then plenty, plenty Portagee!")

Their rise from the bottom and absorption into Island society, along with the inevitable fact that they were olive-skinned and dark-haired, forever branded the Portuguese as Locals on the lower end of the prewar hierarchy of race, class, and status. Any other self-classification attempt drew outrage from their peers. "He calls himself *European,*" whispered a Local woman after I had met a friend of hers, "but he's just a Portagee!"

Like the Chinese before them, the Portuguese intermarried heavily with the Hawaiians, producing a new Island personality phenotype, the boaster and big talker. Later this very distinct type got mixed up with the ethnic humor associated on the Mainland with Poles, resulting in the all-purpose joke about the hopeless dummy forever getting into scrapes. In Hawaii, these jokes took a baroque and complicated twist and usually involved a Hawaiian, a Japanese, a Paké, a Manong, and always last, a Portagee. Thus was Portuguese transformed, in the mysterious crucible of Local, to Portagee.

Long after plantation days people of Portuguese descent still carried the full burden of their ambiguous classification. Portuguese influence remained strongest in food, most notably breadstuffs: sweet bread, or pao doce, now called Hawaiian sweet bread, and malasadas, hot fried dough made from potato flour and rolled in sugar (terrific when served piping hot; cold, a gut bomb of the first order). But as for the pressing question, What *is* a Portagee, really?—a concern that reflects the intense Island need to categorize and classify racial and ethnic differences, an unquenchable curiosity that has produced a society of amateur sociologists, anthropologists, geneticists, and social psychologists all rolled into one—there has still been no satisfactory answer.

I knew one old-time Portagee, George Santos, a pig farmer. Pig farms had once been an important feature of Island life. In a custom reflecting infant mortality rates in the old and very old days, a baby was not named or celebrated as a real person until it had survived to reach one year of age, and it was ritual among Hawaiian families to drive out to a pig farm to select the main course for their baby's upcoming first-year birthday party luau.

George Santos had formerly raised his pigs out on Ehukai Road in Kalama Valley, the dry Leeward plain behind the famous Oahu bodysurfing spot Sandy Beach. George had lost his land in 1970, when all the Local farmers were kicked out for a suburban housing project. (This incident and the protest that followed, led by Larry Kamakawiwiole, were the first organized resistance to land development and laid the foundations of the Hawaiian land rights movement.)

After George got evicted, he had no place to go with his pigs, and so the City and County of Honolulu gave him a facility with concrete sties in the uplands above Pearl City. Student volunteers, organized by some of the Farrington Hall boys from the university, helped George keep the pigs going. But the new place was too cold and wet; the pigs kept getting sick. Also, with the advent of fast food in the Islands (the first McDonald's opened in Hawaii Kai in 1970), the quality of the slops he picked up in the early morning hours from the Waikiki restaurants had sharply deteriorated: they were thin and watery, with Styrofoam and bits of plastic and always, it seemed to me, the odd bit of ham or bacon floating on top.

In all, George had maybe two hundred pigs. Many of the baby pigs, shivering under naked light bulbs in the damp concrete sties, were dying of pneumonia. George himself wasn't in good health; he had a heart problem and the whole uprooting from his familiar turf in Kalama Valley, where the three bedroom–two bath town houses and the golf course were now going in, had just been too much for him. Mainly you got the feeling around George and his pigs that another small way of life with its intricate, delicately woven web of associations was going, going, gone. The students could give George some of the help he needed, but maintaining the pig farm in these alien conditions was like hooking up a terminal patient to a hospital machine: despite all efforts it was going to be over soon and there was nothing anybody could do about it.

George loved talking to the pigs. And the fact he was their executioner as well as provider didn't stop the pigs from going wild with joy every time they laid eyes on him. When George walked in the shed, the great creatures lumbered up happily in their stalls, shook their huge furry heads, propped their forelegs clumsily on the gate, and shrilled at him like a pack of bewitched humans. Meanwhile, feeding them, George kept up his nonstop Portagee rap—"Eh! Be good or I going luau you!"—this fate of course awaiting them anyway, good or not good.

In my time the Islands contained odd tiny pockets of unexpected (if that is the right word) resident ethnic groups: the Navajo, for instance, brought to the Islands during World War II so they could broadcast military information back and forth across the Pacific in their native tongue. Because the Navajo language was synthetic in structure and thus at the other end of the linguistic spectrum from Japanese, the latter were deceived into thinking it was code, not a real language—so the story runs— and thus were never able to "break" it. After the war the Navajo looked around Hawaii and saw a good thing. A handful stayed on.

Every so often the Navajo and a scattering of other Native American tribes threw a fair in Thomas Square with booths selling *sopaipilla,* a sweet bread that went over big because, as a Local person explained to me, it was really an Indian malasada. A few people always showed up in sweaty buckskins and cockroach-ravaged headdresses, a bizarre counterpoint to the Hawaiians' own feather cloaks and helmets of the very old days. The hawk noses, slant eyes, chiseled features, and orange-brown skin of the Native Americans, in fact, made a provocative contrast to the rounded (if not outright mashed) noses and purplish-brown skin of the Hawaiians.

The sight of an unfamiliar group of dark-skinned people immediately sets the compulsive Island imagination to work: What combination of Local genes would you have to put together to come out with a Native American? Maybe a Samoan for size and cheekbones, a Paké for the slant eyes, and some kind of ethnic haole for the nose (it was a rare Islander who could distinguish, among haoles, Jew from Gentile). And, finally, copper-colored makeup. In all probability this could have been the original recipe back there in Asia; Amerindians, if you stopped to think about it, were the first Mainland Locals.

What else did the Navajo have in common with the Hawaiians, in that gentle filtered light under the banyan trees of Thomas Square, their adopted tropical home? They had a certain heavy dignity, an inaccessible sadness in the eyes.

The gypsies? As always, another story. All over Oahu in the late sixties, they were most dramatically in evidence at their base of operations down on Hotel Street, telling fortunes in the shabbiest of storefront façades. Typical grouping: one or two attractive young women flanked by a bevy of crones (the men were never in sight). Their olive skins and colorful outfits resembled the people in folk costumes you saw marching every year in the Holy Ghost Society Easter parades, a circumstance that sometimes caused Locals to confuse the gypsies with the long-suffering Portagees.

I'm not sure how many years the gypsies had been there before I got to Hawaii—I don't think it had been very long—but one thing is certain: by the time I moved back in 1977, they were gone. Transported into thin air. Did they keep moving west into the Pacific, I used to wonder, establishing beachheads in Guam, Tahiti, even—unlikely thought—proper English colonial New Zealand, where they were likely to be accused of kidnapping babies? Or did they draw back into their established enclaves in Oakland, Los Angeles, the Central Valley, finding the weird magpie Local culture of Hawaii not enough of a drab foil for their splendid gypsy ways? Maybe, as for the rest of us—what with the gentrification of downtown and the organized interests behind the Waikiki sleaze—Hawaii just got too expensive for them?

What do I remember? Oh, how those gypsy women loved to stare! Their shrewd, penetrating once-over was so totally unlike the round-eyed impassive curiosity of Pacific Islanders. "The eyes of all Polynesians," remarked Robert Louis Stevenson, "are large, luminous, and melting; they are like the eyes of animals and some Italians." He was right, Polynesian eyes are beautiful. But they don't glitter, not like gypsy eyes.

Close up, the various races and cultures of the Pacific are so utterly different that it was always a surprise to me how outsiders confused and mingled, say, the Maoris of New Zealand with the aboriginal inhabitants of Australia (or the most grotesque gaffe of all, in Local eyes—Pacific Islanders with Asians). I quickly learned that three very distinct groups inhabited the islands of Oceania: *Polynesians* (the "hula" people: Hawaiians, Tahitians, Marquesans, Maoris, Tongans, Cook Islanders, Easter Islanders, and assorted others), *Melanesians* (the more negroid inhabitants of the Solomons, New Ireland, New Caledonia, other groups of the Western Pacific), and *Micronesians* (the smaller, more Asian-featured inhabitants of the Northwestern Pacific—Ponape, Palau, Guam, the Trust Territories). Then you had the Filipinos (both modern and aboriginal), and the aborigines of Australia and New Guinea. The latter carried the distinction of being the only people who got to their Pacific homes on foot. Aboriginal occupancy of Australia dated from the time this continent was still connected to the landmass of Asia, a mere forty thousand years ago.

I was to have only one split-second glimpse of the fabled Garden of Eden behind Local, namely, the "true" prehistoric—and a foreign prehistoric at that—via a rare meeting with Australian aborigines. The abos came to my party with the Australian haole I persist in thinking of as their keeper, the good young man from the Department of Aboriginal Affairs who was shepherding the fellows through a series of concerts celebrating Australia Day in Hawaii. Someone else had invited the group, but not a sign of them until after midnight, when everyone else had gone home. Looking idly out the kitchen window as I did the washing up, I saw a sight that made me freeze. Walking up the street were four of the weirdest human silhouettes I had ever seen—tall, very tall rangy forms, neither African nor American black, with profiles of fairytale cragginess. In the Islands, where everyone prides himself on superhuman powers of ethno-racial acuity, these people were showstoppers: Who *are* you?

The abos marched in—with dijeridoos, their drone pipes, I noted excitedly—and sat down, subdued and polite, in the living room. The young man from the department inquired if we had anything left to eat or drink. In the kitchen he explained to me that he was sorry they were so late but the fellows had wanted some girls and so they had gone to Hotel Street first.

Definitely, the fellows weren't interested in the remains of the black bean soup; worse, there was no wine left. We sat in silence. I asked them about the trick of cooking turtle meat inside a dugong carcass I had read about on the Great Barrier Reef—they were from the Northern Territories—and this was agreed to: Yes. It was done. Then I asked if they wanted to hear the music of the Hawaiians. This suggestion being greeted with mild enthusiasm, I put on a Gabby Pahinui record. As the 1940s slack-key rhythms oozed out and Gabby began singing in Hawaiian about the clean sheets in the Royal Hawaiian Hotel, an attack of self-conscious Western reverse racism struck me like a tidal wave and I blushed deeply at the thought of polluting the ears of bona fide representatives of the Dreamtime—so bona fide, apparently, they couldn't be left unchaperoned in a big city—with this musical chop suey. At the same time my imagination was furiously engaged in re-creating what possible cross-cultural sexual encounter had occurred between these anorexic giants and the enormous scowling Samoan transvestites, with their pounds of makeup and sleeveless dresses cut to reveal bulging tattooed biceps, who paced up and down Hotel Street in a show of sullen availability.

The abos listened politely to Gabby. All too obviously this sort of music didn't interest them. When the record was over they stood up, still notably quiet and subdued, along with the young man from the Department of Aboriginal Affairs. The strange silhouettes vanished into the night as mysteriously as they had come and I was left to digest the implications, as they appeared to my Subject's sentimental mind: Were the aborigines spiritually disoriented by the Western urban intensity of Honolulu or, as a cynical friend opined, "all fucked out," or was it maybe a little of both?

Mainly it was the steadfast gaze of Polynesian Pacific Islanders I met on the streets of Honolulu—in the ancient laundromat on King Street in Moiliili, for example, only a half-step up from pounding your clothes on a rock, where a full load could be washed for a quarter and dried ten minutes for a dime. There were two times to stay away from the place: when the Tongan family came and engaged all thirty washers for the dirty clothes of the kinship system, and when the haole madman talking furiously to himself and wearing only a newspaper tied around his waist with string (so as to wash *everything*) also ran all thirty machines, but with only a single item—a sock, a pair of shorts— churning in each one. Once I found the Tongan family and the haole man in the newspaper *malo,* or loincloth, there at the same time: here under one roof the exaggerated twin poles of Island life, haole rugged individualism versus the Polynesian extended family! How they were sharing the washers was not clear but my turn would not be coming up soon, that much was certain.

11

Songs of Happy Families

Oh those Polynesian families, the bosom of the *ohana*, or extended family, more than the scenery made Hawaii the right place for backward movement, regression to the womb. Missionaries were startled to find the Book of Genesis their converts' favorite part of the Bible. How the Polynesians from Rarotonga to Rapa Nui loved reading, over and over, "And Abraham begat Isaac"—it was the very mirror of their own genealogical chants. Robert Louis Stevenson described a Marquesan chief's eagerness to master a typewriter so that he could transcribe the whole list of his family, with his own name carefully hand-lettered at the bottom.

A Samoan student of mine once told me, with a certain embarrassment, how he had boasted to his mother as a boy that he would have a hundred and fifty children for her. Now that he was a man of nineteen, he said, he realized what a foolish dream that was: "Five to eight is about right."

For the old Hawaiians as for all the old Polynesian societies, the metaphysical center of things, the innermost locus of emotional and spiritual life, was not "heart" or "soul" but "stomach," *opu*. Thus you have the *opu kanaka*, the descent group, or "belly man"—literally, the belly of the kin group inhabited by the whole crowd of swallowed Jonahs, where (to revert to a more

Local image) the vaunted "sanctity of the individual" is mashed flat as a rotten mango under the distended luau foot.

This primacy of family exerted a fatal attraction on the average nuclear-family–sprung Mainland haole of my time, who projected a romantic vision of Garden-of-Eden happiness onto the batallion-sized Hawaiian and Samoan families he saw lolling companionably on adjacent mats every Sunday in Kapiolani Park but failed to understand that his very standpoint as a free and unattached observer, his "objectivity," would be ground to a pulp in the family maw were he really and truly to *belong,* as he thought he longed to do. Case in point: the Peace Corps volunteer who married the Manuan girl he met during his posting. At the wedding, attended (and hosted) by about three hundred of her blood relations, he had a brief and terrible vision of the lifelong sociofinancial obligations he was incurring that very moment to every one of them. (He never recovered from this revelation and they were soon divorced.*)

But on the idyllic side of the ledger, oh, the romance of happy families! (This phrase has a slightly different, more innocent and old-fashioned inflection than Freud's "family romance.") Maori elders on the *pa* in New Zealand who grabbed little children to take to bed just as you would a pillow or stuffed animal. The Samoan brothers and sisters, that flock of gentle angels in an old Jeep who sang me the song of the turtle and the dolphin in perfect five-part arrangement as I hitched a ride with them from Waimanalo back to Honolulu. The old church on Punchbowl resounding with *himine,* hymns, in the same gorgeous harmonies.

One beautiful afternoon in the days before I learned how to drive, the greatest of Hawaiian minstrels got on my bus at the Hawaii Kai stop. I nearly fell out of my seat. Gabby, *the* Gabby Pahinui, master living slack-key guitarist and singer, riding the Waimanalo bus like the rest of us mortals?

---

*This archetypal Peace Corps experience holds a poignant, century-old echo of the lives of the South Seas traders. In a story by the Australian Louis Becke, a sea captain chaffs the Scots trader on Majuro: "What's the matter, Macpherson? . . . Have you married a native girl and found out that she is related to everyone on the island, and you haven't house room enough for 'em all, or what?"

Of course Gabby was riding the bus; so were most of the other great noncommercial, non–Las Vegas Hawaiian musicians. He was lucky not to be hitchhiking, in fact. Gabby Pahinui worked full time for the Oahu Department of Sanitation (that is, he was a garbage collector). Most of the others had equally modest full-time day jobs. For the dedicated, Hawaiian music was hardly a big-money vocation.

Before I came to the Islands I loathed the syrupy Muzak I associated with fat plumbers from Nebraska on holiday with their loud shirts, cigars, and muumuued wives. To the hard-edged sixties sensibility, Hawaiian music was like sinking into a tub of warm oatmeal, the embodiment of fifties blandness and mediocrity. But a funny thing happened when I got to Hawaii. I listened to this same music and liked it. Really liked it. In just the way that aloha clothes, so garish and vulgar in the thin watery Mainland sunlight, looked vividly, perfectly right in their native territory, Hawaiian music sounded great in Hawaii. Especially when the true practitioners like Gabby, whom I had never heard of on the Mainland, played songs like the sublime "Hualalai." Even hackneyed standards like "E Ku'u Morning Dew" sounded okay as long as the singer didn't act like he/she was auditioning for the opening slot at Harrah's Tahoe.

Hawaiian music, though unique to Hawaii, wasn't exclusively Hawaiian; it was Local, it was poi dog, chop suey, a mixture of full-on chanting from prehistoric days, Dixieland and ragtime pop music techniques grafted onto song standards of nineteenth-century Hawaii, grass skirts borrowed from the Tuamotus, and its trademark musical instrument a typically Local mutation of European and Hawaiian: the ukulele.

Berated virtually from the first moment of Contact for their "Europeanization," the resilient Hawaiians steadfastly continued to display their intense intellectual curiosity and ability to draw from other cultures, as the highly flexible medium of this music demonstrates. Even as their own society crumbled to bits around them, their unquenchable interest in new things allowed the Hawaiians to transmute the classic hula forms into the *hapahaole* landmarks of the new society:

Uluwehiwehi 'oe i ka'u 'ike la,
E ka Royal Hawaiian Hotel.

A he nani la, ke hulali nei,
A he nani maoli no.

You are festive to see,
  O Royal Hawaiian Hotel.
  Beauty gleaming,
  True beauty.

The last Hawaiian queen, Liliuokalani, a noted composer of many hundreds of songs, or *meles,* was inspired by her first sight of a lawn sprinkler, for example, to write a playfully sophisticated little ditty delicately transformed by the *kaona* (hidden meaning) devices of the classic hula into a love song with physical and emotional frissons ("Slow down a little / That I may drink," etc.) Abby Kong and Johnny Noble composed a hula to honor the coming of electricity to Kaneohe that represents a typical blending of the stateliness of the old hula, its celebration of natural places and forms, with the coming wonders of the new:

  Light flashes at the Kaneohe
  Cooperative society at Laniwai.

          Chorus
  The Puakea rain,
  The peace of Laulani,
  And the coolness of the Koolau.

  Koolau-poko is famous
  And lights go on at Kaneohe.

It's instructive to remember that these pretty songs, along with all their later Tin Pan Alley and tourist variants, are the offspring on one hand of the lively multiracial and commercial potpourri of Mainland American music and, on the other, of a formal literary and musicological tradition more than a thousand years old—a genealogy as confusing but vital (and maddeningly unavoidable, for the hapless heirs who desperately wished they were either all one or all the other) as those produced by the union of brash, opportunistic New England sailors with stately Hawaiian princesses.

Huli, hula. To get to the prehistoric hula, the "real thing" that preceded slack key, you had to peel back a lot of Local overlays. For me grass skirts, teriyaki chicken, and revolution were indissolubly linked because these are words that share the Hawaiian root *hul-* (Proto-Malayo-Polynesian *suliq*). *Huli-huli* chicken, like Portuguese sausage a staple of Local fund-raising drives, is turned on a spit. In the later seventies *huli* came to refer to Hawaiian political activism in the context of "overturning." *Huli* also refers to the curled leaf of the taro: when you are picking the plant in water, first you grab the mother in the center, then the baby taro sprouts ringed around it come out easily. So, then, in keeping with the root meaning of "turn" or "motion" you have the sublime, majestic, playful, and frightening hula, the pan-Polynesian storytelling chant simultaneously interpreted through the body movements of hips, torso, hands, and arms.

My own contact with the prehistoric hula came through the performance of the late Iolani Luahine, whose devotion to the art, as the heir of a trained handful of secret practitioners who kept the tradition alive during more than a century of missionary censorship and repression, helped begin the great revival of the original pre-Contact dance with its formal *halau*, or schools, among modern Hawaiians. These *halau* provided a complete mental and physical training within a religious framework for their disciples, who entered at age five or six and dedicated their lives to the art. Traditional hula interpreters were raised in isolation with the understanding that they had no family, only their art. Iolani, no exception to this stern rule, was noted, though, for her *kolohe*, or "rascal," personality.

I have two memories—one profane, the other sacred—of Iolani Luahine. The first time she was dead drunk, waving a Primo bottle and doing a parody of a farewell hula for a departing plane on the Hana airport runway after the 1970 Hawaiian Music Festival. The second time was a hair-raising performance of the old chants, accompanied by her niece Hoakalei Kamau'u on the stage of the McKinley High School auditorium in Makiki. Here was my first revelation that the old ritual was not meant to be pretty and charming like modern "Local" hula but, on the contrary, fear-inducing. The facial expressions accompanying these very old hula were seductive and ferocious by turns, and never more terrifying than when the performer smiled. Watching

66

Iolani this time I understood as never before that a great big grin, in the ancient ceremonial context, was about as friendly as a rictus, and that the gods of old Hawaii were not very nice.

After seeing Iolani's dance I wanted to read the texts of the ancient hula, but it was hard, lacking a sound knowledge of Hawaiian, to lift the curtain of Western sensibility and get a close look at the real animal. Through inadequate and bowdlerized translations I had tantalizing glimpses of an impressive opus. The closest Western equivalent to hula are possibly the Troubador lyrics, but the hula composers surpassed their Provençal counterparts in complexity of sexual, religious, and topographic punning. The worldview of the old Hawaiians as expressed in these chants and stories was also much larger, combining in the same lines cosmology, specific features of the natural landscape, sociopolitical comment, sexual gossip, and jokes.

My first bookish bridge to the hula of the very old days was *The Unwritten Literature of Hawaii,* by Nathaniel Emerson, originally published by the Bureau of American Ethnology in 1909. A physician turned amateur scholar who performed heroic efforts in recording great hula works that would otherwise be lost, Emerson was a sensitive and knowledgeable interpreter who yet presents the fascinating spectacle of a man at war with himself. First, we have his lush and terrible translations of the sensual originals:

> Whence art thou, thirsty wind,
> That gently kissest the sea,
> Then, wed to the ocean breeze,
> Playest fan with the bread-fruit tree?

Lest his patent deep sympathy with the spirit of the old Hawaiians lead a genteel audience to the unfortunate conclusion that he had "gone bush," however, Emerson was forever qualifying his basically perceptive and intelligent insights with the standard boilerplate of the days of Social Darwinism: "The most advanced modern is better able to hark back to the sweetness and light and music of the primeval world than the veriest wigwam-dweller that ever chipped an arrowhead. It is not so much what the primitive man can give us as what we can find in him that is worth our while." Coming from the source it does—a total devotee of a prohibited "native" art—the disclaimer rings a bit defensively. At the time he wrote his was an unsanctioned hobby, and as a child of missionaries he must have been uncomfortably aware of the fact.

Emerson tried his best to justify, according to the lights of his day, the all-pervasive sexuality of the hula lyrics: "How, then, could the dramatic efforts of this primitive people, still in the bonds of animalism, escape the note of passion? . . . It may be said of them all that when they do step into the mud it is not to tarry and wallow in it; it is rather with the unconscious naivete of a child thinking no evil." But reading the ancient hula texts even in Emerson's versions makes it clear that if the subject itself of a *hula* or *mele* (a chant without accompanying dance) were not outright sexual, at the very least it had to be rendered as sexual allegory: one cannot avoid feeling that the Hawaiians did love to "wallow in it," and with a great deal of grace and wit. The obvious conclusion seems not to have occurred to Emerson: that, in sexual matters, his subjects were the sophisticates and he the naive recorder.

The delicate ambivalence of his Hawaiian informants in the face of intrusive haole curiosity was never better, or more unwittingly, captured by Emerson than in his earnest efforts to track down the *kaona,* or hidden meaning, of these lines:

Perilous steep, is the climb to Hanalei woods;
To walk canny footed over its bogs;
To balance oneself on its ledges,
And toil up ladder of hanging roots,
The bulk of my guide overhangs me,
His loins are well-nigh exhausted;
Two beautiful shapes!
'Neath this bank I crouch sheltered from rain.

As a number of interesting images fill the reader's mind, Emerson comments: "One asks what uncouth or romantic love adventure this wild mountain climb symbolizes. All the Hawaiians whom the author has consulted on this question deny any hidden meaning to this mele."

It is easy enough to laugh at outdated attitudes while forgetting how each age holds its own mirror up to other cultures and the past. No matter how free of ethnocentrism the observer feels himself to be, he remains the prisoner of his own time and culture. It becomes an equally easy trap of the twentieth-century sensibility to focus on the sexual aura of the hula at the expense of the panorama of natural, social, political, religious, and other meanings so subtly bonded into a single set of images by their Hawaiian creators.

Every now and then, though, disturbing little reminders of the sexual flavor of premissionary Hawaii did surface, not in books but the real Local world—in the number and social acceptability of homosexuals, for one thing. After our first Tahitian dance class in a small close room, a female Mainlander friend complained: "Gee, an hour of twenty women shaking like that and a feminine hygiene deodorant salesman could have made a fortune off us!" She was only too right. While provoking the wit and imagination of their audience with intricate lyrics, the clever Polynesians had not neglected to include olfactory as well as visual stimuli in their beloved hula.

12

Plate Lunch

The old Polynesians regarded the *opu,* or stomach—or more precisely, the lower intestine—as the location of their life force. By my time the Hawaiian sacrament of nourishing the sacred spot had come to depend heavily on a strictly Local amalgam known as plate lunch. This Island soul food, available at all the drive-ins, was a mishmash or, more appropriately, chop suey of different ethnic foods: teriyaki beef or char siu chicken, two scoops rice, macaroni salad.

Regardless of origin—Hawaiian, Asian, Filipino, American, Portuguese, or whatever—Local cuisine was not big on greens. Many Local males I knew—the old-fashioned kind who were not stoned vegetarian surfer-hippies, that is—ate only meat, fish, rice; any other diet was regarded as unhealthy. Spam was a big favorite. So were pork and bean sandwiches with mayonnaise. Even when Zippy's Saimin Lanai finally installed its salad bar, some things stayed sacred: salad never, never came with your plate lunch.

A Portuguese man who had grown up on Maui in the days when his family still had their own brick outdoor oven for baking pao doce recalled that he had never eaten a single green vegetable while growing up because his mother thought they made children sick. In compensation, he and his brothers and sisters

70

had fed secretly, instinctively as animals, on the wild green grass that grew in the fields over Makawao—a forbidden treat their mother whipped them for if she caught them at it.

This Local carnivore tradition dated from the old and very old days. After an audience with the four-hundred-pound Queen Kaahumanu in the early 1800s, a diminutive Japanese visitor made this horrified entry in his diary: "She lies on her back and eats a dog a day." Among the tall, big-boned Polynesians in their precarious island agricultural economies all over the Pacific, to be fat was, and still is, a mark of beauty and prosperity. Visual verification of this cultural bias may be had anywhere from Samoa to Kapingamarangi, but for the statistically minded I have before me a recent news item:

Air New Zealand and Polynesian Airlines have been forced to reduce the number of passengers on flights in the South Pacific because of the size of Polynesian passengers. King Taufa'ahau Tupou of Tonga, for example, weighs 299 pounds. "The average passenger on these flights tends to be heavier than passengers on most other services," said Air New Zealand official Vern Mitchell.

To keep within international limits, the story notes, "both airlines must leave 13 seats empty of 113-seat Boeing 737s and increase the weight allowance from the usual 169 pounds per person to 205 pounds."

In the pantheon of Local foods starch came in a strong second after meat. In my time Hawaii was probably the only place in the world chili con carne was served over rice; it was the only state in the Union where more rice than potatoes was consumed per capita. Millet and grain were unknown in the Pacific Islands before European contact; poi, the starchy paste made from taro root, was the Hawaiian staple of the very old days. Other Polynesian settlements—the Society Islands and the Marquesas, for example—used breadfruit, which grew better in those more tropical settings than in temperate-zone Hawaii. The sweet potato was also widely distributed, but it was never as popular as taro, or *kalo* in the Hawaiian orthography, a plant for which Hawaiians had over 100 different species names.

I once watched a haole anthropologist get himself in trouble on a Honolulu television show by doing a midden analysis based on garbage can contents of two city districts. Viewers were treated to a rare glimpse of anthropological fieldwork in action as he rummaged happily through the cans, intent on his prizes as a Bowery wino. The chosen districts were two valleys, Kalihi (low income and mostly Hawaiian) and Manoa (university haole), so everybody knew the score before the analysis even began.

Like a kind of eerie brand-X-versus-our-product commercial, on one side he had piled up the Spam containers and evaporated milk cans, *opihi* shells, *wana* spines, Hungry Man frozen TV dinner boxes, Eskimo Pie wrappers, daikon roots, Chips Ahoy cookie sacks, cases of Primo beer bottles. On the other side, lettuce and cabbage leaves, coriander roots, carrot tops, chicken necks and potato peels, ends of whole-grain bread loaves, wine corks, wrappings and rinds from blocks of cheese (a haole delicacy considered disgusting by conservative Asians and for a long time available only in the ethnic food section of Hawaiian supermarkets).

At first our expert managed to stay on safe ground. "Primarily a meat and starch diet here, contrasted to a more—" he stopped, one felt, just before uttering the culturally judgmental word "balanced," and started over again—"vegetable-oriented diet. One group drinks beer, the other wine. The people on this side use the more expensive packaged and canned convenience foods, whereas these people seem to take more time and care in preparing their food fresh . . ." Hot water again, and there was nothing for it but to cut to the real commercial, which was probably for McDonald's.

When the talk show came back on the anthropologist and his two piles of garbage had disappeared. I always wondered if it was because Local viewers had taken offense at what had turned into a thinly veiled nutritional lecture, the kind you get in old-fashioned Department of Public Health brochures that show pie-chart graphs of the Daily Seven Food Groups. On balance, I rather think they did not. Regardless of what *he* said, most Local folk would have known for a fact that the meals whose remnants found their way into the upwardly mobile garbage cans were dangerously lacking in bulk.

Island appetizers, another staple of Local cuisine, were known by the generic name *pupu*. (To avoid unfortunate Mainland associations with cowpies, it's necessary to say the word lightly, liltingly: *pu!pu!*) The Hawaiian word for hors d'oeuvres referred originally to the succulent morsel scooped raw from a seashell. In its Local manifestation it was a catchall label for the staggering array of sashimi, teriyaki beef, fried shrimp, chicken wings, and the like served free as you ordered rounds of beer. In long-gone places like the Kuhio Grill in Moiliili or the Aloha Grill on Nuuanu Street, the waitress purchased the pupus from the kitchen with her own money; you bought them, at a healthy profit for her, by means of your larger-than-usual tips. But somehow, as the succession of treats came through the kitchen doors to your table, one delightful greasy surprise after another, they seemed gloriously *free*. And, needless to add, a meal in themselves.

Once, having lunch at one of those places with two haole men friends, I left the table briefly as we were being attended by the tiny old Japanese waitresses who were a fixture of the old-time Hawaiian restaurant world. When I came back, my friends were hunched red-faced and choking over the table, but not from the food. It seems that once the female was safely out of range, the old ladies in their green polyester uniforms had zeroed in like vultures on the two handsome young fellows, inquiring shrilly what sort of pupus they desired: "You like hair pie?" Cackle, cackle. "Pussy on toast?"

I gaped at the two balding, wizened crones now innocently positioned by the kitchen door. Oh, they were funky folk, these old Waikiki hands, especially the ones who had weathered World War II and all those servicemen. Making haole boys blush, their specialty. For them my return to the table signaled "back to business." One bore down on our table with a plate of beef hekka. Face etched in stone, she set it before us. Our pupu.

Goat soup, another delicacy. Ed Bilderbach, Alaskan hunter and fisherman, caught salmon off Cordova in the summer and wintered in Hawaii, where he motored out in the interisland channel waters to net Kona crabs. In his spare time Ed liked to bow-and-arrow hunt wild goats on the Big Island (back home in Alaska it was grizzlies), and once he threw a gigantic goat luau, cooking up his kill by wrapping it in *ti* leaves and burying it in an *imu*, or earth oven, just like the Hawaiians did with their kalua pig.

At the end of the evening the three or four earthen pits were still full of meat-covered carcasses—it was no vegetarian's dream, that banquet. Though I had eaten only a little of my kalua goat I hated seeing all the meat and bones go to waste, so I asked Ed if I could take the remains with me to cook up into stock. Favorably impressed with the thriftiness of this idea, he organized the project and an hour later, three heavy garbage bags slung over my shoulder, I mooched on home like old Witch Hazel.

Next morning I threw the meat-covered bones and a few pounds of onions and carrots into a ten-gallon institutional-size stock pot. Soon the contents boiled merrily. The aroma now filling the kitchen, however, was not quite that of chicken or potato-peel broth. No, it was rather pungent. Your middle-class prejudice against wild game is showing itself, I lectured myself. Be flexible. This is *real* flavor.

After another hour I could no longer stand the smell—a few times the memories it aroused of the stinking mountain goats in Haleakala Crater even made me gag—so I shut off the heat and let the contents of the enormous cauldron cool down. It'll be fine once it's strained, I thought. I'll have the base for ten or fifteen soups and stews.

Straining was no picnic, either, involving as it did tedious exchanges between five or six other pots and one packed garbage bag full of cooked bones and soggy vegetables. Finally the cleaned-out stock pot stood on the stovetop brimming with viscous dark brown fluid. I didn't do anything more with it, didn't even taste it, till Ed came over that afternoon.

He lifted a spoonful to his mouth. "Hoo-ee," he said.

I shook my head as he stuck out the spoon for me. Somehow I knew it was goodbye consommé and egg flower soup.

"You know what you got here?" Ed said after a pause. "Goat soup." And he was right.

Eating in Hawaii carried with it strange associated customs. For one thing, you had to do something with all the mess generated by your plate lunch and/or takeout pupu; out here the drive-in had been an entrenched institution long before fast food ever hit the Mainland. This problem raised the dread specter of

Plate Lunch

littering—in California, a crime on a par with murder and incest;
in Hawaii, a way of life. The broken zoris I saw my first day in
Honolulu were part of a bewildering array of discarded junk
strewn along Island sidewalks and roadways. Like the old cars in
Hawaiian front yards that rusted into skeletons and ultimately
metamorphosed into a kind of accidental planter for vines and
small trees, most of the trash disappeared in the speedy process
of disintegration most everything organic undergoes in a tropical
climate.

(I can already hear a chorus of disapproving voices rising—
"Yes, but what about the plastic straws and the Clorox bottles,
the unbiodegradable substances and—"If this was your reaction,
do not read on.)

Kanaina and Brian took me to the Local gastronomic mecca,
Zippy's Saiman Lanai—not the later California-ized version with
the ferns and the salad bar, but the old basic Zippy's. Our plate
lunches, or dinner by this time (it was dark, I remember; this was
a crime I could never have contemplated in broad daylight),
came nested in the usual plethora of cardboard trays, cups, nap-
kins, plastic forks. As we pulled away from the parking lot, I
noticed both boys rapidly rolling down their windows. My heart
froze as each nonchalantly pushed a square foot of paper prod-
ucts and half-eaten manapua out the window into the—*environment*. Brian noticed my expression. "Dump 'em," he said.

I was young and wanted to try everything. But littering was
the limit.

Brian said, "It'll make you feel good."

Heart pounding, I gave the remains of my box lunch a timid
push over the edge of the window as we sped off down—was it
King Street or Beretania? I couldn't bear to look back but, as I
settled in my seat, I was overcome by a strange sensation of
lightness, as of a burden lifted, the feeling they always say you
experience when breaking one of the major life taboos. I knew
the worst about myself now and I didn't care—as long as I wasn't
caught.

I believe Melville must have been thinking about littering
when he wrote in *Typee* about the "easy unstudied graces of a
child of nature . . . enjoying a perfect freedom from care and
anxiety." Getting rid of trash the easy way—with a light, careless

toss—is exhilarating, fun, relaxing, joyous even. For a split second it had made me "feel celebratory," as I had heard a colleague in the U.H. English Department say about reading a poem. That's why people like to litter. That's why being civilized along the whole range of human behavior carries with it a high psychic price tag.

13

Valiant

I'm not sure how it is now, but anytime during the seventies you could stand at a busy streetcorner in Honolulu—say, Keeaumoku at Kapiolani Boulevard—and ask yourself the following question: What kind of car is most often driven by gray-haired Japanese males not wearing suits and ties? And you, as seasoned longtime resident and informal market researcher, would know that whatever car this might turn out to be would also be the cheapest, easiest to fix, most durable and reliable piece of transportation not just in the Hawaiian Islands but *the whole world.*

Because its owners—those old Japanese guys in T-shirts and shorts with their nets and spears and reef slippers stuck in a plastic bucket in the back seat, heading back from Holiday Mart to their bungalows in Pauoa or Kaimuki, the tin-roofed houses that had a bathtub with a *koi* swimming in it out in front, under the mango tree—they weren't anybody's fools. They didn't buy to impress. They bought because something worked. And kept on working. One car, that's it, like getting married, as the graffiti down in the Queen's Surf women's room says: "4-Evah." So it better be good.

Now the answer.

A 1962 Plymouth Valiant, with the "duckbill" body, slant-six cylinder engine, push-button automatic transmission, Edsel-

77

type front grill, and fake Thunderbird-style molded tire carrier on the trunk. Favored colors: white, red, powder blue. Hot as Hades inside because the windows were so tiny, its radiator too small for a tropical climate—the old pros quickly reinstalled a heavy-duty Death Valley–caliber rad—but believe it. A Valiant is 4-Evah.

The original Mainland prole car, most of the early sixties Valiants didn't even have radios (though their fraternal twin the larger Dodge Dart did), but so what? Let the old guys clue you in: this car worked. The Valiant was the American Volkswagen bug, and it took not materially spoiled Mainlanders but thrifty ex-plantation *akamai* Hawaiian Japanese-Americans to identify this admirable product, buy it, enshrine it in their open-air carports for the next twenty-five years as the body dissolved in rust and the faithful engine, like a sturdy old heart, just kept pounding away.

When last noted in 1980 by this observer, even the Oahu Water Supply Board's fleet of staff cars were Valiants, albeit later models (junk after 1968 when they went to eight cylinders, but bureaucrats, like most everybody else except the old guys, are unwisely concerned with appearances, not with what's really good).

My first car in Hawaii, which was also my first car "evah," was a 1962 Buick Special whose rust condition at the moment of purchase, after a decade of Island life, was close to terminal. I bought it from a young resident at the new U.H. Medical Center who was married to the daughter of a colleague of mine in the English Department. Like most every other major expenditure of mine in Hawaii, the Buick cost $75. I did not have a license when I bought the car—picture the anomaly of a twenty-six-year-old Californian who didn't know how to drive—and so the two-block solo trip from his modern apartment building to my tin-roof house on Punchbowl was an adventure in terror.

I had ten driving lessons from ten different friends, so as not to burn anyone out. Finally I felt ready to take the test. The DMV examiner looked askance at my heap, especially when I explained that the passenger door did not open and he had to crawl in through the driver's side. But the fact that Myra Tomonari came down with me was a mark in my favor—in those days haoles were viewed, not without reason, as holding themselves apart from Locals—and so the DMV man did not stop the test, as he could have, because of a substandard vehicle.

I passed. Armed with a bottle of water to cool off the radiator, I began my tentative explorations of the highways of Oahu, where you could drive no more than forty miles in any direction. Rumor had it that H-1, Hawaii's first freeway and the pride of the Islands, had been built by eighteen different contractors on eighteen different political payoffs, which was why the on ramps and off ramps were the length of driveways and had, directly over them, different names from the signs announcing them two miles before. Because these truncated entrances feeding directly into the main flow of traffic called for maximum acceleration, I quickly learned which ones the Buick was capable of and which it wasn't.

The Buick and all my later old cars were serviced at the Union station on the corner of University and Beretania. My mechanic was a silver-haired Japanese who looked like a philosopher king, and he knew how to fix the Buick at precisely its level of need and my ability to pay. When the tail pipe had rusted to the point where there was no longer enough of it to bolt onto the body, Harry welded the remains onto the underside of the car for $12. I never had a repair from him that cost more than $30. Around the corner was Ken's Tire Shop, where I outfitted my cars with used tires, $7 and $8 plus installation. I never had a flat. These old guys were thrifty, and they were honest. The gas station was like the Goodwill. You could afford to go there, and what you got you were happy with.

The Buick Special's power problem finally became so acute that later, when I moved from Punchbowl to Manoa Valley, it was a struggle coaxing the car up the steep little rise (an old volcanic cinder cone) where my street, Pamoa, formed a T intersection with Alaula Way. My friend the anthropologist Jim Mac-Donald, who lived at the other end of Pamoa, had an ancient station wagon that stalled whenever he hit the brakes. The inevitable day came when I was inching the Buick up my side of the cinder cone while, unknown to me and out of sight, Jim was powering up the other side. Since braking was mutually out of the question, we had a Road Warrior–style confrontation at the intersection, swerved like pros, and roared neck and neck up both lanes of Alaula.

In our circle this episode was widely held to be as amusing as the time the two most aggressive young male bucks of the English faculty accidentally backed their identical VW bugs full speed into each other from opposite ends of the dirt parking lot below Kuykendall Hall.

When finally the tired Buick could no longer cope even with backing out of the driveway, I unloaded it for a '64 Dodge Dart, standard shift but with the same slant-six engine as the fabulous Valiants. This car had a long, ungainly blue body and was sold to me for $100 by my surfer friend Brian Lieberman. My first trip in the Dart was—naturally—to Queen's Surf. But when I took my regulation straw mat from the back seat of the car and unrolled it on the beach, a startled gecko and three cockroaches raced out of the folds. Panicking when they hit the hot sand, they ran round and round in pathetic, frenzied little circles. I managed to scoop the mat under them and release them over on the grass next to the big luau pit under the banyan tree, where I hope they prospered. It seemed Brian and his friends had used the back seat of the Dart as a garbage can, and although he had scrupulously cleaned it out before selling the car to me, some traces of wildlife still remained. (Years later I remembered these poor creatures when, as I drove over the Golden Gate Bridge in yet another blue '64 Dart, several land snails bravely adhering to the hood were blown off by gale-force winds and sailed straight over the railing like little suicides.)

These old Hawaii cars of mine were the occasion of many pleasantly hassle-free—as we liked to say then—encounters. One time, after my own jolting back-up collision with someone in the Manoa Safeway parking lot, the other driver and I, circling the damage, gradually became aware that we owned analogous vehicles. When I allowed that I seemed to have slightly scraped the side of his '63 Rambler, my young haole counterpart gallantly responded, "Well, it's got plenty of other dings!" After a pause he added, "Your fender looks like it's gouged." This was my cue to say "This car *came* gouged!" and I did. Whereupon we shook hands on the spot, wished each other a nice day, jumped in our scraped and gouged vehicles and took off.

Valiant

My ultimate Hawaii car, sold to me by handyman extraordinaire Mel Darneal, was the envy of all the old guys at the gas station: a '64 Valiant station wagon with a red interior, a tape deck installed by Mel that he had bought at the Kam Drive-In Swap Meet, and an electric back window *that still worked.* Because of the chrome ridge that ran down the center of the hood, I wasn't able to transfer my favorite hood ornament, installed by Mel on my previous cars—a fabulous chrome flying goddess with green plastic wings that lit up with the headlights, mail-ordered from the J. C. Whitney catalog, $7.95—but never mind, I now owned the Mercedes of Hawaiian junk cars.

When I left the Islands I gave up my treasured white Valiant because, like most cars exported directly to Hawaii, it didn't have a heater. I sold it to Joe Kennedy, who turned it into his Archaeological Associates staff car, complete with impressive logo. Unwisely Joe had a new engine installed that was too powerful for the noble Valiant, and when he started it up the car shook and trembled like an octogenarian with a heart transplant from an Olympic athlete. The Valiant finally got so shaky it was exiled to driving up and down Crozier Drive on the North Shore. I was fearing the worst when unexpected good news came from Joe: my car had been purchased by none other than Buzzy Trent, *the* Buzzy Trent, that legendary fifties surfer from Santa Monica who rode the forty-foot North Shore storm waves. Now, he says, Buzzy Trent lives on Pamoa Road under the same little rise, and he probably finds it very handy storing his surfboards in the back of the Valiant—I'm sure the electric window still works—and he is the best last owner I could ever want for my faithful car, peace to all.

The following incident from Herb Caen's San Francisco *Chronicle* column produced a nostalgic quiver in my soul when I came across it in my later California years:

On Sept. 20 Jim King's '68 Plymouth Valiant—so austere it doesn't even have a radio—was stolen. The police recovered it 10 days later. As he was driving home, with the sun in his eyes, he pulled down the visor to find this typed message taped to the inside: "Dear suckhead: Meatball and I would like to express our gratitude for the use of your car on our

81

vacation in Disneyland. Thanks for keeping it in top condition. All we had had to do was add one qt. of oil the whole 800-mile trip. We were very annoyed that there was no music but the gas mileage made up for the inconvenience. (Signed) The Happy Transvestites."

Somebody besides the old Japanese guys, I was glad to see, knew what was good.

Driving up Kapahulu in the very first of the old cars, the '62 Buick Special, I learned an important lesson in Local on-the-road etiquette, to wit: in a world where power and status are measured by physical as opposed to psychological or economic intimidation, make no moves you aren't prepared to back up completely.

I had stopped under the freeway to let some children pass on the crosswalk when suddenly, of its own accord, my car began violently rocking up and down. I turned around to find looming behind me a flatbed truck so enormous I couldn't even see into the driver's cab. The bed was loaded to the brim with coco palm trimmings. As an expression of impatience this truck was, unbelievably, *humping* the rear end of my car. Without thinking, I stuck my left hand out the window and "flipped the bird."

This carefree gesture, acquired in the rarefied world of Berkeley sixties student life, transformed the vehicle behind me from a simple nuisance into an engine of destruction very much like the vengeful truck in the Spielberg movie *Duel*. Zooming ahead in the next lane, it crossed a grass divider to get in front of me on the freeway entrance, and together—for it had cut its speed drastically to keep me blocked behind—we inched out into the blur of traffic. At this point the truck and its invisible driver confounded me by stopping dead in the middle of the freeway. The Buick wasn't great on acceleration—that's why I always used this freeway entrance, slightly longer than some of the others, to get enough momentum going—and I knew I couldn't pull around the truck fast enough to get away. So I sat and waited.

Suddenly the truck began moving again, but this time instead of going forward it was reversing. Full speed, straight into me. Slam! The jolt was hard enough to rattle my fillings. The truck pulled a few ceremonious feet forward and reversed again: Pow!

This time the impact buckled the hood. The truck started up again and drove off down the turnpike in a dignified and unhurried manner.

With shaking hands I managed to write down the license plate number and then drive home, where I called the police. Officer Watanabe, who came to my door to question me, heard my story without comment—I had to tell him I had given them the finger, which embarrassed me and made me aware for the first time that all the habits I so eagerly picked up in college perhaps ran counter to my own inner biases—and then dialed the DMV for the truck's registration. He repeated the name—ethnic origin concealed here to avoid stereotyping—but did not write it down, I noticed. He turned to me. "Those ----s, they got a quick temper, yeah?" he said. "You got to be careful with them." He put his notebook away. "I go see these guys Monday, I talk to them." Sure, Officer Watanabe.

It was not until after he left that I realized the full measure of my good fortune. Because I was female, I had received a relative tap on the wrist—or hood—from the driver of the mysterious coco palm truck. If I'd been a man I'd have been beaten to a pulp. So what if my car had a bent hood now? God knew the Buick had other problems. The main point was, I'd survived a serious error in real-life judgment. Beyond my dreamy underwater existence was a real world out there waiting to be come to terms with. Once in a while, as a displaced character wandering through this exotic movie set—*The Road to Papeete,* starring Dorothy Lamour?—I made a wrong turn and suddenly came out on the makeshift plywood backing, the stinking trash cans, the asphalt parking lot. But I wasn't ready to stride out yet, no, let's get back inside the set, back underwater—a little more time, please, I only just got here, it hasn't been long enough yet.

TO THE
BERNICE P. BISHOP
MUSEUM

14

My Reading List

In Hawaii the Book of Nature flourishes. The other, manmade ones succumb to powerful predators. Silverfish eat the paper, cockroaches go for the traces of human sweat on the covers. Hardbacks warp and mildew, paperbacks fall to dust.

With eyes at first only for the Book of Nature (and its student manual, the Book of Acid), in time I turned back to those real books whose covers were sprouting paisley designs just as the cuffs of my Mainland suede jacket developed cowboy fringes. At home, on the beach, I was reading, reading. The books drew me from my own adventures in the world before my eyes into its complicated past. Under my wonder and delight pressing questions had begun to form: What came before Local? How did all these people get here, and what had it been like then? I was off on a new Pacific voyage.

It was a slow start, lolling on the beach with gaudy nickel paperbacks from the Nuuanu Goodwill. The yellowed pages gave off a musty smell that mingled with the familiar Queen's Surf odors of salt water and suntan lotion. The cheap glue bindings disintegrated, sending printed leaves tumbling down the beach until the surf snatched them out of the air and sucked them under.

The books that managed to stay in my hands furnished me with some interesting Island sociological history. There was *The Re-*

volt of Mamie Stover, by William Bradford Huie, a forgotten classic in which is recounted, among other interesting facts, the ingenious "towel count" devised by the Internal Revenue Service to calculate the takings of Honolulu brothels during World War II. In the same vein, *Honolulu Madame,* by "Iolana Mitsuko"; lots of good ethnic angles here. Old copies of *Pacific Islands Monthly,* a bizarre mixture of political reportage, yachting information, and riveting backdoor gossip from the various island groups of Oceania. Nordhoff and Hall's *Mutiny on the Bounty,* the *Iliad* of popular Pacific literature. And, of course, James Michener's *Hawaii,* full of wit, energy, and information.

My first serious reading came from the Goodwill, too, in the form of the paperback collections of Hawaiian and South Seas literature expertly assembled by A. Grove Day of the University of Hawaii, who with his colleague Carl Stroven was able to present a fascinating range of literature about Polynesia in its historical context: *A Hawaiian Reader, Best South Seas Stories, The Spell of the Pacific,* and many more. I went on to Day's more scholarly collections published by the University of Hawaii Press: *Mark Twain's Letters from Hawaii; South Seas Supercargo,* a collection of stories by the great forgotten Australian writer, Louis Becke; and others. Forty years of effort by this scholar saved English-language literature of the Pacific from the oblivion of library stacks and rare book rooms and made it available with no compromise in taste and accuracy to the general public. I also discovered the Hawaiian historical novels of O. A. Bushnell, which enterprising Mainland paperback publishers often reprinted, like Day's anthologies, with lurid "South Seas" covers (*The Return of Lono,* his novel about Captain Cook, became *Peril in Paradise* in its mass-market manifestation).

My reading quickly sorted itself out into a rough chronological sequence. Though the Hawaiian Islands have lived and died a hundred incarnations, in the end there are only three major human time periods:

The Very Old Days	eighteenth century and earlier: the thousand-odd years before European contact, the "prehistory" of the indigenous Polynesians *cum* Hawaiians

The Old Days nineteenth century: the Hawaiian kingdom and its ragtime interlopers, whalers, missionaries, Chinese fieldhands, the flowering of a unique cultural amalgam of old Hawaiian with European/American, along with the tragic decline, through disease and Western encroachment, of native Hawaiian leadership

Now, or Modern Hawaii twentieth century, even though here there are innumerable subdivisions. Early Now starts with "Annexation" (1893), when Hawaii was commandeered by business interests to become a colony of the United States, through World War II; Late Now extends from Statehood (1959) through Californiazation (1969–present)

I had a map now for my new journey into Polynesia, and dominant, distinctive voices from each of these three eras—the very old days, the old days, and "now"—as my guides. The voices of the very old days were Polynesian. The voices of the old days were those of visiting Westerners, explorers and literati. The voices of the late twentieth century, as Subjects and Objects reversed roles once again, would be Local.

The reality of the Hawaiian prehistoric was so utterly opposed to the period that followed on its heels in a few decades of cultural convulsion after Captain James Cook's visit in 1778 that it was hard to believe any connections at all could exist between two worlds. Yet there was continuity, rich continuity, once the eyes were trained to find it. As I grew more and more obsessed with identifying these threads, tracing them through to the present, I moved on, hit or miss, to the primary sources. My path led me from Queen's Surf and the Nuuanu Goodwill first to the university library and then, inevitably, to the Bishop Museum.

15

The Ground Floor: Fishhooked

On the rainy winter day the bus brought me to the corner of Kalihi Street and the Likelike Highway, a tiny old Paké woman struggling on managed to stick her umbrella up my skirt as I was climbing off. To a chorus of high-pitched Local giggles from my fellow riders, grown men and women all, I dismounted to my first glimpse of the Bernice Pauahi Bishop Museum.

Here was the big gate perversely opening to the rear of the main building. A rare specimen of stone Victoriana in Hawaii (its nickname, "Dark Shadows," I was to hear later from the archaeology students), the former estate of the Hawaiian princess Bernice Pauahi, once the site of the Kamehameha Schools, had been converted to a memorial museum in 1889 by the princess's haole husband, Charles Reed Bishop. During my first days in the Islands the museum was famous to me solely for the reason that Kanaina had excitedly spotted a pipe in the Chinese section with lumps of petrified opium clearly visible. Now I was ready to take a look at the other artifacts.

In the main hall I found my three periods of Hawaiian chronology materialized like a kind of Renaissance memory palace. The ground floor held prehistoric displays grouped around a traditional Hawaiian grass hut in the open court; two tiers of balconies were devoted to the nineteenth and twentieth centuries, respectively. Over this entire allegorical "lifehouse" of Hawaiian history hung an enormous facsimile cutaway blue whale looking heavy enough to drop on our heads any minute, thereby striking the right note of Melvillean menace. This, at any rate, was the neat image my imagination preserved. When I returned years later, the layout in no way matched my memory palace: there were iron nails on the ground floor, wooden gods on the third balcony. Is the act of remembering only another act of creation, or had they just swapped everything around?

"Prehistoric" with its echoes of Ice Age hunter-gatherers rings oddly as a description of eighteenth-century Hawaii. The term, however, accurately describes a culture in which records are not kept in writing and the past is conceptualized in mythic and symbolic, not factual, sequence. In the case of the pre-Contact Hawaiian Islands it meant a rigid, hierarchical society of chiefs and commoners with a staggering list of proscribed or *kapu* behaviors. (*Kapu* is missionary orthography for the same word that was written down as *tapu* in Tahiti and that we know as "taboo.") Contrary to local color stereotype, there was nothing you would call *relaxed* about this culture, but some of its abundances are indicated in the following comment from a history of the famous Chiefs' School at Lahainaluna written by a nineteenth-century Hawaiian: "The chiefs had many honored attendants, many intimate friends, many foster children, many lovers, many stewards, many guardians of the gods, many favorites, many women, many warriors ready on call." (They also indulged, according to this account, in a great deal of the "game called thigh on thigh.")

In the Bishop Museum the very old days were represented by such items as the outrigger canoe or *wa'a;* gods; volcanic basalt adzes; *ulumaika,* or bowling stones; wooden refuse bowls tastefully inlaid with the teeth of enemies; and fishhooks, fishhooks, fishhooks.

You had the gods, of course. The principal players were Ku and Hina, the male and female ancestral fertility deities, followed by three other major gods (Lono, Kane, and Kanaloa), goddesses such as the well-known Pele of the volcanoes and Laka, goddess of the forest and patroness of the hula, plus a host of godlets and ancestor spirits. A few tattered survivors of this impressive pantheon were riding out eternity in the Bishop Museum cases: Kalaipahoa, the poison god. A wicker god. A snarling feather god with shark teeth and mother-of-pearl eyes. Scariest of all, the anonymous wooden idol that looked like a can opener. These battered objects of worship, carrying only the vaguest echo of their former powers, reminded me that the two Polynesian words to gain widespread currency in English and other Western languages were *mana* and *taboo*—divine sanctity and the prohibitions safeguarding that sanctity, respectively.

Mainly, the ground floor of the Bishop Museum was about fishhooks. The real buried treasure of Hawaii was not gold doubloons but just these mundane objects. From delicate miniatures to huge whalebone meathooks, prehistoric Hawaiian fishhooks came in all sizes. They could be carved from shell or bone, the latter most commonly pig or dog but in rare ceremonial fishhooks, human—made from your defeated battle foe's leg bone and thereby possessing his mana. They could be carved in one piece and knobbed or notched at the point, or carved in two pieces and knobbed or notched at the join.

If you were dreaming of the pharaoh's sarcophagus, it took a while to get excited about a mere "tool," but eventually I did. Fishhook as *idea* permeated the Polynesian mind; it was a conceptual tool as well as a concrete one. A Hawaiian variant of the famous story of Polynesian mythology relates how Maui, the Polynesian trickster god, pulled all the islands together by catching a great fish with his fishhook *Manai-ka-lani* ("Come here from the heavens")—but the islands separated again when Maui stopped paying attention and the great fish escaped. Fishhooks at the mythic level have a *kaona*, or hidden meaning: they are spurs and goads in the long slow process of the development of human consciousness so beautifully chronicled in the *Kumulipo*. The myth showed that for the ancient Hawaiians (as later for me), consciousness was constantly in danger of slipping back into the sea again.

The ground floor was also about Polynesian migration. After running across the same broad-boned faces, the big bodies, virtually the identical language and customs all over the Pacific, Captain James Cook was moved to ask, with a certain amount of exasperation, "How shall we account for this Nation spreading it self so far over this Vast ocean?" Linguistics and archaeology tell us the Polynesians, like the other inhabitants of the Pacific, came originally from Southeast Asia. Over a fifteen-hundred-year period the outrigger people spread from Malaysia, Indonesia, and the Philippines into the islands of Western Polynesia—notably Tonga and Samoa. Around the time of the birth of Christ the navigators pushed on to settle Eastern Polynesia—the Marquesas, Tahiti and Easter Island, then Hawaii, New Zealand last. Their root Malayo-Polynesian language flowered into all the Polynesian languages as Latin did into French, Spanish, Italian.

But the idea of origins is a powerful one that tends to wrench thinking instantly into the mythic mode. No amount of rationality seems to quench these mythmaking desires, especially among scientists. As handed down by the Polynesian migrants themselves, the official mythic version of where they came from (an Avalon-style island called Hawaiki) is no more self-serving than the romantic hypotheses concocted by turn-of-the-century Western anthropologists, who, in projective Object identification love with the Polynesians, wanted very much to make them "white": hence a burst of theories they were the lost tribe of Israel, of "Nordic" descent, and the like. (In my time even the hippies spun their own post-Christian Aquarian myths of Hawaiians as descendants of the lost continent of Mu.)

Europeans fell hard for the Polynesians, all right, wanted to be hooked up with them in a way that did no violence to their own inner conviction of racial superiority. But why Polynesians and not Melanesians or Micronesians? For a not-so-subtle reason of racial bigotry, I suspect: like the latter two groups a genetic mixture of Asian, white, and black, the big, powerfully built Polynesians were not as dark-skinned as their closest relations the Melanesians or as short and Asian-looking as the Micronesians. Even Cook commented that the "negroid" Melanesians were "less attractive" than the Polynesians, some of whom were quite fair-skinned. And the following nugget of wisdom offered by Charles Bernard Nordhoff in *Faery Lands of the South Seas* (1921) sums up the popular and scholarly Western biases of more than a century:

The better sort of white man is ready to admit that God, who presumably made him, also made the native, and made of the Polynesian a rather fine piece of work. . . . Even today it needs no effort of the imagination to see two distinct types among the island people: men and women of the kind one considers typically Polynesian—tall, clean limbed, and light brown, with clear, dark eyes, straight or waving hair, and heads not differing greatly from the heads of Europeans; and another kind, of a negroid or Melanesian cast—short, squat, and many shades darker in complexion, thick-lipped and apish, with muddy eyes, kinky hair, and flattened, undeveloped heads. And, strangely enough, after more than a century of missions and leveling foreign influence, the dark and awkward people seem still to fill the humbler walks of life.

The irony is, though, that by fifty years after Cook the island populations of the Pacific, literally decimated by disease, had already begun wholesale intermarrying with newcomers. They looked more and more like "us" for the simple reason that this, in part, was what they had forever become, genetically as well as culturally: part European.

But the secret of Polynesian origins also shines through a small visual detail of material culture, namely, the lei. This single charming artifact is not specific to Hawaii or Polynesia but is found all over Asia, Southeast Asia, and the Indian subcontinent. Almost a third of the world, in fact, is united by a ceremonial garland of flowers worn around the neck, on the head, and on wrists and ankles. These flower necklaces were not much found in the traditional West, with the important exception of that ancient Greek head lei, the laurel wreath.

In Hawaii and the other Polynesian societies of the very old days, the concept was adapted to the material at hand on these Pacific islands: bone, feather, nut, vine, seed, fern, a few modest native blooms like *ilima, mamo,* and the Hawaiian ginger known as *awapuhi.* The modern flower lei came, paradoxically, with the arrival of the foreigners and their plants from all the continents of the world: crownflower; tuberose; jasmine, or *pikake;* plumeria; carnation; vanda orchid; bougainvillea; and the vine roses

94

beloved of Hawaiians, lokelani and roselani. One book I consulted listed more than one thousand distinct types of Hawaiian leis.

A ground-floor case held the Hawaiians' most prized object of personal adornment—the lei called *niho palaoa,* a stylized whalebone fishhook pendant suspended in a heavy swatch of human hair. Strange to consider, this fierce, oppressive artifact worn only by the highest chiefs was not just grandfather but cousin and brother to the fragrant garland of *pikake* hung around my neck, with a kiss, on my birthday—long-forgotten hook to the continent of Asia, a necklace around the Pacific.

The *Kumulipo*

> Very dark is the ocean and obscure
> A sea of coral like the green heights of Paliuli
> The land disappears into them
> Covered by the darkness of night
>   Still it is night

A spiritual principle united the ragtag collection of remains on the ground floor. This principle was preserved and expressed in the greatest *mele,* or epic song, of them all, that masterpiece of ancient Hawaiian literature, the *Kumulipo.* A poetic work of some 2,102 lines, this genealogical creation chant pictures the natural world, and the spiritual realm behind it, as an extension of the family.

The word *kumulipo* means literally "dark source," with a subtle image of darkness, or *lipo,* as, in the words of its translator, the distinguished scholar Martha Beckwith, "dark from the depth of a cavern, or from the depth of the sea." It implies a space concept and at the same time one of degree of shade as applied, for example, to the change in color of the ocean as one gets away from the shore into deep water.

The origins of the world, according to the *Kumulipo,* lie in primordial night, which is also in some way underwater. This fertile darkness generates its opposite, life, and the watery night gives birth to all manner of creatures. The land is born out of the ocean, and the first living organism to emerge from this mating is the coral polyp.

In this Polynesian Genesis, I discovered, every living thing on land is the guardian of its counterpart under the sea, and creation proceeds as a gradual but inexorable movement from darkness to light, underwater to air, night to day, as the sea-land pairs unfold:

Born was the 'A'ala moss living in the sea
Guarded by the 'Ala'ala mint living on land
Man for the narrow stream, woman for the broad stream
Born was the Manauea moss living in the sea
Guarded by the Manauea taro plant living on land
Man for the narrow stream, woman for the broad stream

The *Kumulipo* offers a fascinating Linnaean categorization of the natural order by linking the pairs of animals and plants above and below by the similarity of their names. In the beginning was the Word: in the very old days, language was the *a priori* ordering principle of the universe. As the linguist and Hawaiian scholar Samuel Elbert has pointed out, the early Hawaiians "like the Stoic Greeks . . . thought their names were universals with inherent nonarbitrary meanings. The meanings had power and explained the universe." A chant like the *Kumulipo* imposes the structure of language on the known world and thereby establishes the connections between living things.

This *Kumulipo* universe is dynamic, not static. Beneath all the pairs of contrasts runs the primary duality of dark and light, *po* and *ao*. For an interminable period, though, there is a barrier, an obstruction to further development—"the god enters, man can not enter"—and we are stuck in *ao*, the primordial night of underwater, a mirror-reflection of the world of air. "Still it is night," the chant repeats endlessly. But at last, slowly, we move out of the darkness and the inevitable and satisfying resolution emerges.

Naked was man born in the day
Naked the woman born in the upland
She lived here with man

Born was Creeping-ti-plant to man
Born was Expected-day, a female
Born was Midnight, born First-light
Opening-wide was their youngest
These were those who gave birth
The little ones, the older ones
Ever increasing in number
Man spread abroad, man was here now
   It was Day . . .

The *Kumulipo* presents humans, daylight, and air as emerging simultaneously in the natural world, a metaphor suggesting the quality that distinguishes us from other living creatures, namely, consciousness.

The self-referential unity of this old Hawaiian universe, however, was about to change drastically—had already changed, in fact, before the version of the chant that has come down to us was made. Not only is the *Kumulipo* simply what it is—a magnificent specimen of sacred poetry and natural science rolled into one—but it acts, by a traditional attribution, as a symbolic bridge between prehistory and Contact, between the ground floor and the second floor of the Bishop Museum. Queen Liliuokalani, the last Hawaiian monarch and a notable composer and scholar in her own right, identified the *Kumulipo* as the chant recited at the Hikiau *heiau,* or temple, at Kealakekua Bay, Hawaii, as Captain James Cook was greeted by the priests as the god Lono in 1779. Whether or not it is historically "true," this possibility still creates a conjunction of eminences something like having a tradition that *Beowulf* was recited to William the Conqueror the first week he set up housekeeping in the British Isles. And the final lines of the *Kumulipo*—

Ended is the line of the first chief of the dim past
   dwelling in cold uplands
Dead is the current sweeping in from the navel of the
   earth: that was a warrior wave
Many who came vanquished, lost in the passing night

—hold the small dark prophecy of the complicated fate that was to be set in motion by this meeting.

16

Captain Cook by Hook or Crook

Climbing the stairs to the second floor meant passing symbolically through the invisible barrier of Contact and the ghost of
Captain James Cook. I feel I have spent most of my adult life no
more than a stone's throw away from one of Captain Cook's
landings. In a curious way he stands as the inventor of my Pacific,
sets the boundaries of the world my imagination inhabits. In his
three Pacific voyages undertaken in the years between 1768 and
1779, Cook never ventured as far south on the North American
coast as California (though Sir Francis Drake did before him), but
there are very few other places in the Pacific Basin he didn't get
to. From the Great Barrier Reef to New Zealand to Hawaii,
Tahiti, even Antarctica, his mark is everywhere; his journals the
understated (hence doubly exciting) record of the "first look."

The newcomer to the Pacific quickly gets caught up in the
mass voyeurism around Contact, that irrecoverable point in time
when European first encountered societies of humans, plants,
and animals evolved some thousands of years in isolation. The
museum itself had sponsored a memorable exhibit of "artificial
curiosities," Pacific artifacts collected by Cook and his crew that
represented the final point of their pre-European history. For
from the instant a Pacific Islander first touched cloth made of
cotton, breathed air carrying influenza germs, opened a book,

drank water carrying mosquito eggs, everything changed. Nothing would be the same again. None of the hundreds of thousands of European and Americans who followed his path to the Pacific would have the kind of encounter Cook and his men did. And this fact has titillated us ever since.

Who, for instance, would not have wanted to be the one to pen the first Western sighting, in Australia, of this strange, nameless animal (from Cook's journal of his first voyage, July 14, 1770):

> The head neck and shoulders . . . was very small in proportion to the other parts; the tail was nearly as long as the body, thick next the rump and tapering towards the end; the fore legs were 8 Inch long and the hind 22, its progression is by hop[p]ing or jumping 7 or 8 feet at each hop upon its hind legs only, for in this it makes no use of the fore, which seem to be only design'd for scratching in the ground&c. The skin is cover'd with a short hairy fur of a dark Mouse or Grey Colour. Excepting the head and ears which I thought was something like a Hare's, it bears no sort of resemblance to any European Animal I ever saw; it is said to bear much resemblance to the Gerbua excepting in size, the Gerbua being no larger than a common rat.

Newness and unfamiliarity trick the eye of the observer as we instinctively try to twist the object back within the framework of the known and described. The objects of our perception alter, their forms harden and conventionalize, in direct proportion to the numbers of successive pairs of eyes gazing on them.

Nor were very many after Cook privileged to see their own amazement mirrored in the faces of the human inhabitants of these new islands. Of the Hawaiians, Cook remarked: "I Never saw Indians so much astonished at the entering a ship before, their eyes were continually flying from object to object, the wildness of thier [sic] looks and actions fully express'd their surprise and astonishment at the several new objects before them"— which they tried to "grasp" in that charmingly literal way which was all too soon to prove Cook's undoing.

Eagerness, an intense and hungry intellectual curiosity—especially in Hawaii, doubly vulnerable because only a few years before Contact the islands had been united under one ruler for the first time and a complicated religious structure had been overthrown—these traits were characteristic of the touching, tragic openness of Polynesians, so unlike the clannish, bellicose attitudes of the more grudgingly impressed "natives" of other regions visited, then overwhelmed, by Westerners. Reading Cook's account of the *Endeavour*'s reception, I share in the delight, wonder, and fear the Hawaiians' overwhelming hospitality provoked in his Anglo-Saxon heart: *"all imaginable marks of friendship and submission"* (italics his). Two hundred years later I was to know the same feeling on Molokai.

By the time Cook returned to the island of Hawaii—appropriately enough at Kealakekua Bay, or "pathway of the gods"—the Hawaiians had formed the idea that he was none other than their god Lono. Cook did nothing to disabuse them of this belief, allowing himself to be presented to the images on the *heiau* platform in a great ceremony (during which two of the priests chanted "a kind of hymn," the song Liliuokalani believed was the *Kumulipo*).

A great scholarly controversy has always raged around this point, missionary commentators especially attacking Cook's ethics in accepting the mantle of godhood. Certainly his deification made it easier for him to manipulate the Hawaiians and also, whatever the supremely pragmatic captain's private feelings on the matter may have been, fit the average Westerner's inflated self-image all too well. By the eighteenth century *Homo europeansis* might have been ready to abandon his position at the dead center of the universe, but not at the top of the ladder of Creation—no, not by a long shot.

The sad, gory details of Cook's death: stabbed in a confused fracas arising from the theft of a boat, reflecting Hawaiian resentment about having to feed the "gods" from their overtaxed food supplies and from their justified growing doubts about the Westerners' immortality after watching the latter's shrunken bellies swell on their own desperately needed provisions. Several days after Cook's murder a Hawaiian paddled out to the *Endeavour* to inform one of his hastily appointed successors, Captain James King, that he "had something for me belonging to Captain Cook," whereupon the man passed over "a small bundle wrapped up in cloth." Unwrapping the package, King was horrified to discover

> a piece of human flesh, about nine or ten pounds weight. This, he said, was all that remained of the body; that the rest was cut to pieces, and burnt; but that the head and all the bones, except what belonged to the trunks, were in the possession of Terreeoboo, and the other *Erees* [*aliis*, or noblemen]; that what we saw had been allotted to Kaoo, the chief of the priests, to be made use of in some religious ceremony; and that he had sent it as a proof of his innocence and attachment to us.

Two days later "a Chief called Eappo" told the Englishmen that

> the flesh of all the bodies of our people, together with the bones of the trunks, had been burnt; that the limb bones of the marines had been divided among the inferior chiefs; and that those of Captain Cook had been disposed of in the following manner: the head to a great Chief, called Kahoo-opeon; the hair to Maihamaiha; and the legs, thighs, and arms to Terreeoboo.

Highest honors, in short: dismemberment, deboning, and partial burning, which was customary procedure for the disposal not of gods but of worthy enemies in battle (the long bones of a rival chief, being full of *mana*, or spiritual power, were especially prized as fishhooks). But we do well to remember that sacrifice and death are part of a god's job description the world over. Cook and his men, adherents of a genteel Protestantism, found themselves in a place where the human relationship to the spiritual world was perceived as concrete and immediate. Selective ritual cannibalism was part of Hawaiian and other Polynesian religious rites. Eating the blood and body of the god? All very well as metaphor, even as the Papist rite of consuming (so much more euphonious than "eating") wine and wafer. On the literal level, a bit much.

As nearly as can be determined, no portion of Captain Cook was actually eaten. I find my own view of the unfortunate event, however, coinciding to some extent with that of the missionaries, namely: If Christ died for man's sins, then Cook died for Western European hubris. And if, as seems likely, the great Pacific navigator was recycled in part as a shark hook, in the larger scheme of things such a cultural exchange—considering the devastation European contact was about to wreck on the Islands—can only be regarded as a fair one.

It has become a late twentieth-century convention to sentimentalize the superior goodness and wisdom of the lost cultures of the Pacific, the Americas, and Africa in the face of their cynical exploitation by the West. This idealizing represents the guilty backlash of self-criticism by the more sophisticated segments of Western nations against their (at best) condescension toward and (at worst and far more frequent) indescribably vile treatment of "native" races the world round. But it must be admitted that the Polynesians showed themselves just as ready to equate higher technology with moral and spiritual superiority as their canny visitors were. Cook gave nails to the Hawaiians. No sane human being is going to deny that an iron nail is a powerful shortcut in establishing control over the natural environment. Nor will that person deprive himself of the immense savings in time and labor such a tool provides.

But it is impossible to "borrow" an artifact from a technologically specialized culture without setting off a virtually endless chain of consequences. The nail itself was to prove a kind of *mana*-filled Western fishhook that dragged along with it a whole world, not just hammer and boards but cotton dresses, influenza, newspapers, railroads, and another sacrificed god, Jesus Christ.

102

17

Second Floor:
Queequeg's Hook

The first balcony of the Bishop Museum was given over to nineteenth-century Hawaii and Polynesia, but the whole cavernous exhibition hall with its dark koa wood cases and *ki'i* god figures instead of saints hovering high in the cornices embodied the spirit of the "old days," a weird mixture of Victorian Gothic and traditional Hawaiian—the post-Contact Hawaii of missionaries, sailors, and adventurers, the imported cattle and horses along with cowboy *paniolos,* dashing *pa'u* riders. Here was the distinctive Hawaiian *holoku* that was to serve as combination dress, bathing costume, and shroud. Hawaiian women were made to wear these modified New England nightgowns for all situations, including swimming, in which they had previously gone naked. Catching chills in the wet heavy garments, they picked up the flu and died in amazing numbers.

A single display case held the split personality of those times: huge crude koa wood poi bowls side by side with Queen Kapiolani's china fish plates. If the modern mind reels from the contrast, what must it have been like for the nineteenth-century Hawaiian *ali'i* or aristocrat, shuttled back and forth between the universe embodied in these two sets of utensils?

Looking at the relics of the old days, a great wave of hope quickly followed by hopelessness washed over me: the population, reduced by the usual diseases—flu, measles, chicken pox— from 300,000 at Cook's contact to an unbelievable 50,000 after ten years of visits from European sailing vessels, bravely embraced the new culture—what else could they do?—and in the next decades managed to produce the distinctive amalgam that was nineteenth-century Hawaii. One watches the historical events unfold with a small portion of delight and a much larger portion of despair engendered by hindsight. Hawaii, the land and the people, latches onto things so quickly, intensely. In the old days they got as excited about books as they were later to get about cockfights; reading and writing were a bona fide *passion* for nineteenth-century Hawaiians. "No place where *public* education so widely diffused," Mark Twain had remarked in his private notebook. "Children of ten—all read and write." In 1889 Robert Louis Stevenson observed how little attention his arrival caused on Kona because the inhabitants were forever occupied reading their mail, the Hawaiian-language newspapers, and whatever else came to hand:

> One hundred and ten years before the ancestors of these indifferents had looked in the faces of Cook and his seamen with admiration and alarm; called them gods, called them volcanoes; took their clothes for a loose skin, confounded their hats and their heads, and described their pockets as a "treasure door, through which they plunge their hands into their bodies and bring forth cutlery and necklaces and cloth and nails"; and today the coming of the most attractive stranger failed (it would appear) to divert them from Miss Porter's *Scottish Chiefs,* for that was the novel of the day—*Na 'Lii O Sekotia*—so ran the title in Hawaii.

The demand to read and write grew so rapidly, and the instructional materials were in such short supply, that missionary teachers often had only one Bible for a class of twenty. Old pictures show groups of adults crowded around the Holy Book, with those on the opposite side of the teacher learning to read just as fluently upside down as the ones looking over his shoulder.

During the country's American acculturation, literacy and education in Hawaii declined drastically; far from enhancing such benefits, the U.S. colonization stamped out a lively, creative, aggressive *hapa*-Hawaiian society that was busily producing its own fusion of Polynesian and Western cultures. For a split second of historical time they had just enough of the new to excite their intellects and imagination, producing a much-altered but still Hawaiian-dominated culture—then *too much*, plus too much death among the leadership as well as the population as a whole, tipped them over the edge, both in acculturation and in socioeconomic power, into an interminable twilight of impotent and decorative minorityhood. (Of course Hawaii should have stayed autonomous, should have been a kingdom today, like Tonga, but it has always been too accessible; like all things possessing great beauty it remains forever too much a target of powerful outside greed to have held onto this privileged status.)

The second-floor exhibit cases, full of crowns, shiny medals, and fur-trimmed cloaks, reflected the introduction of a whole bogus European concept of "royalty" that reached a baroque and decadent fever pitch under the reign of the "Merry Monarch," David Kalakaua, who struck medals in direct proportion to his insecurity about his own rights to the throne. Underneath the pathetic trappings a great destruction was taking place: a century-long tragedy, all those truncated lives and dashed hopes, as painful to look at as a battlefield full of dead bodies, and just as impossible to do anything about. The whole vibrant culture, a brand-new life for the language, the hope for what Hawaiians could do with it and their autonomous island kingdom were gradually suffocated by the appalling mortality rate and the increasing economic and cultural cooption by waves of incoming haoles. The young king Liholiho (Kamehameha II) and his queen, Kamamalu, grotesquely dying of measles on their state visit to England—hope stamped out at every turn, with heartbreaking regularity, by early death, early death, early death. Eventually the American planters led by the pineapple magnate Sanford Dole made their move and ousted the last Hawaiian monarch, Liliuokalani. By the end of the century Hawaii was a colony of the United States.

Besides O. A. Bushnell's poignant novel of the Hawaiian monarchy, *Ka'a'awa,* my own two emblematic Western texts on the discovery, destruction, and reincarnation of old Polynesia were

Herman Melville's *Typee* and *Moby-Dick*, respectively. Of all the accounts, true and fabricated, of the white man–native encounter, both these works had a special meaning for me. In the relationship of Ishmael and Queequeg, I sensed, Melville had managed to solve, within himself, the Western side of the Pacific Subject-Object problem. By granting a Polynesian full and unconditional humanity, Melville had promoted himself to the same status, became fully human in a way no self-consciously superior or inferior Subject, in the face of his Object, can ever be.

The first Westerners the Hawaiians saw were English sailors. Within an eyebat of this meeting, and notwithstanding getting off on the wrong foot with Captain Cook, they and the other adaptable, intellectually curious, seafaring Polynesians were popping up as crew—first involuntarily, through the notorious practice of "blackbirding" or kidnapping, then of their own accord—on European sailing ships all over the Pacific in the early 1800s. Meanwhile the sailors were busy making their own more drastic incursions into the islands of the Pacific.

So: *Typee: A Peep at Polynesian Life* (1846), Melville's early sketch of life in the Marquesas Islands as told by an American sailor. The old Hawaiians, Marquesans, and Tahitians were closely related genetically, linguistically, and culturally—in a word, they were kissing cousins. Converting Melville's weird renditions of Marquesan into Hawaiian is a compulsive habit I've never been able to break: *poee-poee* is *poi,* of course, except that in the Marquesas the starchy paste is made from the more plentiful breadfruit instead of from taro root. *Awa,* their exclamation of sadness, is Hawaiian *auwe; ki-ki,* eat, is Hawaiian *kai,* or, as food, *kau.* Typee itself, the valley and the people, would be Taipi or Kaipi.* Kory-Kory, the narrator's rescuer, could easily be Kole

*Before his own pilgrimage to the Marquesas in 1905 Jack London recorded in *The Cruise of the Snark* a similar obsession: " 'Taipi' the chart spelled it, and spelled it correctly, but I prefer 'Typee,' and I shall always spell it 'Typee.' When I was a little boy, I read a book spelled in that manner— Herman Melville's 'Typee'; and many long hours I dreamed over its pages . . . I resolved there and then, mightily, come what would, that when I had gained strength and years, I, too, would voyage to Typee."

But concerning Melville's "grotesque misspellings" of Marquesan words, the earlier (1888) visitor Robert Louis Stevenson was less sanguine: "At his christening . . . some influential fairy must have been neglected: 'He shall

Kole, like the Oahu mountain pass the Japanese flew over on their way to bomb Pearl Harbor.

Typee is told as a true story. Casting himself as Tommo, a ship-jumper stranded with a companion among the cannibal Marquesans, Melville like every other sailor embellished his tall tale with the inevitable claims to have had, among other special favors, the love of the king's daughter Fayaway (a name I could never turn into Hawaiian). In *Typee* reality and romance are maddeningly mixed. A vivid and ethnographically accurate detail of life on a Polynesian high island is suddenly undercut by sentimental platitudes: "There seemed to be no cares, griefs, troubles, or vexations in all Typee," Melville proclaims, "the heart burnings, the jealousies, the social rivalries, the family dissensions and the thousand self-inflicted deceptions of refined life . . . are unknown among these unsophisticated people."

Reading these lines more than a century later on another Pacific high island (namely Oahu, which Melville loathed in the mid-1850s as already hopelessly overdeveloped by Westerners), I was willing to accept, even endorse, the idea that Polynesians had then and still had a highly visible character trait that is best described as a certain ineffable *goodness* or at least charisma of kindness. But that lives lived in pretechnological times lack psychic complications? That the Golden Age is to be found in the absence of books, nails, electricity? This naive belief lives on in the guilt-ridden tributes of many late twentieth-century Westerners to "ethnic spirituality." In the end, the statement "They are better than we" is the same as "We are better than they"— and does no more justice to the emotional complexities of any human life or any human society.

The young writer's frequent classical allusions in *Typee* are an uneasy mix of sincerity and mockery: outriggers floating on the water like swans, "sweet nymphs who sported with me in the lake," and the like. This corrupt language constantly intrudes between us and the object of Melville's attention, blurring his clear vision of the islands. In the same way, irony is derived from

---

be able to see,' 'He shall be able to tell,' 'He shall be able to charm,' said the friendly godmothers; 'But he shall not be able to hear,' exclaimed the last" *(In the South Seas).*

the juxtaposition of heroic rhetoric with everyday native doings: a tribesman wrapped in tapa "like a valiant Templar in a new and costly suit of armor." Or the healer, a "savage Aesculapius." Or their sleeping habits: the inhabitants of Typee Valley are said to "pass a large portion of their time in the arms of Somnius." All ingenuous goodwill on the surface, with the implicit contrast—namely, between the sublime Western diction and the ridiculous native behavior—geared to provoke a superior chuckle.

After a long and condescending description of his tagalong friend Kory-Kory's body tattooing, which "suggested to me the idea of a pictorial museum of natural history, or an illustrated copy of 'Goldsmith's Animated Nature,' " Melville then has his narrator artlessly profess: "But it seems really heartless in me to write thus of the poor islander, when I owe perhaps to his unremitting attentions the very existence I now enjoy." Thereupon follows a tribute to Kory-Kory that is just possibly designed to reflect as flatteringly on the praiser as on the person praised—that so-familiar Western put-on humility, the obligatory obeisance to the faithful "savage valet," Gunga Din or whomever, mainly intended to show off the lord and master to best advantage.

But oh, from the twenty-five-year-old author of *Typee* to the thirty-one-year-old author of *Moby-Dick*—what a change was in the works! By itself *Typee* is a half-breed sort of creature, a strange mix of unique and commonplace. In relation to Melville's greatest Pacific mural, however, it stands as the necessary cartoon, a crucial dress rehearsal in which the young author, still submerged in the literary formulas of his day, was able to purge a great deal of conventionality—clearing his blowspout of the detritus of popular culture, as it were, an absolutely essential step in the development of his own vision.

In Queequeg we have no less than the first—and only—heroic portrait of a Polynesian in Western literature. The passage from Kory-Kory to Queequeg marks the transformation of "savage valet" into friend, social equal, and moral superior, an occurrence that reflects a profound change in Melville's own attitude and his complete reorientation toward Western civilization's Other, or Shadow, that is traditionally projected onto the dark-skinned native.

In marked contrast to his treatment of the most visible mark of Kory-Kory's Polynesian Otherness—namely, his tattooing—in *Moby-Dick* Melville dispenses immediately with the coyness of his *Typee* narrator and has Ishmael say of Queequeg: "For all his tattooings he was on the whole a clean, comely cannibal. What's all this fuss I have been making about, thought I to myself—the man's a human being just as I am . . ." Later the body ornamentation that was such an occasion for sly fun in *Typee* is transfigured like so much else in *Moby-Dick* into the sublime riddle and mystery of flesh, a bold human inscription in the Book of Nature:

And this tattooing, had been the work of a departed prophet and seer of [Queequeg's] island, who, by those hieroglyphic marks, had written out on his body a complete theory of the heavens and the earth, and a mystical treatise on the art of attaining truth; so that Queequeg in his own proper person was a riddle to unfold; a wondrous work in one volume; but whose mysteries not even himself could read, though his own live heart beat against them; and these mysteries were therefore destined in the end to moulder away with the living parchment whereon they were inscribed, and so be unsolved to the last.

Melville had an uncanny knack for capturing key details of old-days Polynesian culture. By any number of details and personality quirks, a reader acquainted with Polynesians spots in Queequeg the genuine article: He is, first, a Marquesan, since these islanders along with the Maoris practiced facial *(moku)* and body tattooing far more extensively than any other Eastern Polynesians. (And it is clearly a Maori embalmed head, similarly tattooed, that Queequeg carries in his satchel and sells to a Nantucket barber; the traffic in Maori heads was a thriving nineteenth-century Pacific industry.) Melville, however, makes a point of telling us that the shaven-headed harpooner comes from an island called "Kokovoko," remarking: "It is not down in any map; true places never are."

Robert Louis Stevenson's observation about the disease-ravaged, dispirited post-Contact Marquesans makes an interesting gloss on Queequeg's absorption in his coming death: "The coffin, though of late introduction, strangely engages their attention. It is to the mature Marquesan what a watch is to the European schoolboy." Stevenson narrates further tales of Nukuhivan men digging their own graves in which to lie like pious medieval abbots contemplating their own mortality.

Queequeg's grand obsession thus had real-world models, but the symbol is magnificently double-edged. The distinctive outrigger canoe, or *wa'a,* the great symbol of Polynesian fate in their voyaging and navigational achievements, was universally described as "coffin-shaped" by Western writers. It will be an easy conversion, in Polynesian terms, from Queequeg's coffin, with all its echoes of the great plagues of Western disease decimating nineteenth-century Polynesia, to a vessel that floats on the open ocean.

Undeniably, the lingering *Typee* aura of Noble Savage hangs like a Nantucket mist about Queequeg, whose "very indifference speaking a nature in which there lurked no civilized hypocrisies and bland deceits." And Ishmael does—amazingly—prostrate himself before the latter's "harmless" tiki god. But unlike the human connections in *Typee,* the most remarkable feature of the Pacific Islander's relationship with Ishmael is its unmistakably easy affection, *pace* those critics who stress its homosexual flavor. In this "cozing, loving pair" Melville produces an utterly convincing depiction of spontaneous grace arising between absolute equals. Just as his fellow Pacific traveler Mark Twain managed later with Huckleberry Finn and Jim, Melville was in fact at work on his own synthesis of Opposites. Ishmael is that most fortunate of men who, by blind luck, happens upon, and briefly "marries"—to the immeasurable psychic gain of both parties—his Other, his secret sharer.

The true center of *Moby-Dick,* after all, is not the schoolboy posturing and quasi-Shakespearean soliloquies on the bridge but rather the great mystic visions of what lies under and beneath the *Pequod,* the "wondrous depths, where strange shapes of the unwarped primal world glided to and fro." Our guide and intermediary to these wonders is not Ahab but Queequeg the harpooner, and the strangest circumstance of all is that in Queequeg Melville has—through his symbiotic sensitivity to all things Polynesian—unwittingly recast one of the most famous characters of Pacific creation myths. The way Queequeg bears his weapon constantly at his side might remind a Western reader, in a ruined *Typee*-like simile, of an Arthurian knight with his sword. But a Polynesian of the very old days would see at once that the fisherman-prince Queequeg carries the talismanic hook that will capture the biggest fish of all, the lord of the underworld, just as the god Maui used his mighty fishhook *Manai-a-ka-lani* to haul whole islands out of the sea, thus creating the known world of the Pacific. (And these islands, like the white whale, after a tantalizing surfacing in daylight were often to drop off Maui's hook and slip back into the sea.)

Like Maui—and like Melville himself as creator of the world of *Moby-Dick*—Queequeg carries the mythic burden of capturing and raising up what lies mysteriously beneath and out of reach so that it may be exposed to consciousness. In the *Kumulipo*, what lives below stays below, even though symbolically bound to its counterpart on land; in *Moby-Dick* what lives below must, after a brief surfacing, return to the depths along with its cargo of human sacrifice.

This mass regression under the waves—which means drowning for all but Ishmael, for whom it serves as a kind of baptism—means the latter has incorporated some of Queequeg's identity into his own being by the very means of his survival. Ishmael is reborn by default as the Polynesian who must navigate his alter ego's well-provisioned funeral outrigger, his new self's own cradle, alone into Western consciousness. In this way lost Polynesia is reincarnated in Melville's imagination, and by extension in ours. It's the big fish harpooned in *Moby-Dick* that didn't get away.

18

Third Floor: Local Versus Local Color

Why did not Captain Cook have taste enough to call his
great discovery the Rainbow Islands?

—Mark Twain, *Roughing It*

Reaching the top floor of the Bishop Museum made me think of
Robert Louis Stevenson's "Isle of Voices." Wandering among the
mannequins garbed in the sepulchral wedding and formal costumes of the Immigrants—Chinese, Japanese, Portuguese, Filipino, plus a few stray haole missionaries and whalers—I knew I'd
arrived in the late nineteenth and early twentieth centuries,
when all those ghostly Voices materialized in the Pacific with a
vengeance. The floodgates were flung open and the other cultures and influences poured in over the bodies of dying Hawaiians. And these imported vines flourished, one race and ethnic
group after the other, multiplying like the lantana and blackberry that choked out the native plants in a kind of biological
imperialism that wryly paralleled the human invasion.

That memory of the Robert Louis Stevenson story drew in the
whole Troika. If no Pacific traveler escapes the ghostly presence
of Captain James Cook, no literate Californian who ventures
west can escape the late nineteenth-century Troika of Twain-
Stevenson-London. The Pacific books of Mark Twain, Robert
Louis Stevenson, and Jack London sat side by side on my book-
shelf, covers rubbing intimately against Cook's *Journals,* because

112

all described real voyages to Hawaii and the South Seas. But what an abyss separates the eighteenth-century navigator in his *Endeavour* from the three celebrity-writers*—Twain first, in 1866, on the steamer *Ajax*, then Stevenson in 1889 and London just past the century mark in 1907, on their chartered and/or custom-built pleasure yachts *Casco* and *Snark*, respectively. In sensibility this literary trio stands much closer to us, a full century later, than they do to Cook the century before.

All three were tangled up with Northern California, too: Twain as a reporter for the San Francisco *Morning Call;* RLS, whose wife Fanny hailed from Oakland, putting in time as the "Silverado Squatter" of the Mother Lode country; London the native son all over the Bay Area, from the Oakland Library where he learned to read to the Bay itself where he sailed as a young man with the oyster pirates and where his prototypic hero Martin Eden drowned himself (the novel *Martin Eden* was written on the *Casco*, en route to Honolulu), to his pre-Hearst San Simeon up in the Valley of the Moon, where he chose death by other means than drowning.

The nineteenth century witnessed the birth of the literary cult of personality as we know it today. For Stevenson and London, golden *Wunderkinder* who were both to die around age forty, their writing careers at the time of their Pacific adventures had long since stopped depending on the content of their works and now were based solely and rather shakily on the charisma and fame that had accumulated around their names. Both already a bit jaded and ghostlike, these two young men soon to die; both renewed, their decline temporarily halted, by exposure to the powerful vitality of the Pacific (London poignantly closed his account, *"See Hawaii and live"*). Each parlayed his jottings on Hawaii and the Pacific into sizable sums of money from magazines and publishers.

Their reportage is charmingly, professionally written, but the odor of irrelevance, of glibness even, rises off these pages of

*Twain was not yet a celebrity when he sailed for Hawaii, but he would be when he came back, thanks to his exclusive scoop of a clipper ship's burning; the trip also provided the material for a lecture tour, "Our Fellow Savages of the Sandwich Islands," which launched his career as a public humorist.

intelligently observed set pieces on surfriding, volcanoes, the leper colony at Kalaupapa, and so on (though I cherish Stevenson's account of a Marquesan chieftess who lifted her dress to rub her bare bottom, moaning with astonished delight, on the velvet cushions of the *Casco*).

Mark Twain's descriptions, in contrast—and by vocation and avocation he was at this time in his life far more the paid hack than Stevenson or London—still leap from the page, robust, idiosyncratic, full of life, with sharply etched characters, scenes, phrases like "the tumbled, wrinkled sea." As his unexpurgated notebooks testify, Mark Twain writes just the way you'd expect a red-haired man to. The Hawaiians knew all about this sort of fellow; in the very old days, before intermarriage mixed everything up, they and the other Polynesians typecast their own *ehu* people, reddish-haired with lighter skin, as fiery, ambitious upstarts descended from Pele, the volcano goddess.

But Twain fell into the same celebrity trap, the strange self-disposal machinery of the successful American writer that later chewed up London. By his own testimony Samuel Clemens yearned for the Islands the rest of his life, but I found the flaccidity, the professional calculation, of the famous "prose poem" he delivered at a New York dinner many years later deeply dismaying:

No alien land in all the world has any deep strong charm for me but that one, no other land could so longingly and so beseechingly haunt me, sleeping and waking, through half a lifetime, as that one has done. Other things leave me, but it abides; other things change, but it remains the same. For me its balmy airs are always blowing, its summer seas flashing in the sun; the pulsing of its surfbeat is in my ear; I can see its garlanded crags, its leaping cascades, its plumy palms drowsing by the shore, its remote summits floating like islands above the cloud wrack; I can feel the spirit of its woodland solitudes, I can hear the plash of its brooks; in my nostrils still lives the breath of flowers that perished twenty years ago.

This is as distant from the physical reality of the Pacific as a view of the Pyrenees rendered by a minor painter of the Royal Acad-

emy. Here we are right back in toastmaster's paradise along young Melville and his sporting Greco-Polynesian nymphs in the valley of Typee—in platitude land, the saddest place of all. For all Twain's rebelliousness, the undertow of nineteenth-century sensibility caught him in the end, drew him back under, via his immense popularity and fame, as surely as the late twentieth century has been trapped in its own back eddies of mannered, cinematic spareness. *He* knew this, of course—to his own despair—but his contemporaries did not. (How clearly those of a later time can spot the mechanical regurgitations of the group consciousness, as an age's own member-victims cannot!)

The Troika wrote Pacific fiction of the local color variety. Both London and Stevenson produced a burst of late stories with Hawaiian and South Seas settings; Twain started a novel whose first-person protagonist was a Hawaiian in the Molokai leper colony at Kalaupapa (also the scene for stories by London and by Fanny Stevenson). Here the Subject/Object relationship remains inviolable, the material stays distanced, manipulated with tricks of plot and character that could often be plugged into any other "native" habitat: Africa or Asia or South America. The refusal of these writers to surrender completely to their material cheapened their relationship to it and limited the artistic merit of the result. In contrast, the greater artist Melville like a gentleman did the right thing by his South Seas "material"—he married it. That is, he transformed this outer landscape in the crucible of his imagination into a personal symbolic language of tremendous resonance. (London, Stevenson, and Twain had separately left their true primal landscapes back home, of course.)

As a Pacific emblem, though, Stevenson's "Isle of Voices" has points to recommend it. This tale concerns a Molokai *kahuna* (or "wizard," as RLS the generalist calls him) who makes magic trips to a dream beach where he collects shells that turn into silver dollars. The setting is emphatically and accurately nineteenth-century Hawaii: there are flanking portraits of Victoria and Kamehameha V on the *kahuna*'s respectable middle-class parlor walls. His son-in-law, fleeing the *kahuna*, winds up in the real-life Tuamotus, where he finds the inhabitants shunning a mysterious beach full of "voices"—French, Russian, Dutch, Tamil, Chinese—which is none other than his father-in-law's secret place,

where sorcerers the world over come to harvest the magic shells that turn into money.

This story of a beach so very much like my own Waimanalo, swirling with a Babel of disembodied foreign Prosperos who engage in a ghostly battle with the flesh-and-blood inhabitants, reads like an eerie subtext on the colonization of the Pacific. It's all there: the greed of the rest of the world fastening on these beautiful isolated islands, the dollars their beaches were ultimately to pour forth, and the ongoing confusion of the islanders over just what it was, exactly, these outlander spirits were after— shells? pearls? an ordinary white sand beach?

The more I read of the old South Seas popular fiction—a genre whose heyday stretched roughly from the 1850s to the 1930s— the more allegorical I found it in terms of stock characters and recurring motifs. You had the copra traders, the blackbirders, the whalers, the gullible and/or cunning natives, the beautiful half-breed females who always died young. There were the two captains, Cook and Bligh, mythic emblems of Good and Evil. There were the island Paradises, thousands of them. Ultimately no more standardized, interchangeable literary fare exists than "local color," a kind of literature in which, paradoxically, the most specific becomes the most general because all such stories are founded upon that ever-present "omniscient" Western perspective that reduces its material to variants on the formulaic white man–native encounter.

But World War II changed the political map of the Pacific forever, and transformed its literature as well. The local color tradition (so closely tied here as elsewhere to the colonial sensibility) ended with James Michener, the new (and, interestingly, only) major proponent of this fiction in the radically transformed postwar Pacific.

What about the Objects, now—more or less—their own Subjects again? The first barrier I hit in trying to read modern Pacific Islands literature is the direct legacy of nineteenth-century colonialism, recast as publishers' marketing areas: Americans don't get to read New Zealand or Western Samoan or New Guinea or Fijian literature because they are outside the zone of ex–British Commonwealth copyright and vice versa. A Londoner may read the entire works of the Samoan writer Albert

Wendt; Wendt's calabash cousins in Hawaii cannot. Ironically, however closely related the inhabitants of the former British, French, Dutch, and American imperial holdings in the Pacific may be by virtue of race and indigenous language, a French-speaking Tahitian and an English-speaking Hawaiian have a much harder time communicating now, when they can fly, write, and telephone, than they did in the days of the outrigger.

Maoris and Western Samoans have fared better, in a way, than Tahitians or Hawaiians or American Samoans because their colonial fate was to be incorporated into small countries that support national literature as an identity factor. Consequently Witi Ihimaera, Patricia Grace, and many others in New Zealand, for example, enjoy identifiable existences as writers. Hawaiians, swallowed up in the belly of American mass culture right along with all the Island literati of every other race, are in worse shape. The unique Local sensibility is fermenting to produce its own tradition but faces the various gulfs between old oral modes, American mass culture, and the formidable Western literary tradition embodied in their only vehicle of expression, the English language. Literature rises out of tradition; "creating" a tradition is almost a contradiction in terms and poses endless problems at the basic levels of language and influence. Forging the language and the new container of the tradition is a difficult, thankless task carried on in obscurity. Even now, though, the rice pot is boiling. Hawaii will have its great Local—not local color—writers.

Back on the third floor, mentally blotting out the ornate ethnic getups from long-forgotten Mother Countries, I clothed the mannequins instead in the T-shirts, shorts, and zoris that constitute the universal late twentieth-century Local folk costume for all concerned. Ancient Hawaiian is dead, I thought. Long live Local, long live Now.

But a sense of suffocation arising from the spectacle of suffering and death, plus nostalgia for the grand illusion of Paradise ("before it all got spoiled"), drew me back again to the very old days. In defiance of all reason I turned and walked down the staircase—quickly past the second floor, that scene of unspeakable suffering—to the ground floor, the world of Hawaiian prehistory. For me as for many before, the glamour of lost Polynesia

117

won out over the sturdy modern truths embodied in the peasants and fortune seekers of half a dozen other races.

What motivates young Westerners to cast off the imperial cloak of Subject to merge and identify with the Object? Idealism, mostly, though they are unaware of the lack of enthusiasm with which their adopted ethnic group regards them. This charade of haoles in costume instinctively repulsed me, but then what was I up to myself? From this question I resolutely turned my face. Every time I surfaced in Now, I ran into nothing but uncertainties, embarrassing doubts. More, much more, could still be mined from the past, the times before my time, "before it all got spoiled," inside the safe, set boundaries of the dead-past-saving. The rich universe of ancient Hawaiian history had crooked its finger, and I came running.

In front of the fishhooks, next to the god that looked like a can opener, I made a decision. I would keep on reading the Book of Nature. But now I was determined to read it in a systematic way. This decision moved me not just from the third floor to the first floor but from the front of the Bishop Museum to its bowels, via the rear-door entrance to the Archaeology-Anthropology Department. Here, reviving a childhood passion, I volunteered for Bishop Museum archaeological surveys. My brand of dilettantism was a principal source of free manual labor for these underfunded enterprises and they signed me on at once.

The project that summer of 1970 was a contract archaeology survey of Moanalua Valley on Oahu. This survey was intended to precede construction of the legendary H-3 freeway (a third route over the Koolau mountains supplementing the Pali and Likelike highways that has stayed legendary, i.e., never built, to this day). The twisted aluminum wreckage from a twenty-year-old airplane crash at the head of the valley lay beached in the dry stream bed where we sprawled, exhausted, every lunch hour after hacking away at guava trunks with the museum's dull World War II army surplus machetes. (The matching backpacks, made of reinforced steel slats painted olive green and weighing at least ten pounds even before anything was loaded on them, made you very admiring of the physical prowess of our brave soldiers in the Pacific island jungles.)

After a few weeks' sweaty work among the rubbery-limbed

guava and *hau,* the archaeologist in charge offered me a deal: The museum needed workers on a real dig over on Molokai. Did I want to go?

Did I? On a real dig? Yes, I did. I wanted to sift red Hawaiian dirt through the screens, sort through the sticks and broken shells and waterworn pebbles until that elegant man-fashioned curve of Fishhook leaped out from the rubble of Nature's more casual creations. Hawaii had hooked me and I was deep underwater. Now, just as I seemed to be immersing myself still further, the opposite movement had subtly set in. Though the island of my still-forming consciousness had not yet broken surface, I was beginning to feel the pull. Out of blindest instinct, I was searching, eagerly searching, for a hook to hoist myself up with, to haul myself out of the long Polynesian night—and in this contrary way the fishhook reeled me to Molokai.

MOLOKAI:
FORK IN THE TREE

19

Haole No More Money

When my Aloha Airlines plane landed at the tiny airport outside Kaunakakai that summer of 1970, the most I had known of my destination was the Local expression "Molokai suitcase," denoting a wrinkled grocery bag stuffed full of poi, leis, and packets of bleeding meat. Molokai in reality was an island suspended between two eras: pre-Hilton and pre–Rent-a-Car, but also, in a lingering way, postwar and very soon to be postplantation. After the workers had finally won their hard-fought battle to unionize, the Island pineapple and sugarcane industries had fallen into sharp decline. Competition from cheaper labor forces in foreign countries meant they were about to be supplanted by a tourist industry previously concentrated in Waikiki. Plantation paternalism was giving way to the new paternalism of multinational investment and land development; in the boardrooms of Honolulu, Los Angeles, and Tokyo the financial interests that decided the future of Molokai were busy laying out their plans. And, half a heartbeat before the massive migrations of those duller avians the tourists, a motley vivid flock of hippies were just now lighting down in the Outer Islands—the first Mainland haoles besides G.I.s that Outer Islanders were destined to get a good close look at. Because of its "bad" beaches, Molokai was one of the last Outer Islands to go. But the forces of drastic change had already been set in motion long before that June morning I stepped off the plane.

At the end of the sixties the Outer Islands were rather like Hawaii before Cook. The Molokai people especially had a good thing going in the insular ethnic amalgam that was their world. The closely knit population of five thousand greeted each other, as they passed on the island's single highway, with a dignified lift of the hand. They indulged in all manner of old-fashioned pastimes. They listened to the radio and chewed Choward's violet-scented lozenges, a product my grandmother might equally have enjoyed in turn-of-the-century Arkansas. The high school had an active chess club. The combination locks sold in the general *cum* army-surplus store in Kaunakakai all opened with the same set of numbers.

At the same time, the Molokai people craved new sensations. It's easy to forget now just how bored some were, how eager for unfamiliar faces. They hung around the airport watching to see who got off the plane. They fell on strangers like long-lost relations. And they had memories like elephants, with total recall of a day's chance meeting three years later. If you, a young haole carrying a backpack, happened to be walking past their house, the screen door flew open to joyous greetings, your forehead was tenderly patted, misty plastic bags of ice-cold Tahitian mangoes were pushed into your hands. And, if this were your desire, you could let yourself be dragged inside for three solid days of force-feeding and storytelling.

Yes, just like the pre-Contact Hawaiians, those Molokai people were on the lookout for something new. Their TV sets with the uncertain reception from Honolulu showed them things they didn't have. Like the Kauai people and the Maui people, they were ready to be better off economically, ready to get out from under the stifling plantation oligarchy. But they weren't ready for what they were going to get. Opportunities came for some, but not for all. For, in the long run, was being a busboy or tour driver, Object to somebody else's Subject, that much of an advance over fieldhanding?

The two archaeologists Tom Riley and Pat Kirch—only students themselves, as I soon discovered—had come to fetch me at the airport in an ancient Land Rover. From Kaunakakai, the island's only town, we drove about twenty miles to Pukoo, located halfway between the West End and the East End. Sausage-shaped Molokai was oriented on an elongated east–west axis instead of a northeast–southwest one; instead of having its Windward and Leeward sides conveniently demarcated by a mountain range like the other major Hawaiian islands, the island had a Leeward West End and a Windward East End, and every evening the trade winds blew gale force through the middle— namely, Pukoo.

Pukoo was a small settlement of houses scattered along the beach and mountain side of the island's single highway. Its main claims to fame were (1) a still-functioning prehistoric fishpond (now raising mullet, and protected from poachers by its shotgun-wielding female owner) and (2) the Peace Corps training camp, a ramshackle collection of barracks that was to be our home for the summer. The camp bore many traces of recent Peace Corps occupancy: inside, blackboards covered with Samoan conjugations; outside, a jungly thicket of trees dotted with half-built latrines and replicas of sleeping houses where the Peace Corps volunteers were expected to make the most difficult cultural transition of all: from screened to unscreened windows.

The Bishop Museum occupation of the camp overlapped the last week's stay of a Boy Scout troop from Oahu. My first morning in Pukoo began with a thunderous pounding on the door of my cubicle; the boys had mischievously told their scoutmaster a laggard was still in bed. Deeply embarrassed, he insisted on making me a strawberry waffle in the open-air cookhouse hung with "hands" of ripening bananas where he toiled with the other two scoutmasters to feed their spoiled charges, most of whom, as suburban kids, were barely able to make it up the Kalaupapa cliff trail to get their hiking badges.

The adults got their own back, however, with a luau straight out of *Lord of the Flies*. It seems that, in time-honored Hawaiian fashion, a pig had been purchased the first day of their arrival in anticipation of the last big banquet. In an outrageous but typically confused mix of old and new sensibilities, the scoutmasters had allowed the boys, middle-class Americans of Japanese descent and not a farm lad among them, to make friends with their future lunch, pet it, feed it, and, inevitably, name it. Came the day before the luau, the boys were obliged to participate in the manly act of butchering their pet, with each boy allowed one hack with the knife. Not surprisingly, tears fell among the carnage.

Once the Boy Scouts were gone—carrying with them God knows what sets of memories—fifteen excited Molokai High School students moved into the camp and our summer officially began. For the next six weeks a constant stream of visitors—the kids' relatives, other archaeologists from Oahu, the archaeologists' friends, my friends, friends of friends, all sorts of colorful characters including the scientist who may or may not have accidentally ignited half a field in Halawa by tossing away a cigarette—flowed in and out of Pukoo. There was plenty of room in the barracks and more, for the thick-skinned, out in the sleeping huts. In all places sheltered from the winds, the Molokai mosquitoes made their presence felt.

Like everything else from the outside, the two-year Bishop Museum archaeological expedition had created a mild sensation on the little island, being widely regarded, to the bemusement of the two graduate students and one undergraduate in charge, as the last word in big-time Honolulu sophistication. Moreover, the museum had hired high school kids of Hawaiian descent for purposes of "cultural enrichment." Everybody wanted on. Digging trenches for the Bishop Museum was a lot more glamorous than the usual summer employment for Molokai teenagers— picking "pine" in the Dole fields.

On the way from the airport to camp that first day we were stopped in the street in Kaunakakai by an older haole man. I was still in the throes of digesting the major thrill of a few minutes before: when we had stopped in Kane's Bakery to pick up bread for the camp, I had heard the people next to us speaking in *real Hawaiian*. (Tom theorized outside that they were talking Hawaiian because they were discussing us and didn't want us to understand.)

The pale, white-haired old man before us had two sullen and mortified dark-skinned teenagers in tow. "These are my sons," he explained. "You didn't hire them, but you should have. They're good workers, if they're watched. They've got just enough of that Scotch-Irish fighter in them . . ." A morose look

came over his face and he trailed off without finishing the sentence. No fighter himself, Scotch-Irish or any other kind, he was
physically a wreck; both his lower legs were so enormously swollen he could barely walk. But he was persistent in a dogged sort
of way, willing to humiliate his sons and himself to get them a job.
Tom promised to give the boys first consideration if anybody
dropped out. We walked back to the Land Rover. The father
stared after us; his sons looked away.

This fellow, it seemed—like a good anthropologist, Tom knew
all the gossip—had been married to a Hawaiian woman who had
left him to bring up the kids by himself. Once he was no longer
married to her, he lost their Hawaiian Homestead house, which
only people of at least half Hawaiian descent were eligible for.
Now he got by as a substitute teacher. The Outer Islands had a
name for this kind of person and I learned it that first day on
Molokai.

20

Halawa Valley

Already in its second year when I arrived on Molokai, our dig was located in Halawa, a classic Hawaiian wet valley at the end of the East End highway. People had been living in Halawa—in archaeological jargon, it had been a "continuous habitation site"—from about A.D. 500 to 1946, when a tidal wave inundated the Islands and left a salt deposit over all the coastal valleys, ruining the taro crop. That and the radically changing Territorial economy were the trigger for the mass exodus out of all the Windward wet valleys of Hawaii to the towns and plantations.

In Halawa Valley one man had stayed behind. This was the valley's self-appointed caretaker and greeter, Johnny Kainoa, a charismatic figure in baggy shorts who stood poised every morning at the bottom of the road with outstretched hands and a magnetic smile. He and his wife, Pauline, lived in a neat wooden frame house at the mouth of the valley among the other empty houses, the remains of three churches, and a schoolhouse. Relatives of the old Halawa residents came down on weekends to tend the homes and the church.

A contained sadness rose out of these deserted tin-roofed bungalows with their well-kept lawns, gaudy croton plants, and Surinam cherry bushes fronting the main dirt road. Farther back in the valley was the stone terracing of the impressive system of taro agriculture that in some form or other had amply supported the human occupants of Halawa for well over a millennium. Back even farther, about a mile and a half up the trail, the main waterfall Moa Ula steamed down the cliffs into its big pool, source of the wide stream that bisected the valley, making one distinctive hook—*halawa* means "bend" or "curve"—before feeding into a shallow bay. (Except on Kauai, the only island to rate "rivers," every Hawaiian wet valley has its "stream," even though in winter some of these torrents far surpassed Mainland rivers in their flow.)

As in all the formerly inhabited Windward valleys of the Outer Islands, imported plants escaped cultivation, grew wild and untended in Halawa: avocado, orange, papaya, banana, mango, coffee. The farther back in the valley you went, the more native the vegetation got. Thus, in the upper reaches you came upon the mystic mountain apple, *ohia-ai,* and its translucent, watery, rosy-skinned fruit, the living essence of Hawaiian wetland fertility. Huge bird's nest ferns uncurled mysteriously in the forks of koa trees. In the very old days the Hawaiians used the black fiber from the center of these leaves as the ornamental weave in their lauhala mats.

What, finally, is a native plant? In Hawaii all forms of life are émigrés. Plants were simply the first organisms to arrive, in the form of seeds borne by the trades or birds' digestive tracts. Later, domesticated plants were brought in the Polynesian seafarers' outriggers: taro (Hawaiian missionary orthography: *kalo*), sweet potato, *ti,* breadfruit.

In the old days Halawa was noted for its taro. In his classic work of Hawaiian ethnobotany, *Plants of Hawaii National Park Illustrative of Plants and Customs of the South Seas,* Otto Degener recounts one turn-of-the-century observer's description of being almost blinded, as he looked down into the famous Halawa Valley from the ridge trail, by the profusion of huge, healthy taro leaves glistening like mirrors from one end of the valley to the other. After fifteen hundred years of cultivation all that remained in my time were the extensive terracing systems and, here and there in the jungle of overgrowth, a few stray light-green shoots. In the streams there was also a great deal of wild *ape,* the false taro whose dark-green leaves slant up just like true taro.

Of the other native vegetation in Halawa, there were (1) the *koa* and *kukui* trees, whose leaves combine to make the distinctive silvery green–dark green pattern of most upland Hawaiian valleys. In the very old days koa wood was used for canoe building; the hard black nut of the kukui tree produced greasy oil that provided fuel for light. (2) The *noni* tree, tall with big round *hau*like leaves. (3) The clusters of *ti* plants around the old house platforms and even *halapepe*, a rare *ti*like plant that produced little red berries. (4) The parasitical *'ie'ie* vines, a vegetable cobweb shrouding ground and trees. (5) The fragrant white-flowered Hawaiian ginger, or *awapuhi*, smelling so much like honeysuckle. Unlike Chinese ginger, the mild root was unsuitable for cooking; in the very old days Hawaiians used the sap of the flowers as a shampoo. In the heavy shade under the java plums and mangoes that choked the valley bottom grew (6) the *ho'i*, the Hawaiian yam with its aerial tubers and distinctive heart-shaped leaves. On the other side of the stream the trail was blocked by (7) a *hau* labyrinth, the springy-limbed tree with small yellow flowers that proliferated into its own self-contained jungle of branches. (8) Only a few breadfruit trees. A staple in the more tropical South Sea Islands, this knobbly-skinned starchy fruit the size of a basketball was scarce in temperate-zone Hawaii.

Typically, a Hawaiian wet valley isn't bright flowers and fragrant smells like a travel ad. It is rather a subtle blending of Greens, every hue of Green imaginable, overlaid with the ever-present but not unpleasant odor of organic decay—wet leaves, rotting fruit, damp earth. But Halawa boasted one isolated, enchanting burst of color: around the old houses still standing near the stream the trees were carpeted, like a second valley floor, with an aerial canopy of blooming morning-glories, passion fruit vines, and pink Virginia creepers.

The fauna of Halawa Valley? Wild pigs. Goats. Deer. Up valley, above the two waterfalls Moa Ula and Hipuapua, tiny native Hawaiian birds. The Hawaiian owl, *pu'eo*. Mosquitoes, fruit flies. Centipedes and scorpions, though not in sufficient numbers to frighten. No snakes. Unlike its surrounding waters, the benign Hawaiian land harbored no predators of humans. This circumstance took some getting used to. A childhood in Florida made me flinch, my first years in Hawaii, each time I saw someone in shorts and zoris plunge into swampy knee-deep stream water with careless disregard for water moccasins, alligators, copperheads, coral snakes, or leeches.

Halawa Valley's other notable natural feature was Mrs. Akina. Was she related to one of the kids? I don't remember. In the old days her family lived in Halawa, and she often came back to visit. I first came upon stately Mrs. Akina sitting up to her neck in Halawa Stream, sailor hat perched rakishly on her gray hair. Under the water her enormous bra shone whitely through her transparent T-shirt. Slowly the leonine head swiveled to regard me, and this was the first true pair of Hawaiian eyes, except Kanaina's, I had looked deeply into—large, liquid, kind, unbearably kind. The aloha streaming from them was foreign to me; yes, that amount of spontaneous love was unsupportable, delighted and terrified me standing there in thunderstruck confusion as I was made aware for the first time, age twenty-four, of my own irredeemable puniness in love, but there was hope for me, hope for everyone, too, in Mrs. Akina's eyes.

21

On the Backpile

Twisted into filmy overlapping curtains by the rising trades, every afternoon the famous Halawa rains tumbled and twirled out of the valley. Sometimes they stopped short at the sharp bend that concealed the waterfall Maka'ele'ele; sometimes the well-known *ua nihi pali,* "rain creeping on the cliff," swallowed the beach in gentle gray wetness. At our test pit on the grassy dune tops at the beach we could set our watches by these Halawa showers: 3:45 P.M. sharp.

Digging, then sifting the dirt we had dug, we lifted off one after another of the dark-gray cultural layers marbling the dunes until we reached the lowest and earliest: postholes and firepits of an oval habitation, an uncommon shape in Eastern Polynesia. The backpiles swelled around the meter-square pits as we sorted quickly through pieces of wood, *opihi,* other shells, and assorted rubble to pounce on the treasure: worked bone (a common material for fishhooks, also, less frequently, for such tools as tapa cloth needles), remains of pig-tusk bracelets, dog-tooth leg bands; worked shells (spotted cowries with holes bored in them, used as squid lures); worked stone (poi pounders, net weights, adzes and adze blanks, obsidian chips, etc.).

Out of the piles of midden (literally, "muck dung," from Old Norse *myki-dyngla,* meaning "garbage heap"; here, shells and bones that were obviously remains of meals, not tools) we also saved random bags from each cultural level for sorting back in Honolulu. By totaling up the relative amounts of *opihi* shells, pig and dog bones, and so on—so the thinking went—the proportions of the prehistoric Hawaiian diet could be gauged in much the way the anthropologist back on Oahu tried to count the Hungry Man frozen dinner boxes in the Kalihi Valley trashcans. Both on Molokai and back at the Bishop Museum I dropped, switched, and generally messed up these rotting paper bags full of vital evidence whose bottoms were always inconveniently falling out. Not my strong suit, quantitative analysis.

Local people—relatives of the kids on the dig, campers up at the park, or the just plain curious—often came down to visit us at the beach trenches. They always brought something to eat, usually straight out of the sea: white crabs in buckets of ocean water; spiny sea urchins, or *wana; opihi* and *pipipi* plucked right off the rocks. All these were to be eaten on the spot while they were still alive and kicking. ("The native is very fond of fish, and *eats the article raw and alive!*" Mark Twain commented in *Roughing It.*) The Halawa Valley hippies, Pauline Kainoa told me, called Hawaiians cannibals for eating raw fish, "but," she said jokingly with that easy Polynesian elegance that makes a society matron look like a gum-cracking carhop by comparison, "we are *decorous* cannibals."

You cracked the crabs and *wana* from the underside and sucked out the contents like a raw egg. There was a taste of brine and tough sea muscle, very pleasant. Sometimes the crown shells were boiled in water, producing a succulent bit of white meat about the size of a pea with a pretty black dot on the top. *Opihi* were only eaten raw—crunchy, salty little tidbits, a sea peanut in its shell, hence a good pupu with beer—in fact, the original pupu, since that word means "shell," or "animal plus shell."

These *opihi* were limpets about the size of a quarter with a round tapered shell shaped like a puckered lampshade. The real nuisance was gathering them, an action sport suited only for the nimble and brave. The best time for plucking the cone-shaped mussels off the tidal rocks was high tide. Preferred tool, a putty knife or screwdriver. You had to slice the *opihi* cleanly off the rock at the first go; otherwise, frightened, it clamped down harder, contracting its muscle, and was almost impossible to pry off. Meanwhile, your head swiveled constantly as you checked the approach of the next big wave. Because the *opihi* live on the sides of the rocks facing the ocean, you had to turn your back to it to get them, and because you were gathering them at high tide, you could very easily go right out with the retreating wave if you weren't prepared at every moment to sprint up the slippery beach to safety. Every few weeks the Oahu newspapers routinely reported this or that person lost off Makapuu Head while picking *opihi*, presumed drowned: compared to other ocean activities, rather a high mortality rate.

Limu, that is, seaweed of all varieties—what Melville was pleased to call "saline salad"—could be harvested right off the beach, a procedure furnishing good mild exercise for old Hawaiian ladies. Miraculously, *limu* stayed the same incandescent green out of the water; scattered bits of undersea color leaped out at you from the sand like exclamation points.

Tiny black *pipipi* lived on the tidal rocks like *opihi* and yielded a meat smaller than the average pea. A point of interest about *pipipi* was that, like so much else in Hawaii, they had a freshwater equivalent, the *hehewai*, that was just a little bit bigger and had a lighter gray shell. Our midden heaps were full of these *pipipi* and *hehewai* shells, the very-old-days equivalent of peanut husks.

Hehewai and *pipipi*. Every living thing in the ocean had its counterpart on land. The lives of these little animals were the foundation of the great bridge between land and sea celebrated in the *Kumulipo*, the mythic parallelism that lies at the heart of the old Polynesian imagination, refining the evidence of the natural world to reinforce the human thought patterns of polarity, resolution; duality, unity.

The backpile was a good place for pondering natural dualities. There was the mongoose and the rat, for example. In the old days the "native" (that is, imported by the Polynesians) *ratus Hawaiiensis* whose tiny bones I was forever picking out of the midden screen had wreaked havoc on grain shipments down at the docks. The mongoose, introduced to the Hawaiian Islands as a means of combatting this menace, like most other imported species quickly found its niche in Island ecology and wildly multiplied.

134

(A debate raged in the newspapers about the correct plural of the word—mongeese, mongooses?—until an exasperated reader wrote in: "Everybody knows the plural of 'mongoose' is *'plenty mongoose'!*")

But there was a problem. The Hawaiian rat was a nocturnal lowlands dweller. The mongoose was out only by day and preferred the uplands. After eighty-odd years the predator and its would-be prey had never met; to survive, the mongoose had been obliged to develop instead a taste for rare Hawaiian birds. And so I grew accustomed to thinking, in the appropriate situation, "It's like the mongoose and the rat," imagination trailing off to that large and shadowy realm of meetings never consummated.

Lunch on the dig was also full of surprises, not all of them pleasant. Our mood-prone Filipino cook provided either splendid plate lunches of teriyaki beef, rice, and kim chee in individually Saran-wrapped Melmac dishes or, if he was feeling depressed that morning, slices of plain white bread spread with a thin gruel of spicy mustard and mayonnaise. No worries, though, because the kids always supplemented their camp lunches with plenty from home: laulau, potato chips, kulolo, five-pound sacks of Chips Ahoy cookies, cases and cases of Diamond Head soda. As in most other Island situations the rule of etiquette for food sharing went like this: Here, take my stuff, but no thank you, I wouldn't dream of taking your stuff, because that way I'd be obligated to you and this way you're obligated to me. When lunch ended and it was time to go back to the trenches, we'd be lying dazed and motionless under the Javanese plum trees, easy prey for the circling blur of fruit flies.

One morning, baking under the hot Hawaiian sun, we were unearthing one-thousand-year-old land snail shells and live centipedes in the same trowelsful of sandy dirt but little else. Up by the Land Rover our fried Spam lunches, sweating under their Saran Wrap covers, cooked peacefully in big cardboard boxes. A radio propped on the backpile blasted acid rock from a Honolulu station; the white ribbon of Moa Ula shone on the green back wall of Halawa. Then a buck wandered out of the nearby trees. Instantly, no words exchanged, the kids jumped out of the trench and ran after him shouting and screaming. The startled buck leaped into the water and swam frantically away from shore. The kids walked back down the beach and, very satisfied with their efforts, took up their work again. Once you panicked the deer into the water, they told me, you either shot him or he drowned, and the tide washed the body back in if the sharks didn't get it first.

I was listening to this explanation as I kept one uneasy eye on the pair of antlers now bobbing bravely through the procession of swells at the mouth of the bay. Neither shot nor drowned, the buck was already in open water and heading straight for Maui. The image endures. Was this an authentic hunting practice or a bit of decadent culture-gap cruelty (for no one present had a gun to finish the poor creature off)? I offer it as memory only, outside the arena of judgment, where all true memories live.

22

Story Behind the Story

It is incredible how soon the account of any event is propa-
gated in these narrow countries by the love of talk, which
much leisure produces, and the relief given to the mind in
the penury of insular conversation by a new topick.

—Samuel Johnson, *Journey to the Western
Islands of Scotland*

Johnny Kainoa was a philosopher who had an opinion about
everything, but he always got back to one point: "For every story
you hear, there's always something else going on," he'd say.
"Look for the story behind the story."

For many years I thought this idea was original to Johnny until
someone told me it came from Paul Harvey, the radio newsman.
Molokai people were great radio listeners. "The story behind the
story" was an interesting idea whoever had thought of it, but
Johnny overworked it. All you had to say was "Nice day, huh?"
and Johnny would answer, with a knowing hitch of his head,
"Yeah, but see dose rain clouds? Story behind the story." Even
the weather made him paranoid.

But somehow Johnny had captured the essence of his home
turf. Nights back at camp in the open-air cookhouse, "talking
story" as the gusty winds of Pukoo rattled the tin roof—archaeology stories, ghost stories, family stories, revenge stories, the daily
Molokai gossip served up sugary and hot like *malasadas*: story,
story, more story than I'd ever heard in my life. And Johnny was
right; every story did have a dozen others behind it, and each of
them a dozen more behind, sideways, and in front, a crazy quilt

of tale-telling, so that finally you didn't know which came before and which after; they all explained, overlapped, and contradicted each other, just like the people who told them, this being the whole point of stories, which, like people, aren't meant to live alone.

Above all, Molokai was a rice pot boiling over with ghost stories, stories going back to and ever so faintly touching that *Kumulipo* fear of the bygone days, when

> Fear falls upon me on the mountain top
> Fear of the passing night
> Fear of the night approaching
> Fear of the pregnant night
> Fear of the breach of the law
> Dread of the place of offering and the narrow trail
> Dread of the food and the waste part remaining
> Dread of the receding night
> Awe of the night approaching

—when, as a girl told me her grandmother had told her, so many spirits surrounded you when you walked out on the road at night that they suffocated you, which was why everyone was glad, when Christianity came, to switch to just One; it made things easier and a whole lot less frightening.

Pukoo itself had three ghosts. A woman in white walked on the highway. A dead Chinaman swung from the rafters of the old stone house across the road that had once been owned by the famous von Tempsky family. And a creature lived in the big *haole koa* thicket: woman by day, giant squid by night, in the old days she used to creep down to the pens by the beach to eat the pigs. These creatures came out on nights when the moon and stars were blotted out by clouds. Since even by my time there were no more pigs at Pukoo, only the bulldozed hotel site, how the squid woman and the others continued to manage was no longer clear.

One East End family allowed a brother-in-law who was not a blood relation to clean out their well. A few nights later the mermaid paid the brother-in-law a visit. The mermaid was very pretty. She had white hair and smoked a cigar. She liked men.

The brother-in-law woke up to find her pulling the blanket off his bed. He jumped up and ran out of the room. The mermaid drifted next door, where she tried to suffocate the baby. The whole family got on their knees reciting prayers and obscenities. After the old grandmother had said the Lord's Prayer backward ten times in Hawaiian, the mermaid finally went away.

Molokai must have been one of the last places in the Islands you could hear people speak in ordinary conversation—as opposed to the Madame Pele stuff handed out either to impress tourists or as deliberate revivalism—of the *mo'o,* the giant lizard of Hawaiian mythology. According to East End legend, the little lagoon west of Pukoo that was being dredged for a hotel had a resident *mo'o* already responsible for the death of one man and the injury of another when a bulldozer tipped over. It was a great example of the old forces of imagination mobilized against the new, how the supernatural functions as an allegory for the collision of cultures. And guess who won? Even though it managed to cause some damage, in the long run the *mo'o* did not stop the hotel.

I was never very clear on what a *mo'o* was supposed to look like. In the very old days Hawaii had no lizards of any size or kind (your friendly house lizard Mr. Gecko was a late arrival). If one were able to determine, for instance, that the *mo'o* figure was pan- and even proto-Malayo-Polynesian, one might spitball a bit and say it was a legend carried from Southeast Asia, where big lizard bones from the very, very old days could be dug out of the ground for all to see, but really, who knows? Even if big lizards had never existed, somebody would have invented them.

Mainly I remember how the word was spoken, all by itself, with a slightly exaggerated widening of the eyes, in a semihokey lowered voice—*"Mo'o!"*—embodying all the paradoxes of simultaneous belief and skepticism that torment those sentenced to life imprisonment in the Grand Canyon of fault lines between cultures.

Then you had the *heiau,* the very-old-days place of worship. The first I ever visited in the Islands was Ililiopoe, halfway between Kaunakakai and Pukoo. In a jungle of overgrown java plum and guava behind a cow pasture a huge platform of mildewed green lava rock reared suddenly above the trees. For a split second, the spurious thrill of discovering the great Mayan ruin: Climb up the sloping side that vanishes into the treetops and you will find the Templo del Sol or whatever, five hundred perfectly hewn steps rising to a sacrificial altar.

But no, this was Hawaii, the rocks stopped fifteen feet up and what you had, impressive enough in its own way, just like the fishhooks and bone needles instead of skulls carved out of crystal or the king's ruby, was a huge flat platform about the size of a basketball court, with indentations still visible for the long-vanished "god sticks," the carved wooden statues of the gods with protruding tabs at their feet that were inserted in these holes somewhat like the plastic chess pieces on miniature portable boards. Big ceremonial *heiau* like this one would have needed a passel of attendant priests. Walking on this broad, surprisingly even surface just above the level of the treetops, I was struck by how neatly the eggplant-sized lava rock was graded into smaller and smaller stones, their interstices filled in with coral rubble for easy walking just like in the old house platforms. A *heiau*, I realized, was nothing more than an enormous house platform for the gods.

Halawa Valley itself had the remains of two smaller, older *heiau* that stood sentinel on opposite sides of the valley mouth commanding a wide view of the ocean and the cliffs. These would have been kin group or fishermen's *heiau*, parish chapels as compared to the regional cathedral. The Halawa Valley *heiau* bore the unlikely names of Mana and Papa, a circumstance that provoked a stoned flurry of spurious mythmaking among several microgenerations of Halawa hippies.

Though Halawa's ghosts had ebbed with the receding tide of its full-time occupants, each trail in the valley had once had its own chant to be recited against bad spirits; the famous Twelve Winds of Halawa were still identified by name. Even in my time a driver who eased his car down the dirt road into the valley could hear his name spoken out loud at the bend where the road crossed an ancient Hawaiian footpath. In the empty tin-roofed houses a mirror fogged, a child cried, a white dog ran down a decrepit hallway.

I met the dead of Halawa Valley in broad daylight. My first skeleton was huddled under a house platform a little way up the talus slope. As I brushed away loose dirt with a whisk broom the shape sprang out at me: a child crouched in the earth like an ancient bird about to spread its bony, orange-stained wings and fly. In the Solomon Islands, Tom told me, male family members were buried under one side of the house, the ancestor or sacred side, as distinct from the profane or female side, where the ordinary living took place. People avoided walking on the mats on the sacred side of the house. It was impossible to say which section this corner of the house platform had been, equally impossible to determine the sex of the skeleton while it was still married to the ground.

We recorded the pathetic remains and covered them with a flannel rag weighed down with lava rocks. When the whole platform had been excavated and photographed, the dirt would be filled in again with the bones remaining *in situ*. This was after all a new era of archaeology, geared to sensitivity to Local feelings. Many people on Molokai had either lived in Halawa Valley themselves or were related to those who had. The municipally illegal custom of burying deceased kin in the backyard was still widespread. Nobody wanted to think his grandfather's skull was going to spend all eternity labeled and numbered on a basement shelf in the Bishop Museum. To the Molokai people these remains were Subjects, recent ones, not Objects.

The first year of the Halawa dig, the archaeologist Gil Hendron was sitting in Kane's Bar in Kaunakakai one night having a peaceful beer when a big Hawaiian man came up to him. At first Gil didn't understand what he was mad about.

The man said it again, louder. "You fuck with them bones?"

He was enormous. Gil knew the answer. "No!"

"You fuck with them bones," the man went on in a voice laden with menace—and here the pronoun was the surprise, "they come back, bust you up!"

"Coming back" was fairly standard practice for the dead of Molokai. By all accounts, its ghostly population was as large and vocal as the living one. Dead relations swarmed like bees around the households of the East End. You couldn't keep them away, it seemed; they pressed in all around you clamoring their requests trivial and profound. All day long in the trenches the kids regaled me with these stories; in the evenings visitors like Mrs.

Akina and others picked up the thread. Many East Enders came back, they told me, and for all kinds of reasons. One boy's grandfather came back because the cows from Murphy's Puu o Hoku ranch were trampling his grave. A mother came back to her three daughters as a loud wind in the night, but they were never able to determine her wishes.

In one of the precious camp paperbacks, a dog-eared copy of Claude Lévi-Strauss's *Tristes Tropiques*, I read the great French anthropologist's account of an Amazon tribe's beliefs about the afterlife: "The souls of Nambukwara men are incarnated, after death, in jaguars; but the souls of women and children vanish into the air and no more is heard or seen of them." If nothing else, my informal census of the Molokai ghosts served as dramatic rebuttal of the Nambukwara spiritual hierarchy. On the East End, at any rate, as many woman and children came back as men.

Back at camp we had an ancient Bishop Museum slide show, complete with tattered typescript of commentary to be read aloud to numbered slides, that had been packed along with the World War II metal backpacks and other ancient gear from the museum basement. Assembled by the revered anthropologist Kenneth Emory sometime in the forties or fifties, this visual document of the Polynesian outlier Kapingamarangi had been sent along to be shown to whomever on Molokai might be interested. Priceless ethnographical record though the slides doubtless were, their anonymously written narrative was firmly entrenched in that unmistakable prose style institutionalized by the *National Geographic:* (1) A big catch brings happiness to Tinei and his young companions. (2) As storm clouds gather in a tropic sky, the unspoken fear: Will the nets hold? (3) The wedding feast is a time for rejoicing, and so on.

Yet something in these hackneyed phrases moved me, suggested the frame for the story of my own life—for as soon as I had laid eyes on Halawa my heart was busy taking pictures just like Emory's. Everybody has a story behind the story. What shape was mine taking, in a tin-roof shack on Molokai? I thought about the Pacific and myself, the images and the psychological reality. What, exactly, did a Pacific drowning do to you? A selfish urgency informed my need to know. Did it kill you or transform you? Did it guarantee you a new life and enhanced being, like Ishmael? Or were there more sinister possibilities?

Drowned Queequeg had an uncle of sorts, name of Dirk Peters, Indian pal of Arthur Gordon Pym, literary alter ego of another unlikely seafarer, Edgar Allan Poe. Among the battered paperbacks passed from hand to hand around the Pukoo camp—reading matter was in such painfully short supply that we tore them in half to speed up the process—was *The Narrative of Arthur Gordon Pym of Nantucket*, a weird mixture of quasi-scientific summaries of real outer-world Pacific voyages by early explorers and an inner-world dream-allegory of the voyage to oblivion, in which events are constantly imagined (the plausibly irrational mode), then explained (the implausibly rational mode). The passive, swooning hero is a perfect vessel for this battle of intrapsychic forces in which Poe's *con*structive reason is always hurrying breathlessly behind, but never quite catching up with, his *des*tructive, death-loving imagination.

Unlike Melville, Poe had no anchor in gritty details of stripping whale carcasses, blood and lymph material running in the scuppers, and so on. There are no real toads in this imaginary garden: Poe's is an expressionist Pacific, a screen for the projection of inner psychic processes. The end of the narrative coincides with the voyagers' arrival in the southern polar regions (that is, the region of polarities, the poles of white-black), where they sail into a "limitless cataract" of white vapor pouring down from the sky, with huge white birds circling overhead that utter the same mysterious cries as the natives on an island they recently escaped. Just at the moment they are about to disappear into this whiteness, "there arose in our pathway a shrouded human figure, very far larger in its proportions than any dweller among men. And the hue of the skin of the figure was of the perfect whiteness of the snow." End of Pym's Pacific voyage, though Poe appends various maddening fussy notes pertaining to the former's unexplained survival from this mystic denouement and equally unexplained later death under other circumstances.

Rushing or, rather, getting sucked into whirlpools, cataracts, and *not getting out*—this was, after all, Poe's specialty. This flagrant pursuit of rebirth in death had its secret appeal for me, too. Clearly, Poe held a different attitude toward the "metaphysical" drowning experience than Melville (who was quite familiar with *The Narrative of Arthur Gordon Pym* and may have used it as a model). For Poe drowning is enticing death, but for Melville it is rebirth.

Melville's more robust sensibility turned the apotheosis of Arthur Gordon Pym into quite a different experience for Ishmael, though practical considerations of narrative may also have been involved, to wit: It is hard to read the conclusion of *Moby-Dick* without harboring the suspicion (voiced by others before me) that Melville, whipped into an apocalyptic frenzy that impelled him to sink the *Pequod* with *all* its hands, realized to his horror after penning that immortal last sentence—"Now small fowls flew screaming over the yet yawning gulf; a sullen white surf beat against its steep sides; then all collapsed, and the great shroud of the sea rolled on as it rolled five thousand years ago"—that he had drowned his first-person "point of view" right along with everybody else. A mighty whack of hand to forehead, then the hasty resurrection of Ishmael in the one-page "Epilogue": "And I only am escaped alone to tell thee."

So, bobbing in the ocean, Ishmael is pulled inexorably into the whirlpool left by the swallowed-up *Pequod:*

> Round and round, then, and ever contracting towards the buttonlike black bubble at the axis of that slowly wheeling circle, like another Ixion I did revolve. Till, gaining that vital centre, the black bubble upward burst; and now, liberated by reason of its cunning spring, and, owing to its great buoyancy, rising with great force, the coffin life-buoy shot lengthwise from the sea, fell over, and floated by my side.

All in all, a neat save, and a deeper affirmation, as well, representing as it does Herman Melville's instinctual backing away from the seductive black center of the Poe maelstrom.

My own soul felt caught between these two models: Poe's, in which you slide gloriously down the drain, and Melville's, in which you also slide down but are spit out again, gloriously transformed. All this time, though, a third model nipped at my heels: William Golding's, in which you drown and come back but shouldn't, because you are dead. (Poe was equally partial to

"coming back," of course, but only out of the ground, not the sea.)
In *Close Quarters,* Golding's narrator confronts a sailor he had
thought lost overboard:

> "Wheeler! You are a ghost. You were drowned, I said!" . . .
> "Yes, sir. But only after three days, sir. I believe it was
> three days. But you are right, of course, sir. Then I
> drowned."
> My hair prickled. His eyes rose now to meet mine. They
> never blinked.
> "I drowned, sir. I did—and the life in me so strong!"

Here was a sobering prospect. What if the whole transcendant
drowning experience backfired and turned me into some kind of
living zombie? Instead of becoming that new transfigured thing
I yearned to be, suppose I walked out of the water at Waimanalo
a ghost with no home, no past, and no future? Westerners can
lose their souls as easily as "natives"—more easily, because we no
longer know we have souls and thus lack the rituals to protect
them. Two hundred years' hard training had made Wheeler's
dilemma a subject the Hawaiians knew a little something about.
I had a lot to learn yet, and I was taking my first real instruction
here on the island of Molokai.

23

Molokai, Isle of Passion

In the unlikely event that no visitors came to the Pukoo camp, gossip dried up, or beer ran out, an evening run to Kaunakakai in the Land Rover was in order—sometimes even a visit to the only movie theater on the island, which was outdoors but was *not* a drive-in. A carryover both from the military presence in the Outer Islands during World War II and from the old planta- tion culture, it was a passing tradition in the new tourist indus- try–dominated society; except for a few holdouts like the Kaneohe and Haleiwa theaters, these places were gone on Oahu by the time I got there. In these termite-ridden palaces one dollar got you a sagging seat in a musty old hall with a roach- eaten velvet curtain and a couple of croton plants, miraculously alive without sunlight, decorating the stage. There were rustlings under the seats you didn't investigate. Either Island-style market research or a true spirit of cultural equality made it the custom to change the bill every night, providing a show for each major ethnic and/or interest group: Monday was samurai, Tuesday was Chinese martial arts, Wednesday Filipino, Thursday porno, Fri- day horror/sci fi, Saturday one slightly used Hollywood action film, and Sunday chop suey.

The Kaunakakai theater consisted of high school bleachers erected on the bare red West End dirt facing a large screen under which a white door marked the only "restroom" facility. As you watched the movie to the sound of mosquitoes grilling on the electrified rods strategically positioned above the bleachers, the door underneath flew open at unexpected moments and a blast of light and a loudly flushing toilet drowned out the sound and giant images overhead. Occasionally, even though this was the dry side of the island, a downpour stopped the show and everybody ran for cover.

Next to ghost stories, the kids liked retelling movie plots in the trenches the next day. Jim Brown and Raquel Welch in *100 Rifles* was an interracial combo that went down well with the Molokai audience. The opening scene, featuring dozens of dead Mexican rebels hanging on makeshift gallows, caused grunts of surprise among the impressionable Outer Island viewers of those inno- cent days. A burly Hawaiian man in front of me muttered, "Huh! Just as soon hang you as look at you!" (This remark immediately triggered in me the memory of an analogous moment during a screening of *The Pawnbroker* in a shabby-genteel Toronto movie theater: As a black kid brazenly rolled a lawnmower into Rod Steiger's Bronx pawnshop, an Anglo-provincial voice behind me whispered, in tones of deepest horror, *"Stolen!"*)

But just in the people around us there was plenty of story- behind-the-story. Take the old photos, for example. What they were was clear enough, only too clear. The story behind them eluded. These tiny sepia-tinted snaps, ancient and wrinkled, were passed around by the plump, light-skinned teenager who never quite met your eye. He didn't belong in the camp; he was somebody's relative or friend, one of the people who came around in the evening when the kids were playing ukes in the cookhouse or baby-sitting a child or two who had been dropped off for the evening. The others didn't seem to like him. Hoping to impress with these photos. His trump cards.

Asian men in uniforms, executioners and their victims. Corpses, corpses, and more corpses, always in the same careless attitudes of death regardless of the means of dispatch: hanging, rifle squad, indeterminate causes among the rubble of cities. The moment before a beheading, sword frozen over the neck, as formally poised as a wedding portrait.

My great-uncle, the boy explained. In China during the thirties. He took these pictures. Lots of commotion, yeah? "The Manchus," Tom whispered, but this was no explanation, either.

Then you had Butchie Dudoit with his permanent wave, his scarlet fingernails, and his revolving squad of *mahu* drivers, a different boy almost every day, chauffeuring us back and forth from Pukoo to Halawa Valley in the big Land Rover. Oh, those Molokai *mahus!* A nostalgic reminder came many years later when a beautiful blond man in the car ahead of me turned off on Market Street in San Francisco. All too clearly the California Department of Motor Vehicles board of censors had never been to Hawaii. The personalized license plate of his red Alfa Romeo read, in impeccable pidgin: "1 MAHU."

Among old-time Outer Island churchgoing Hawaiians, homosexual behavior was a lot more accepted than it was or is on the Mainland. The *mahus,* or male homosexuals, were an integral part of the very old life, and there was plenty of it left when I got to Molokai: All summer long the beach park at Halawa was full of *mahus* camping with a gaggle of seven-year-old boys who were always introduced as their nephews—which they may well have been, as I never knew them well enough to sort out what the complicated family and sexual allegiances might have been. Among the adults, however, it was always clear who was "one *mahu*" or "one tomboy"—as in, "Lani, yeah, she one tomboy."

By tradition all the waiters at Kane's bar in Kaunakakai were *mahu,* though not the clientele; they joked and flirted with their straight customers, who teased them and pinched them on the rear. I remember, hazily, heated discussions on minor points of the transvestitism law: As long as the guy wore jockey shorts under the pink dress, he was okay, yeah? Even today it seems no more than fitting that the Miss Gay Hawaii Beauty Pageant is held yearly in Kaunakakai.

What *did* those Polynesians get up to in the very old days? We had in camp a purportedly daring ethnographic study of the Polynesian outlier Ra'ivavae, written for the popular market by an anthropologist who had spent more time out there than was probably good for him. The back cover trumpeted such titillating excerpts as: "There was something deeper and darker which set this strange land apart. This was an island of passion, of terrible battles and erotic rites. War and sex walked hand in hand in Ra'ivavae." And the San Francisco *Chronicle* had let itself be quoted as saying: "Makes breviaries of sex such as the 'Kamasu-tra' seem like child's primers!"

The anthropologist, in whom the tedious chores of fieldwork had apparently produced, by way of compensation, a prurient obsession with the open, highly sophisticated sexual mores of the Polynesians, was fond of underscoring the "erotic basis of the ancient religion" with remarks like the following, which we enjoyed reading out to each other: "In one site Stokes had dug up a large stone image which was obviously an erect male phallus. And on each side of it he also found a full-size statue of a pregnant woman! The meaning of this would be made clear to us later."

Well, Molokai had its very own Phallic Rock up in the forest on the ridge over Kalaupapa, twelve feet high and pointed at a slant that meant business. The accompanying female stone was rumored to be in the bushes somewhere down the hill, but I was never able to find it. The postcard they sold in the Kaunakakai general store showed—for scale?—an unsmiling little Japanese woman tourist standing next to the huge thing. Dwarfed by it. *Not* touching it. Clutching her camera.

Still, there were limits, as the case of the two Momis demonstrated. Momi Lau, Hawaiian-Chinese, not on our dig but the most beautiful girl on the whole island, was going to attend a small church college on the Mainland in the fall. Cool as a marble statue, Momi Lau had the chaste, elegant manner of an aristocrat turned nun. A Hollywood star looked like a stripper next to Momi Lau. Story behind the story? Momi Lau was madly in love with Momi Morrison, the stocky, part-Hawaiian female mechanic at the only garage in Kaunakakai who had grease under her nails and wore coveralls exclusively. The doings of these two "tomboys" had grown so notorious that Momi Lau's parents were shipping her off the island to keep her out of trouble.

And there was our neighbor in Pukoo, Queenie—not, as the name might suggest, a Molokai *mahu,* but a prototypical Filipino bachelor in his sixties, of which there were many all over the Islands in those days. Most are probably still alive today, twenty years later; they were tough old birds after a lifetime of hard labor. Brought over in the thirties, these last representatives of the practice of importing foreign fieldhands for the pineapple and sugarcane industries of Hawaii were victims of a final twist in racial maneuvering on the part of the employers: the first over, the Chinese in the nineteenth century, were not allowed to bring wives so that they would not reproduce. This constraint was quickly circumvented by wholesale intermarriage with the hospitable Hawaiians to produce what is generally considered the most beautiful genetic blend in the Islands: big Polynesian bone structure with delicate Asian features. Observing these unanticipated results, the owners decreed that the next lot over, who happened to be the Japanese, should be allowed to bring wives from their own country to prevent racial mixing. The picture bride industry, plus perhaps a certain latent xenophobia among the new arrivals, caused a population explosion of such proportions that today in sheer numbers the Japanese are the dominant ethnic group in Hawaii.

Viewing this new outcome, the owners reverted as a last-gap tactic to the bachelors-only rule for the next and final group: the Filipinos. This time the strategy seemed to work all too well. By the time these men had enough money saved up to go home to the Philippines, they were too old and not rich enough to win a bride. Retired from work, they either stayed in their shacks on the plantation or rented cheap rooms in Honolulu, sentimental loners who made ridiculously easy marks for bar girls and other urban predators.

Queenie was a lot better off then his big-city counterparts. He had his own place by the side of the road near Pukoo, a fairly nice house even if the chickens did run through it. An avid fisherman and *opihi* picker, Queenie was one of the old Local bachelors who had lucked out beyond his wildest dreams when the cresting wave of hippies broke gently on Molokai's muddy shores, for there was always, during those never-to-be-repeated times, a young blond female in a madras sundress and puka shell necklace who needed a place to stay. Later he adopted many young hippie boys who stayed at the house to learn his considerable fishing lore. It was a sight you saw all over the Outer Islands during the early seventies: one short dark determined head, a gaggle of tall blond ones bobbing obediently behind like ducklings, all heading for their classroom, the ocean.

In Honolulu the Filipinos carried the stereotype of hot-tempered romantics—not for nothing was Romeo a common male first name—who preferred, among the small minority so inclined, to fight with broken bottles and knives, *sharp* things, as opposed to that old Local standby the baseball bat, the modern Hawaiian war club that also had the advantage of being legal to carry in your car. But Queenie was a gentle character, the sort of fellow who believed, where his heart was involved, that a woman is someone to whom money must be given, every day. Oh dear, Queenie in his baseball cap and brand-new aloha shirt, stars in his eyes, grinning and brandishing a wad of bills. It made me want to cry, thinking about how he must have been taken, but he seemed to *enjoy* being taken; I think that was part of the agony and the ecstasy for him. Though the Polynesian psyche had its own dark corners, Queenie's aloha lacked the sunny flavor of the original Hawaiian kind; some intense Latin-Filipino masochism gave his passion an entirely different twist.

Our camp cook, Rudy, who was also Filipino, took us to the chicken fights (never "cockfights" in Hawaii) on the pineapple plantation up at Maunaloa. The Local heart was a gambling heart, as all those discount flights from Honolulu to Las Vegas testified, and on Molokai gambling was very, very big. I had felt a certain superficial kinship with the chicken fight spectacle because before the 1964 arrest of 800-odd Berkeley students— a.k.a. the Free Speech Movement, I being one of them—chicken fights in the Islands made up the largest mass arrests in U.S. history. A single Sunday afternoon sweep, usually on image-conscious Oahu, routinely rounded up hundreds of men, women, and children. But no way were Filipinos going to give up their favorite animal sport. What's more, like certain oh-so-special plants, animals, foods, and words, chicken fighting was one of those foreign imports that had not simply overrun the Hawaiians. On the contrary: the Hawaiians themselves had run toward it like breathless lovers, clasped it eagerly to their bosoms, and pronounced it their own.

The dirt around the fighting cocks' coops was red and hard-packed. The arena was crowded with men, plantation men, barefoot, in dirty old T-shirts and *puka* pants (that is, full of holes). The women were all behind the food booths selling Filipino pupus: chicken adobo, cubes of fried pork fat, beer. Karma Riley and I, not working in a booth and the only haole women there, knew we were not where we should be, always an important point of Island etiquette—and, increasingly, of personal safety, though in those cordial days before Rent-a-Car tourism, condos, and haole land speculation, nobody bothered to give us the stink eye though there was plenty of politely veiled curiosity (if we weren't hippies or—dream the impossible dream—Honolulu hookers, what *could* we be?).

Dole and Del Monte owned the pineapple fields on Molokai, and their workers lived in modest shacks on the plantation grounds that they were allowed to buy from the company on low-interest terms. Here they kept their fighting chickens, brewed "swipe" (a horrifying firewater made of fermented pineapple I never sampled, one lost opportunity I have no regrets about), and led their cloistered, rigorous existence. High school kids were hired on for the summer harvest. (For this reason you never saw a pineapple at any luau on Molokai; the sight and smell of the highly acidic yellow fruit was universally loathed.)

On the sidelines crowds of men clustered around the gambling games. Big stacks of money, more cold cash than I'd seen in one place in my life, lay piled on the tables. They were betting at *pai dao,* a Chinese game of chance that seemed to involve a kind of domino. Scattered card games were also in progress. The protection wasn't visible, but you knew it wasn't far away. The day I had come in at the airport, the plane from Kahalui had just landed and two Local men got off, each carrying a rooster in a Port-a-Kennel. The only males on Molokai not wearing T-shirts, shorts, and zoris, they were easily identified by their dark glasses and imitation Italian suits as big-time Maui gangsters.

The first fight began. A mob surged toward the ring. Knowing I was there on sufferance only, I stayed put in the rear. Shouts, cheers, and in under three minutes it was all over. One glimpse of a bloody rooster carted off under its owner's arm, that was my chicken fight.

As Rudy would say: "Ah yaw!"

Ah yaw! was an expression I never heard uttered anywhere but Molokai, until I read a transliteration of it in one of those strange James Clavell historical novels so full of oaths and ethnic cursing and realized at last the original source: Paké—I mean Chinese.

Well, that figured. In my time Molokai was one of the few places in the Islands where the Chinese-descended Locals outnumbered the Japanese-descended Locals by a wide margin, and I never found out why. I remember only the Ah Ping store near

Pukoo where the owner, to the concealed giggles of the old Hawaiians sitting on the front porch, played a clever change-making game that separated the rare strayed tourist—invariably flustered and out of his depth in this distinctly non-Waikiki setting—from one thin dime.

Ah *yaw!* (Emphasis always falls on the second syllable.) An exclamation of surprise, wonder, delight, mild grievance with slightly ironic overtones, but without the stronger keening implications of the famous Hawaiian "alas" word, *auwe!* woe is me, so disconcertingly close to *oy veh* in sound and meaning (more fuel for the old theory that the Polynesians were the lost tribe of Israel?). Butchie Dudoit's friend Wayne said *auwe!* when he lifted a full case of Diamond Head cherry soda out of the Land Rover at lunchtime. Rudy said *ah yaw!* when we caught sight of the trailhead as we climbed up the last steep stretch of cliff trail from Kalaupapa.

Kalaupapa was the isolated "flat leaf" jutting out into the ocean under the steep cliffs on the other side of the East End valleys Halawa, Wailau, and Pelekunu. It was still the home of the leprosy settlement that had witnessed, a hundred years before, violent scenes of tragedy, suffering, and death, the martyrdom of Father Damien, during the epidemic that was the scourge of nineteenth-century Hawaiians. In my time, with the disease arrested and treatable by drugs, this formerly shunned no man's land was rumored to be a paradise of old Hawaii, where life had frozen in that mythic moment "before it all got spoiled." The residents ran a mule-ride operation down the steep cliffs that was a big success with tourists. Once, landing briefly on their tiny airstrip in a Royal Hawaiian twin-engine that dropped off the settlement's mail, poi, and the Honolulu newspapers, I had a glimpse like a dream of a man with a disfigured face, a woman missing her fingers. But when I walked down the trail myself and sat on the rocks of this legendary place, the ground was silent, truly dead. The misery and death, so attended to, blessed, sanitized, and scoured away by time, had utterly receded. That old green cemetery under the beetling cliffs held the most amazing story-behind-the-story on Molokai, namely this: You could actually go so far away when you died that you never came back, not for any reason.

24

Cash and Courtesy

There were no foreclosures of mortgages, no protested notes, no bills payable, no debts of honor in Typee; no unreasonable tailors and shoemakers, perversely bent on being paid; no duns of any description . . . no destitute widows with their children starving on the cold charities of the world; no beggars; no debtors' prisons; no proud and hard-hearted nabobs in Typee; or to sum up all in one word—no Money! That "root of all evil" was not to be found in the valley.

—Herman Melville, *Typee*

On Molokai you were expected to behave according to ethnic stereotype. Hawaiians were polite, haoles were rude; Hawaiians were late, haoles were punctual; Hawaiians were generous, haoles weren't. As part of Bishop Museum–community relations, Tom Riley was slated to give a talk to the Hawaiian Civic Club at a hall on the outskirts of Kaunakakai at seven o'clock one weekday evening. At 7:45 the Hawaiians arrived to unlock the building, but to their well-concealed amazement found no Mainland guest speaker angrily cooling his heels in the parking lot. Tom arrived at 8:15. No haole in living memory on Molokai had ever been that late before. He made an awesomely favorable impression.

Hawaiians and the other Polynesians deserved their reputation as one of the politest and most hospitable peoples on earth. But this was not the "natural" courtesy that Westerners like to imagine springs from some Garden of Eden native innocence.

154

Robert Louis Stevenson was socially astute enough to recognize this fact in his South Seas travels. But Jack London, like Melville before him, fell eagerly into the projection: the unequaled hospitality he enjoyed in Polynesia, he averred, was "due to no training, to no complex social ideals . . . it was the untutored and spontaneous outpouring from their hearts."

Pretechnological societies are not simple and natural. They are complicated and unnatural—more so than our own, in many ways. In the Pacific Island context, etiquette and hospitality were an integral function of an elaborate and highly artificial pre–cash economy social structure based on the giving and receiving of favors that were and still are as closely computed as any bookkeeper's ledger sheet. It's dangerous to wax sentimental over the pre-money days, when barter debts could be just as oppressive as money ones, and harder to get out of. (The Icelandic sagas, one feels, give an excellent picture of the "down" side of this ritualized reciprocity.)

The fine art of barter or ritual exchange, self-interested though it ultimately is, requires from its participants tremendous tact, delicacy, and sensitivity, lots of greasing of the social wheels, to function smoothly. A coin or bill, in contrast, does not have to possess these qualities to do its job. Thus, we find a direct correlation between the decline of "manners" and hospitality on one hand and the rise of the capitalist economy that replaced giving and taking, that is, barter, with buying and selling.

This was a point never sufficiently understood by some hippies. Of these young haoles the Outer Island Hawaiians—who were polite, sheltered, and as sensitive to social nuance as a small-town Southern ladies' club of the 1920s—frequently said, "You give them something out of your yard, they say, 'Wow! Free banana,' they give nothing back. All they are is gimme, gimme, gimme, just like Honolulu people." (In the world view of Molokai residents of my time, many of whom had never been off the island, anybody from Oahu, even a Local person, was a kind of haole. As Pauline Kainoa said, "All Honolulu people think about is this": motion of fingers rubbing an imaginary greenback.)

On both sides, though, the bitter ironies lingered. Years after my time on Molokai, I read a Honolulu newspaper item announcing the opening of the Sheraton Molokai over on the old West

End beach land formerly owned by the plantations. Molokai residents employed by the new hotel, the last paragraph noted, were attending compulsory workshops in etiquette and weight-watching.

Ah, and who was teaching whom? It made me think of the ultimate lesson in Polynesian etiquette. I can't remember where I read it, and so this story must remain apocryphal though not, I hope, a figment of my imagination. (I have my doubts because the consumption of "long pig," or human flesh, was usually always strictly ceremonial, not culinary, in Polynesian societies.) It seems to me the instruction was delivered by a Maori leader who had graciously endured the harangues and arrogance of his English missionary guest for weeks on end. (In our gallery of inter-Polynesian stereotypes Maoris, the old Maoris, were reputedly slower to anger than Samoans but, thanks to their constant inter-tribal feuding, far more ferocious once sufficiently provoked.) The visual impression this Westerner made on his patient but increasingly irritated host went something like this: "A black garment, a skinny neck, a red face, an open mouth always talking, talking, talking"—an all-too-recognizable portrait of the less attractive attributes of genus *haole*. Pushed to the limit when the missionary tried to snatch a sacred god stick out of his hands, the exasperated chief ordered him popped in the earthen steam oven, his rusty black coat functioning as a kind of tamale wrapper—and by this drastic measure was finally able to enjoy his first good meal for weeks in silence.

Molokai etiquette had its own rough edges, as the incident of the 110-case luau demonstrated. The party took place next door to the Peace Corps camp in Pukoo, and not that many people were invited—analogous to the Big Island's famous singing Kalima Brothers, who billed themselves as "1,000 Pounds of Melody," and there weren't that many brothers. One of the attendees at this memorable function was Tom Riley, who, after some serious partying, almost caused a major fracas when he tried to depart at midnight. The host turned ugly at the prospect of his hospitality being prematurely spurned and, Tom reported to us somewhat incoherently on his return to camp late the next morning, made him stay till all 110 cases of Primo beer had been drunk; otherwise, he said, he would have gotten beat up.

Even as we all bathed in the spurious lingering glow of primal courtesies and exchanges—reaping all the benefits with none of the responsibilities—by my time the people of Molokai had long since butted heads with twentieth-century economic reality. "Cash crop" had been the elusive Holy Grail of prewar old-time Island economy, what Local families squeezed in the vise between the vast sugarcane/pineapple monopolies and the insufficiency of their taro fields to bring in enough money kept seeking, seeking, failing to find. The marks of these brave attempts were still to be found in the abandoned wet valleys of all the Outer Islands, where unexpectedly you came upon berry-laden coffee bushes poking out of the undergrowth, stray clumps of sisal, untended trees bearing giant mushy avocados.

Up on the ridge above Kalaupapa you could look down into a little culvert and make out a long tear-shaped indentation under a thick carpet of grass: poignant relic of Hawaii's very first ill-fated cash crop. In the old days sandalwood, or *iliahi* as the Hawaiians knew it, was briefly a big industry in the Islands. (By as early as 1845 the scented, close-grained heartwood had been ruthlessly logged out, with no replanting.) This very hole, dug to roughly the dimensions of an average clipper ship's hold, was used to measure shiploads of wood being carried down by mule to the dock at Kamaaloa. Even though a hundred and fifty years of rain had silted up its bottom and sides, the grassy dent seemed shockingly small. Narrow, cramped, landlocked up here in the mountains, looking more like a sunken grave than a prosaic device for gauging cargo, it called up irrelevant memories of Viking burials, the excavation at Sutton Hoo. Earth mirror of those grand sailing ships that loomed so large in my imagination, a sandalwood hull.

The ultimate cash crop proved not to be macadamia nuts and arrived on the scene a generation too late, namely, in the 1970s, long after everybody had given up and moved out of the valleys. To this end, I was present at a historic occasion. Two, actually: the first marijuana-growing bust on the island of Molokai, summer of 1970, and the first community meeting held to discuss this problem.

The year before, in 1969, the first hippies had migrated from Maui to Molokai, literally as well as figuratively in search of greener pastures. They made a beeline for Halawa, where they were welcomed with open arms by Johnny Kainoa, who promptly installed them in a house or two behind his and allotted them land to garden on. Johnny loved to talk and all these impressionable young haoles made for an appreciative audience, one that had never heard his rap before—a real windfall for the hardened raconteur who has long since burned out his original listening group.

The hippies began growing marijuana in their plots right away. It was only a matter of time before Outer Island law caught up with this brand-new offense. One bright afternoon a clutch of excited police officers trooped out to the beach trenches and stood over us proudly waving a sheaf of pungent plants under our noses. "You see this stuff growing anywhere," they instructed, "you come tell."

About a week later the police called a community meeting down at the high school. The lieutenant had a sample "lid of grass" he passed around for inspection to his mostly middle-aged and elderly audience of Molokai residents as he explained the history and use of marijuana. (First bad omen: The lid never came back.) When he mentioned that Hawaii was a natural place for these outsiders to plant their dope because the fertile Hawaiian soil grew anything well, a visible ripple of Local pride ran through those assembled. Guarded allusions to opium use in the old days were volunteered by an elderly Paké—the Chinese connection—but the unexpected high point of the evening came when the sergeant, seeking to impress with his knowledge of official statistics, wrote the resale figures from grower to "street" on the blackboard for all to see.

No one present had the slightest difficulty figuring out that profits of more than 1,000 percent accrued from cultivation of the exotic new crop. The cries of amazement these figures produced soon gave away, one sensed, to some rapid mental calculations among the cannier of the thrifty subsistence farmers. Mistakenly thinking to paint a picture of sinister underworld profiteering, the police had in fact sown an all-too-fertile seed in the minds of some. Out of the first shoots of marijuana nurtured all over the Islands by hippie and surfer Johnny Appleseeds were to come, fifteen to twenty years later, their twentieth-generation descendants, gnarled and bonsaied as English tea roses or Zinfandel grapes, a microgenealogy as prized by their haole and Local growers as anything in the *Kumulipo,* the featured centerfold of *High Times* magazine and now matured to transform Island economy forever. The new cash crop turned the Big Island, for example, into a combat zone of marijuana cultivation that quickly surpassed sugarcane in profitability, initiated high-level ruthless dealings that transformed the criminal world in Hawaii forever, forged ties with its Mainland counterpart, interpenetrated Local and Mainland cultures and economies in ways no one in that room or any of us young haoles blithely lighting up a joint the better to bodysurf, eat "natural" ice cream, or read *The Tibetan Book of the Dead,* ever dreamed possible.

25

Typee Revisited

> Born was the woman Groping-one
> Born was Dim-sighted, a woman
> It was Day.
>
> —the *Kumulipo*

The summer was almost over. The kids were moving out of camp, I was about to return to Honolulu—a metropolis that, after two months in Halawa Valley and the Pukoo camp, seemed as remote as Paris or London—and the resumption of my role, equally remote, as young professor. For in this short time Molokai had become my Marquesas, my very own Typeeland. We were discovering, in an odd conjunction of influences, that the early settlement of oval-shaped dwellings we had uncovered on the beach at Halawa may have first been settled from the Marquesas and not Tahiti as former theories had held. Meanwhile, away from the dig, I had occasion to bite down one of the many unexpected hard nuggets of Polynesian truth in the often inflated fluff of *Typee:* namely, when Melville's narrator Tommo and his shipmate Toby, jumping ship in Nukuhiva, flee over the mountains to the other side of the island and encounter a nightmare series of waterfalls, each dropoff getting longer as they naively attempt to follow a stream from its source at the top of the mountains to the coast.

One afternoon I went hiking on the ridge above Pukoo with Kevin, a haole high school student from Oahu. It was a mysterious place, these misty upland slopes above the riven gulches of the East End. In the dense fog that seemed to steam out of the ground, herds of shy Axis deer grazed among stunted *ohia lehua*. A gelatinous bog covered by a thin skin of grass quaked as we walked over it. Gouts of black soil, traces of wild pigs' uprootings, were everywhere.

Impulsively we slid over a steep slope, shinnied down a convenient tree like a firepole, and found ourselves in a storybook little valley. It seemed much easier simply to walk out of the valley to the main road than to go back up the way we came, and so, following the inevitable stream, we set out through the underbrush. The first waterfall we hit was like something you would find in a Japanese garden: a miniature delight three feet high. We clambered down the slippery rocks and walked along the side of the stream until we came to the next one, which was about fifteen feet high and required a little more skill getting down. Approaching still another dropoff we failed to notice, just as Tommo and Toby had, the "voice of a cataract which had for some time sounded like a low deep bass to the music of smaller waterfalls." We found ourselves at the top of a monster torrent pouring sixty feet straight down onto a jawful of glistening black rocks.

Even for a pair of fools, going farther was out of the question. We retraced our steps back up the valley and tried to climb out a little way below the tree we had slid down. But here again the valley wall turned traitor and we found ourselves elbowing up a sheer incline with nothing to hold onto but bits of dead grass clipped close to the ground by nimble goats. At last I managed to pull myself over the edge. (That's the maddening thing about these Hawaiian mountains, the top has a visible edge, just as the spine of a ridge comes to a point.) There I lay panting, feeling stupid and grateful, shaking all over like the coward I was.

Rereading *Typee* in camp, I was thunderstruck to come upon Melville's minutely accurate description of my own experience. Series of progressively steeper waterfalls are, of course, a feature common to all these high volcanic islands of the Pacific, displaying the same terrible repetitive natural symmetry as the endless up-and-down mountain ridges or the surrealist procession of valley and half-valley edges that unfold along the Napali coast on Kauai. Though I doubt very much whether Tommo and the redoubtable Toby would have survived such a series of jumps in the real world—especially that last 300-foot drop so vividly painted, the actual descent of it so conveniently glossed over—still, Melville saw something, he remembered what he saw and wrote it down, and these hundred and twenty-odd years later I saw what he saw and knew what he wrote was true, true as Gauguin's colors.

Our appetites for adventure whetted by this escapade, Kevin and I decided next to hike the famous Wailau Trail over the mountains. The road ended in Halawa Valley, and the next valley around the bend, Wailau, was accessible only by boat or trail. In between were towering coastal cliffs with waterfalls dropping into *papa haku,* mock or incomplete valleys. Those 3,000-foot sea cliffs, the highest in the world, were so sheer that Tom Riley and another archaeologist, camping the night in one of these shadowed rain gulches, woke up to hear the interminably long falling cry of a goat that had fallen off the top. In the morning they found its shattered body a hundred feet from their tent.

The Wailau trailhead was located on some land owned by a woman in Kaunakakai whose permission we neglected to ask. Her Filipino caretaker came out to the road and told us we couldn't trespass. Then he pointed out how to walk around the land to get on the trail. "She no see you," he added. We decided we hadn't heard this last part because fifteen minutes into the hike we were already staggering under the weight of our sixty-pound World War II metal backpacks; it was a real relief to be turned away. We went out to Halawa instead and hitched a ride around the bend in a fisherman's Boston Whaler.

Because the beach at Wailau was rocky, boats had to anchor in the bay. Kevin and I swam to shore floating our packs on inner tubes. From our low point in the heaving water the deserted mammoth of a valley, choked with blooming ginger, mountain apple, guava, thimbleberry, loomed curiously overhead. A thirty-foot ridge of land blocked most of Wailau's yawning mouth except for the stream, which emptied on the far left-hand side of the bay. In the interior the huge opening took a sharp twist, obstructing our view of the valley head.

This Wailau was a wet valley, wetter than Halawa. It was the biggest, wettest, emptiest valley I had ever seen. Waterfalls ran off the high mountain flatlands down the valley's thousand-foot sides, all feeding into the immense Wailau Stream. In the half mile or so we managed to hack and crawl our way through a tangle of guava and *ohia lehua,* I counted ten waterfalls on each side of the valley, and Wailau was about eleven miles deep. That meant at least two hundred waterfalls of varying sizes poured into this enormous drainage sluice of a valley floor. We slogged endlessly through mud; the ground seemed like one quaking liquefied mass. There wasn't a dry inch anywhere. How could people have lived here? But once, like Halawa, Wailau had been a thriving community.

We had just set up a sagging pup tent on the beach when a new boat appeared in the bay. A white-haired Hawaiian elder waded furiously to shore followed by two young men. It was Walter Naki with two of his twenty children, and he just couldn't believe another couple of haoles had invaded his valley. Last week some hippies had camped right over there; a huge brown finger pointed, quivering, to a spot up the beach. Wailau was a "terror place," Walter warned. Nobody had lived here for years. On and on he ranted in apoplectic fury. But hospitality carried the day, as it had to—unthinkable, not to share dinner ("Here, you take my food but no thanks, I don't want your food")—and that clear, rainless evening by the fire Walter Naki unbent and told us more about Wailau.

Before World War I, he said, Wailau Valley had had its own church and school. Every summer a boat came around from the wharf at Kamaaloa to sell supplies. In winter, when storm surf in the little bay reached fifteen feet, entry by water was impossible and people had to go in and out by the Wailau Trail Kevin and I had tried unsuccessfully to take. Over on the Leeward side people could tell how wet it was in Wailau, whether or not they could take the trail, if a waterfall sprouted in the mountains above Kamaaloa. Children used to walk the Wailau Trail every day to high school on the Kaunakakai side. Walter Naki himself had carried sixty-pound bags of taro root from Wailau to Kamaaloa three times a day.

The Wailau Trail, I found out later, also served Pelekunu, the next valley over. Mrs. Nae, who visited our Pukoo camp, was born and raised in Pelekunu. At the head of their valley, she told us, a sheer drop interrupted the junction of the end of their little valley trail with the beginning of the trail up to the ridge of the mountains. She remembered as a child being lashed to a cluster of sturdy bamboo held down by a person below; her father would be standing on the trail twenty feet above waiting to catch her when the bamboo, released, sprang up with her on it. At the top of the ridge their little valley trail joined the main Wailau Trail. But the Wailau Trail had fallen into disuse and was now sadly overgrown. The year after we were there, a young haole store owner from Honolulu was lost on the trail, his body never found.

Just before we swam out to the fishing boat that was to take us back around the bend to Halawa—for we stayed only a day and a night in this eerie place that seemed on the verge of dissolving at any moment—Kevin and I walked over to the abandoned hippie camp on the beach. A piece of warped plywood plunked down on the rocks, opened tin cans from the Kaunakakai store, burned stubs of incense, soggy wads of toilet paper—these flimsy remains, pathetic as a dead cat, made me want to cry. Wailau was a place everybody deserted. A purple madras bedspread that once had functioned as some kind of brave canopy lay in a soaked mass on the rocks, a long *ohia* stick tangled in its folds. It was the wettest bedspread I had ever seen. Fresh-water wet, rain-wet, wetter even than cloth floating in the ocean. Already its form was blurry, uncertain. Wailau would finish off that bedspread within the week. Annihilate it with wetness.

Down the beach from the valley, walkable at low tide, was a grove of *hala* trees—or pandanus, as the nineteenth-century haole writers always called them. These prehistoric-looking succulents grew in the sand right down to the surf's edge and had sharp, dagger-shaped leaves, smooth barkless skin, and an inedible orange fruit or "key" whose smell, never quite discernible to me, sent old-time Hawaiians crazy; it was their aphrodisiac. The branches of the *hala* trees divided in a simple, archetypal manner and so there was a very primal Hawaiian perspective, like a glimpse of eternity: a bright triangle of turquoise ocean and white sand framed in the fork of a *hala* tree. Others have looked through the fork in the *hala* tree, too; its secrets are beautifully captured in the photographs of Robert Wenkham.

The birth of the soul is considered a second birth, but are you really alive, are you even human, before that second birth takes place? Before I came to Molokai I had had no real life of the spirit. As a very young person I had only begun to taste what lay beyond the narrow limits of my ego. But Molokai had broken this stasis, initiated an inner movement. In the summer of 1970 I was reborn in the fork of a *hala* tree. This is a fact. What is not certain is whether it happened in a dream I dreamed in the shacks at Pukoo or in that real tree I climbed into a few hundred yards down the beach from Wailau Valley.

Somehow, in my dream or in real life—no psychedelic trip this time, I was entirely lucid—I climbed up into the *hala* tree. (I know I did, even though I keep thinking now how hard it would have been to do in "real life" because of the prickly leaves covering the ground, the fragile branches that would scarcely have borne my weight.) Entering that triangle of light was an irreversible act. Crouched in the fork, I felt myself pushed forward, over the other side and, in one of those convulsions of grace that overcame me in the Islands, the bundle of blind impulses that went up the tree came down whole. This wholeness was connected to a world I could not see, marked by secret entry points like the fork of the *hala* tree. But disturbingly, my sense of completeness given to me by this Outer Island, this locus in the physical world, was embedded in it, dependent on it, so that even as my spirit expanded—I felt it do this as we lifted off the tarmac the very next week, bound for Honolulu—it drew in its wake the glowing, possessive, hard-to-shake Molokai ghosts.

FARTHER INTO THE ARCHIPELAGO

26

Jumping-off Places

This is the last place. There is nowhere else to go.
Human movements,
          but for a few,
are Westerly.
Man follows the Sun.

          —Lew Welch, "The Song Mt. Tamalpais Sings"

My primal hesitation about humanhood, Day, persisted. Something in me wanted to stay submerged, did not want to separate and grow. So many adventures still waited underwater, in the long night! After Molokai the next two years were filled with digs, surveys, treks on the other Outer Islands. At some point in time—during the fifties, I suspect—by fiat of the Hawaii Visitors Bureau "Outer" was changed to "Neighbor" and each island was christened with a cute, euphemistic tag designed to deflect attention from its major flaw, vis-à-vis tourism: soggy Kauai (where, as they said in the old song, *Hanohano Hanalei i ka ua nui*, "The glory of Hanalei is its heavy rain") became the "Garden Isle," Molokai with its lousy beaches became the "Friendly Isle," and so on.

The Outer Islands, I found in my explorations, curiously resembled and disresembled each other. What struck me most in all the spots I came to know well was the superabundance of place names. Every rock, every turn of the bend, every rise and fall of the land, every surf break, every variation in the wind and rain had a name. Astonishing numbers of Hawaiian place names survived, even though countless more had been lost and those preserved on the maps were dropping away, too, as the intensely topographic sensibility subsided.

Hawaiian place names are, literally, poetry; their multilayered associations of topography, sexual innuendo, and mythic allusion dominate the chants and hula. Sayings also clustered around specific seas, rains, and winds attached to each island; in the very old days each place carried its own inimitable "halo of delight or sorrow," specific personal, historical, and mythic associations. The act of naming itself, as in the *Kumulipo*, held great power. Speaking the names, chanting them, established cognitive control of the surrounding environment. Old-time Hawaiian storytellers peppered their tales with long recitals of place names, both to authenticate the story as well as to allow listener and teller alike to participate in the joy of hearing an accumulation of well-loved names. Here is a simple example, a song that circles clockwise around the districts of the island of Hawaii, translated by Samuel Elbert and Noelani Mahoe:

Hilo, Hanakahi, rain rustling *lehua*.
Puna, fragrant bowers, bowers fragrant with *hala*.
Ka'u, the wind, the dirt scattering wind.
Kona, the sea, the streaked sea.
Ka-wai-hae, the sea, the whispering sea.
Wai-mea, the rain, the Kipu'upu'u rain.
Kohala, the wind, the Apa'apa'a wind.
Hamakua, the cliff, the tropic birds flying cliffs.
Tell the refrain, rain rustling *lehua*.

The main Hawaiian islands share place names among them—Kailua, Waimea, Mauna Loa. This similarity is pan-Polynesian in the same way that the New England states each have their Concords, Haverhills, and Readings, reflecting the origins of their Anglo-European settlers. Upolu, for example, is a name also found in Samoa, and in all the older Polynesian settlements "Hawaiki" (cognate with "Hawai'i") was the mythic homeland. The familiar Hawaiian place names "Kona" and "Koolau" mean "south" and "north," and thus their cognates "Tonga" and "Tokelau" designate the Pacific island groups lying farthest south and farthest north in the macrocosm of the known Polynesian world.

170

Adding to this sense of cloning and endless serial duplication, most of the main Hawaiian islands, thanks to their volcanic formation, have analogous shapes. All have a Windward and a Leeward, the archipelago being oriented on the northeast–southwest axis. All but Oahu Lanai and Niihau have inaccessible northeastern wet valleys.

For all their maddening, dreamlike similarities, however, each island, and each spot on each island, has its own ineffable essence. During my time I had a proud boast: "Put me down in any valley on any island, and in half an hour I'll tell you where I am." Although nobody with a helicopter ever put me to the test, what if a person was to be airlifted, say, suitably blindfolded, into some anonymous dripping green Hawaiian jungle—how would the identification proceed?

Your first duty, naturally, would be to find the stream, which wouldn't take long in the average steep-sided Hawaiian gulch. Once you were at the stream and now possibly had a clear view of the walls of your valley, the next big clue would be the larger subliminal impression the island itself produced: Kauai, the oldest, where the mountains were a bit more worn down, their edges softened by the weathering of thousands of years, to Hawaii, the newest and rawest.

Now, having guessed your island, you would need to determine if your valley lay on the Leeward or Windward side of a mountain range, and of which range: as a rule Leeward is dry and Windward wet, but most Leeward valleys are wet at their heads. On all the islands the mountain walls are always far sheerer on the Windward side, where the northeast trades and rains beat against them.

Your ultimate guide, however, would be the fact that all these deserted valleys, so alike with their waterfalls, streambanks, prehistoric house platforms, and overgrown taro terraces cloven by the roots of labyrinthine *hau* and guava forests, differ utterly in the way their features are combined. On one level they seem interchangeable. On another, deeper level they are not. For the individual identity of each valley grows out of a unique accumulation of thousands of specific natural features: the insanely sheer valley walls of the Big Island's North Kohala valleys. The hump of land blocking the mouth of Molokai's Wailau Valley that always kept you from mistaking it for the even huger Waipio on the Big Island. The crook of Halawa's stream mouth. The rugged coastal cliffs where Kipahulu Valley on Maui meets the sea next to the lava spillover of Kaupo Gap. The unmistakable way the Windward Koolaus rear up, full of stern green menace, behind Kahana Valley on Oahu.

And the Hawaiians consecrated these details of the natural landscape in names, so that Halawa Valley was not simply Halawa but the sum of its expanding attributes, of—to take only the 1,200-meter stretch of land on each side of the mouth of Halawa stream—Manuwa, Kaio, Pua'alaulau, Hakuhea, Keauhou, Kaaoku, Mooiki, and Kohopapala; of its waterfalls Moa Ula, Hipuapua, and Makaelelele; of its two *heiau* and innumerable smaller shrines, so that, focusing ever more sharply, a limited geographical area opens up a sense of infinite possibility: the continent of Hawaii.

This continent of mine, the most geographically remote island group in the world, was actually an archipelago, a distinctive 2,000-mile-long undersea volcanic mountain chain that hooks far into the middle Pacific latitudes. After the inhabited Eight Islands of the Hawaiian universe—Hawaii, Maui, Kahoolawe, Lanai, Molokai, Oahu, Kauai, Niihau—came the dry Leeward Necker and Nihoa, seasonally inhabited by fishermen in prehistoric times, where Mad Jack Percival from Honolulu once hid out in the early nineteenth century, now a bird sanctuary reeking of guano. Hundreds more miles of water, then numerous bits and dots poked out of the Pacific: the French Frigate Shoals, the Garden Pinnacles, Midway, Laysan Island, Pearl and Humes Atoll.

East, toward America, were more islands in the making. Off the southeast tip of the Big Island, the vulcanological factory was busy manufacturing the next link in the island chain. Naturally, this yet-to-surface Hawaiki already had a name: the Loihi Seamount.

The pre-Contact Hawaiians understood the process by which undersea volcanoes had formed their islands, as a traditional gourd-beating *(pa-ipu)* hula demonstrates. Of this hula the translator, my friend Kenneth Davids, writes: "It is quite clear from this chant and from many other sources that the ancient Hawaiians knew the origin of their land: that volcanic eruption raised it from the ocean, and furthermore, that Kauai, the westernmost island of the Hawaiian chain, was the oldest geographically, and Hawaii, the easternmost and still volcanically active island, the youngest. This knowledge of actual geologic history structures the Gourd-Beating Hula, which follows the geological drama of volcanic conception of the land, beginning with Kauai and moving eastward through Oahu (the second oldest of the four major islands), Maui, and finally Hawaii, the youngest. The language is, as usual, sexually charged."

The refrain, working from Kauai to Hawaii, runs:

> Where the sun comes up there's a pit:
> Pele's hot pit.
> Clouds hang down,
> lightning shoots out,
> shoots out down here,
> shoots out up there,
> crickle crackle
> the stick goes in,
> the stick comes out,
> the first man yells:
> who's digging there?
> It's me, Pele,
> who digs the pit and stokes the fire,
> burning inside Kauai . . .

Whether you thought of Hawaii as an archipelago or a continent, with that land's-end aura oozing from every little airstrip, green pali, and deserted beach, the Outer Islands still had a way of bringing you up short, making you realize you were, in some inscrutable but definite way, at the end of the line. In the very old days the Hawaiians thought so, too. The northwesternmost point of an island, they believed, was a place that funneled the souls of dead people to their ultimate destination, the underworld. On Kauai, I knew, it was Polihale on the Leeward side of the Napali coast. On Oahu, says Martha Beckwith in her classic scholarly work *Hawaiian Mythology*, this *leina-a-uhane*, or leaping place of the souls, was somewhere near Kaena Point, now a rugged, desolate place accessible only by jeep, frequented by fishermen and joyriding soldiers from Schofield Barracks. Originally, every district had its leaping-off place for souls, where a tree—like my *hala* tree?—acted as a path either toward or away from the underworld.

When I returned to California, I confronted, with a shock of recognition, that supreme American *leina-a-uhane,* the Golden Gate: a symbolic westernmost spot of land, its bridge a convenient launching pad to the underworld, the only difference being that here the souls, though lost, were not yet dead when they leaped. The poet Lew Welch, hypnotized by these spots like so many others, vanished into the landscape just north of the Gate. Out of the fork in the tree to baptism or death? This was the tightrope all Pacific young people, haole and Polynesian, walked.

Yes, keeping your footing was important in the Outer Islands. Feet and footgear took on added significance. Because your feet connect you to the ground, they are so to speak your *standpoint* in relation to the world. Shoes mediate the connection. This was an area that gave me problems. When I took up exploring the Islands in the grand manner, I found myself obliged to shoe my feet in the diametrical opposite of zoris, namely, hiking boots. First I mail-ordered a succession of expensive European models from the Mainland. Delicately balanced as Swiss timepieces, these expertly crafted artifacts of suede, leather, and iron epitomized that sterile haole obsession with "perfect" high-tech gear—camping equipment, mountain bikes, skis, and the like—that somehow always manages to miss the mark. They weighed ten pounds apiece and turned my heels into raw meat no matter what quantity of Dr. Scholl's foam pads I pasted on ahead of time. Local folk, who seemed rarely to hike for pleasure* and mostly went into the wilderness to hunt pig, goat, and deer, wore $25 Sears workboots, modest comfortable footgear I ultimately and thankfully reverted to.

*The notable exception—if "pleasure" is the right word—was the Local and Local haole–dominated Hawaiian Trail and Mountain Club, whose members went in for eleven-hour survival treks *"piko* (belly button)-deep in mud," as their circular gleefully advertised. The TMC favored army surplus gear and broiled goat steaks, a sensibility light-years removed from, and highly contemptuous of, the two-hour haoelified Sierra Club strolls with their frequent rest stops and freeze-dried fettucine.

Jumping-off Places

A blister contracted on the sidewalks of Honolulu was one thing; in the Hawaiian wilderness it became quite another matter. The fertile red soil of the Islands teemed with enough staphylococcus to fell an army, infecting the tiniest cut or hangnail. The blisters I brought back from the first summer on Molokai refused to go away, no matter how much I soaked them the "natural way," as the progressive-thinking young doctor at the Kaiser Clinic advised me. In fact, gradually I seemed to have rather more sores than I started out with. Cuts on my arms weren't healing at all. In class my Hawaiian students shook their heads in dismay. I went back to Kaiser, where a different, horrified doctor took a culture. My blood contained not just staph but strep and gangrene. He shot me full of penicillin, swathed both my feet in white gauze, and sent me home.

Since I had ridden down to Kaiser on my bicycle, there was nothing for it but to ride back: my feet didn't really hurt, in spite of the impressive set of bandages that came right down to my straw-and-red-velvet Jap slaps. So I jumped on my white Schwinn ten-speed and pumped away up to Punchbowl. In this fashion I was almost to Green Street when a haole man in a late-model car swerved in front of me with an urgent offer: $100 if I came home with him. This was not an uncommon experience for a young female bicycle rider; once some kids in a car had grabbed my hand and towed me several hair-raising blocks. It was only bewildering never to have gotten quite so specific or so large an offer, before or after, with unbandaged feet.

Hiking in the Hawaiian mountains, I often felt the pressure building under my toenails while making a steep descent with a backpack on. The toe throbbed, the nail turned an alarming maroon; but in a few weeks everything was okay. This happened quite a lot with my fancy metal-toed Swiss boots, to the point where I once found myself completely unable to get them back on. We were camped at Paliku on the edge of Haleakala Crater, a magnificent pit that is not a real crater but rather a series of small cinder cones set within a larger bowl-shaped depression. Our plan was to walk out the Kaupo Gap—where the now-hardened lava had once broken over the lip of the crater and poured down to the ocean—on a slippery, treacherous eight-mile switchback composed entirely of lava rubble, or *a'a* (a Hawaiian word that, according to Local wit, was invented the first time someone stepped barefoot on the razor-sharp volcanic gravel).

What to do? This was no job for boots, sneakers, or even Jap slaps, wedgies, go-aheads, or any effete variations thereof: all my tortured feet wanted were those trusty Woolworth shower slippers always at the ready in the side compartment of my backpack. Slinging on my forty-pound backpack, twenty of which were the boots, I walked, no, *flew* in blessed relief down Kaupo Gap, backpack and all, my foam-light zoris like Mercury's winged sandals, to the flat blue sea below Hana, even though by the time we reached sea level at the old Piilani highway the abrasion of the lava rubble had worn them paper thin and my faithful 39¢ friends ended up where all shower slippers go, namely, in the trash.

The scars from the gangrenous blisters stayed with me. I thought I would have them for life; now, two decades later, they are gone. In their place, by way of eerie substitution, are my two dead big toenails, souvenirs of a much later time in New Zealand when a group of xenophobic "trampers" dedicated to demonstrating Kiwi bush superiority over their luckless Yank companion achieved their goal via a maniacal twelve-hour death march jumping off cliffs and fording rivers in the North Island's Ruahine Mountains, and in this way the Pacific branded my standpoint for good.

27

Maui

Full moon, around midnight, bouncing in a jeep on a back road above Hana—no, that can't be right, no other roads run parallel to the ocean except the main road, the old Piilani highway, but somehow it sticks in my mind we're driving up there on the slope of Haleakala, directly over Hana. Below, to our right, the sea stretches out, one huge flat geometric plane bounded by the dark bulk of Hawaii, the Big Island. The cloudy starless sky breaks over us like a second ocean marbled through and through with streaks of light. Our driver, a young ceramicist named Ira Ono, has turned off the headlights and we are riding under the moon like a dream. Succulents line the road on either side: cereuses. Out of all the year (of five years, of fifty years?), the cereuses are blooming this night. For such monsters, the huge white flowers give off a fragrance of great delicacy; their innards display the complicated symmetry of tile patterns in a mosque. The blooms soak up the moonlight and turn it back in a second, reflected glow: the moon is their sun, feeding them. Headlights loom; Ira switches on his for a brief, glaring encounter. Then we're plunged into the bright night again and our silent mysterious ride, hurtling past cereuses.

December 1971: I went to Maui to make a small field survey of Kipahulu Valley, a restricted area that cut down the eastern flank of Haleakala Crater. As an ecological pocket whose isolation was ensured by the steep dropoff between the upper and lower portions of the valley, Upper Kipahulu was one of the last places in the Islands where the *manu 'o'o* (black honey-eater), the *'iwi* (scarlet honeycreeper), and a substantial number of other endangered native birds and plants survived. Lower Kipahulu was the site of a spectacular set of tiered pools—dubbed "sacred" by an anonymous poet at the Hawaii Visitors Bureau—that fed one into the other down to the ocean. The drop from one pool to the next was not enormous. Still, the ranger's dog I took bathing in these pools scared me witless when he, along with my camera, was sucked over the falls of one into the larger pool below. He survived, much embarrassed; the camera did not.

My field notebook of this walkabout dutifully records signs of house platforms, taro terraces, historic cattle enclosures, but my heart preserves just two images: the bamboo forest and the Hawaiian cemetery.

The bamboo forest was located just above the pools in Lower Kipahulu, where a skinny trail threaded through tiger-striped columns thick as a man's leg. When the wind sieved through this green-and-gold bamboo jungle, the hollow trunks clanked and clattered like a giant wind chime, a most agreeable sensation. But it was hazardous, too, because dead poles hung trapped in the thicket overhead, ready to drop down and knock you senseless like coconuts in Samoa or icicles in Winnipeg.

Maui displayed the same settlement pattern as Molokai: prehistoric and historic occupation followed by wholesale migration to the plantations and towns; the transition period when a few holdouts returned on weekends to tend the taro; finally, abandonment and overgrowth. After a thousand years of cultivation the sites returned, with a sigh—of relief or regret?—to Nature.

My notes contain a long description of the Kanekaula *heiau* complete with post-Contact graves dug right into the rock platform, a most unusual feature, but I have no memory of this place. What still springs vividly to my mind is an intrusion in the small nineteenth-century cemetery on the coast side of the highway: among the weathered tombstones full of sonorous Hawaiian names, two brand-new ones, inscribed "Zippy" and "Zappy" or something like that, these marking the resting place of a couple of Pan American mogul Sam Pryor's beloved pet monkeys.

Pryor was one of a growing number of "Gold Coast" haoles who bought up big pieces of land and built exclusive homes in this impossibly beautiful area south of Hana. Later his friend and neighbor, a world-famous aviator, was to join the Hawaiians and the monkeys in this very cemetery—in a lead-lined coffin at the bottom of a grave of his own design twelve feet deep and lined with huge lava rocks. The eccentricity of this burial went tactfully unremarked in the press. It leads, however, to the unavoidable conclusion that, ultimately and whatever their spiritual motivation, you can't keep haoles (or their pets) out of anywhere. That consuming need to join someone else's ethnic parade carries on even into the hereafter.

But, the imagination urgently inquires, what if by this ill-advised cultural intrusion you the curious and reverent haole ended up in a pre-Contact Hawaiian heaven where all the finicky, elaborate restrictions of the highly structured old society were still observed? As you would have no guarantee of being mistaken, like Cook, for the god Lono, you would be forced to cope with the Prostrating or Burning-Hot Kapu, not to mention the taboo on treading on the chief's shadow and all the other incredibly complicated rules that governed every facet of human behavior in the very old days. No paradise of pagan sensuality, this Alice-in-Wonderland realm of irrational prohibitions and hideous punishments added up, one sensed, to rather an angst-filled eternity.

Maui's major natural attraction, Haleakala Crater, was widely regarded in my time as a "power spot," and consequently tribes of hippies took up residence in the big lava tubes under the crater floor. Once from my campsite I watched two freaks striding purposefully at dusk across the lava field a long way off the trail. The next moment they had vanished utterly. Later, down in the tubes, we found the remains of their campfires. The deserted little valleys beyond Kaupo Gap also filled up quickly with squatter settlements of hippies. In the middle of an archaeological survey I stumbled across a group of my peers, naked golden bodies reclining around a waterfall pool for all the world like Melville's Happars and Typees.

This tableau was being duplicated in dozens of valleys all over the Outer Islands, but it did not lack precedent. Here is Jack London's description, in *Cruise of the Snark,* of a turn-of-the-century "Nature Man" he met on Market Street in San Francisco, a figure who should evoke some lively parallel memories in any Californian alive and breathing during the late 1960s:

> It was a wet and drizzly afternoon, and he was striding along, clad solely in a pair of abbreviated knee-trousers and an abbreviated shirt, his bare feet going slick-slick through the pavement-slush. Every head—and there were thousands—turned to glance curiously at him as he went by. . . . His long yellow hair was burnt, so was his beard, which sprang from a soil unploughed by any razor. He was a tawny man, a golden-tawny man, all glowing and radiant with the sun. . . . "A fool! a fool! I met a fool in the forest!" thought I. And a worthy fool he proved. Between handsprings and whirligigs he delivered his message that would save the world. It was twofold. First, let suffering humanity strip off its clothing and run wild in the mountains and valleys; and, second, let the very miserable world adopt phonetic spelling. I caught a glimpse of the great social problems being settled by the city populations swarming naked over the landscape, to the popping of shot-guns, the barking of ranch-dogs, and countless assaults with pitchforks wielded by irate farmers.

A prescient vision, Mr. London! Demonstrating conclusively, among other things, that the great hippie explosion of the late 1960s did not spring fully formed either from the youth culture of that decade or the introduction of psychedelic drugs; it was, rather, one more tie-dyed wrinkle in a century-long tradition of West Coast bohemian eccentricity, second-rate literary effusions, and utopianism. All the tenets of the New Age—mysticism, vegetarianism, nudism, the model of the "holy fool"—had floated like pollen in the California air for quite some time. Mutating with rock music and LSD to sweep over a whole generation like a new strain of influenza virus, they produced one of those social upheavals that seem to come out of nowhere but in fact are, as psychologists like to say, overdetermined.

A few years down the road London was to run across the Nature Man again in Tahiti, just after the latter had been unceremoniously expelled from Hawaii. "I had a dream," the Nature Man confided to him then. "It seemed that twenty-five nature men and women had just arrived on the steamer from California, and that I was starting to go with them up the wild-pig trail to the plantation."

A scant sixty years later that dream was to be realized beyond the Nature Man's wildest expectations. In the evolutionary cycle of hippiedom, the back-to-Nature stage followed closely on the heels of the movement's first appearance in America. The tropics and especially Hawaii were a popular target. After landing on Oahu and, typically, a stay in Waikiki's Koa Kottages to connect with the drug scene around the International Marketplace, the dedicated freaks made straight for Maui-no-ka-oi.

At first, Local people were intensely curious about the young haoles who seemed to be violating every tenet of the Mainland culture Islanders had been brought up to emulate. Then, like their middle-class counterparts on the Mainland, they came to feel threatened and resentful as the hippies locked into the state welfare and food stamp system. A mayoral candidate on Maui made one of his campaign pledges "Keep *pilau* [dirty] hippies off our beaches." Most Local people had no use for the newcomers' drugs, easy sex, and lack of family ties (for despite their communal and tribal beliefs, most hippies, as sons and daughters of the American middle class, came across to Locals exactly as they were: rampant individualists).

Others took to the hippies like long-lost children. In these young idealists many of the older Hawaiian and Filipino men found eager apprentices for their store of practical knowledge despised by a technological society: fishing, planting, hunting. Many close relationships of mutual benefit were formed. But there were ugly reverberations as well. Resentment boiled to the surface over the wholesale invasion of state and county beach campsites, traditional territory of Hawaiian families who moved to the beach during the summer months. Local gangs began beating up the young haole arrivals. The drug trade, cultivation, and sale, passed in an eyeblink from innocent cottage industry to big-time hustle involving Locals and haoles alike—and, increasingly, organized interests.

Though hippiedom remained a gentle and innocent youthful *rite de passage* for most of its participants, the weird outer fringe made its presence felt on Maui. Borderline gurus and their followers flocked to the island. The abandoned church at Kaupo was broken into; human turds were found on the altar. The dry north Maui cliffs witnessed an infamous group murder-suicide in which the leader, a mentally disturbed pituitary giant, ordered his five disciples to chant while standing on the edge of a 200-foot drop with their eyes shut, holding hands. Then he jumped off, dragging the rest with him to their deaths. A young man and woman leaped—on acid, it was immediately rumored—into the Bottomless Pit in Haleakala Crater, leaving their swaddled baby lying at the rim.

In the long run, though, with the large exception of drug traffic, hippies were to leave far less of a long-term mark on the Outer Islands than the forces of big-time development. As Maui transformed in the mid-seventies from a plantation society to an entrepreneurial venue for hotels, condos, golf courses, yacht harbors, and other Mainland attractions, the hippies dispersed to ever remoter spots (their last and most colorful effulgence would take place on the island of Kauai). My strongest memory snapshot of the last member of subspecies Maui hippie in 1973: an ex-submariner, ponytail to his waist, hobbling on crutches as he thumbed a ride to Kahului. He had broken his leg when the vine he was swinging on at the swimming hole broke, and he did not regard this in any way as an omen.

Other cultures' afterlives did echo in the Maui landscape. Greek mythology, for example, never really in the forefront of my consciousness in Hawaii, popped to the surface when I watched Mikio and his brother, my friends from Honolulu, climb into the bleak little gray-white crevass on the floor of Haleakala. But then my hair stood on end because all at once here was Orpheus, a Japanese Orpheus, disappearing into the Underworld. During the moment of eerie stillness in front of the gaping mouth, so black in the middle of all that white rock, you instinctively sensed the uncanny quality attaching to these openings in the earth.

The Hawaiians liked to think of Haleakala and the other great craters as honeycombed with lava tubes that interconnected as regularly as subway lines. Exaggeration, of course, but it was a very nice thought, and would have been practical, too, like the

Maui

vast underground shopping centers of cities like Montreal. And in the very old days they made varied use of the accessible lava tubes: lived in the seaside ones as temporary fishing camps (the lava tube *cum* garbage pit at Makapuu beach on Oahu), dropped their babies' umbilical cords down the deep ones (the Bottomless Pit in Haleakala), built *heiau* in the wide, flat-bottomed ones (the Thurston lava tube on the Big Island).

Once inside a lava tube you had the not always pleasant sensation, as in the movie *Alien,* of traveling up the intestinal tract of an extremely large fossilized creature of unknown species. Definitely, it was "chicken skin" time, as Locals said of any terror situation, till you got out again. In accordance with my custom of losing amulets, soul pieces, and the like in key Island settings (camera in the "Seven Sacred Pools," graduation watch in Halawa Stream), somewhere under the floor of Haleakala Crater I lost a gold earring, the sharpened stud that eighty-year-old Albert Samuels himself, Dashiell Hammett's employer, had used to pierce my eighteen-year-old ears in his jewelry store on Market Street in 1964—his trembling hands, which nearly gave me a pair of holes somewhere in the vicinity of my jaw, my sole living link to a great San Francisco literary forebear. Now my Mainland talisman had been jealously claimed by Hawaii, a circumstance that added to my anxiety when I discovered the loss. For the overall feeling, in those lava tubes, was one of subtle but mounting claustrophobic panic. Once lodged this deep in Hawaii's guts, you wondered, when did the creature intend to spit you out?

28

Kauai

A dumb stunt, I admit it, diving off that Transpac yacht with Kathryn into the orange rinds, paper cups, and oil slicks of the Ala Wai Yacht Basin in Honolulu—typical haoles, you could see people thinking, taking that kind of health risk.

But it was just an afternoon dip, preliminary to our sunset departure on the Transpac boat we had succeeded in hitching a ride on, the only one with a skipper who was more than happy to have us since he didn't have a flown-over wife to give us the stink eye. The tough part of the 1973 biannual Transpacific race, from San Francisco to Honolulu, was over; the Honolulu–Kauai second lap was the party lap, time to bring aboard the friends, relatives, and hangers-on.

All the yachts, at least fifty of them, sailed out of Ala Wai into the sunset, a phantasmagoria of swollen spinnaker sails reflecting the sinking sun, guitar notes floating over the water, bodies sprawled over deck after deck in the warm evening air, these enormous, noble boats nosing directly West toward the sun. An unforgettable moment of accidental splendor, and almost worth the next sixteen hours of gut-wrenching seasickness I endured after we hit the notoriously choppy seas of the Kauai channel.

Weak as a kitten but ravenously hungry by the time we reached Hanalei Bay, I was sufficiently revived by the prospect of dry land and a big dinner to swim the quarter-mile to shore, for we had managed to miss the shuttle boat to the dock. After showering in the public restrooms on the beach and changing to the dry clothes we had towed behind us in plastic garbage bags, our little group voted to scorn the old-boy boozeout, namely, the official dinner party at a nearby hotel, in favor of a private celebration at the little hippie vegetarian café at the side of the road. Thereupon followed one of the most unsatisfactory meals of my life. Even as I bit into my undercooked vermicelli with its thin pink sauce and rennetless cheese topping, my starved body craved the juicy steaks and french fries being devoured this very moment over at the hotel. Always in the past I had steered well clear of that verithaned Southern California haole side of Hawaii, the yacht club scene. Now, thanks to my atrophied stomach, I discovered I didn't want to be with the gentle people and their sprouts. I didn't want poi and laulau, either. I was dying to be with the old boys, their blue blazers, their deep vulgar non-Local laughs, their martinis. For this twenty-seven-year-old teenager, could adulthood, Mainland style, be far off?

Just the same, like a large number of other young haoles I had some history tied up in the island of Kauai. You could trace the settlement patterns of the great hippie migrations like a modest echo of Polynesian diffusion straight through the Hawaiian chain. From Maui, a subgroup splintered off to Molokai. Many, however, went on to Kauai, which rapidly gained a reputation as the most "spiritual" of the islands. One of the earliest and oldest Kauai communes was Taylor Camp, the ultimate jungle playhouse. This city of treehouses with transparent plastic walls sat perched in the beach ironwoods just before the end of the road at Haena Point on land that belonged to Elizabeth Taylor's brother Howard, who lived on the other side of the highway.

After Taylor Camp came a flood of organized cults, sects, and tribes. There were the Moksha people, not a cult but mostly an extended "family" who had built a concrete-hulled boat in Washington and sailed it to Kauai to make a new home. There was Lomi Farm in Keapana Valley, run by an enterprising Californian as a growth center, which charged its visitors a hefty fee to rise at dawn and pull weeds in the garden in the cause of centering themselves. Lomi Farm was leased to a white-robed guru with a sect called "The Source," who made his charges rise *before* dawn and wake up the neighborhood with some sort of noisy group chanting, the purpose of which was never quite determined; he also forbade the men and women to sleep together except in a special ceremony once a month. The Source made their neighbors nervous when it was discovered that the targets they used for their archery practice were shaped like human beings. Kicked off the island at last for disturbing the peace, their leader was killed the following year while hang gliding on Oahu.

The Hare Krishnas established a strong beachhead on Kauai via various small businesses (health food and secondhand stores) and were famous for their Sunday night feasts, open to all. Every weekend hippies poured out of the north valleys to the trailhead at Haena, where they were picked up by the Krishnas, driven to the Center, proselytized, stuffed with vegetarian food as in a kind of hip Salvation Army cafeteria, then treated to a full-on Krishna chanting rockout, complete with electric guitars and heavy beat. For a long time it was the only reliable hippie social occasion on the island, with the exception of the Full Moon Feast, which the Kalalau dwellers themselves held on their own beach every month—but getting there meant eleven miles of serious trail hiking.

At the back of Keapana Valley was an overgrown fairyland, formerly the Spaulding estate but known to all as Valley House because of the enormous white frame building at its entrance. You crossed a wooden bridge over the muddy river on a cobblestone road lined with massive royal palms. Although the jungle had taken over, the remnants of an impressive array of exotic plantings were still visible. Huge white-trunked eucalyptuses and fan-topped Dutch palms sprang up out of the undergrowth. Behind the ramshackle white house, a surreal vision of former grandeur in tropical decay, was a clearing with big monkeypod trees overgrown with vines and a moss-covered Japanese statue. Banana trees that had not been properly chopped down every year had grown into a tall, scrawny, sterile forest. Out of this wilderness a maze of footpaths led to the various hippie dwellings in the jungle; another path went up to the waterfall. While it lasted it was utterly magic and mysterious, this Amazon community out of Walt Disney and *Last Year at Marienbad*.

The history of Valley House was this: abandoned by Colonel Spaulding, a sugar baron, before the 1920s, the original structure burned down a decade later. A new building constructed near the ruins of the family mansion became army quarters during the war; then, following a classic Outer Island pattern, a gambling casino and (some say) house of prostitution. The house stood empty and the land was leased to a Local Japanese farmer to become the largest lychee orchard in Hawaii. A Health Department psychologist leased the land from the Local Japanese group, or *hui,* that now owned it and turned it into an alternative mental health facility—a healing community, as people said then. The word got out and soon about one hundred people were living in bamboo and plastic huts all over the land; some genuinely crazy, some pretending to be crazy, some just there. They kicked out the Japanese farmer because his lychees weren't organic. Rumors were rife of strange sexual doings in the jungle. The psychologist backed out of the project. Two weeks after my visit some Local kids burned down the main building. The community managed to stagger on several more years before it fell apart.

Kauai's greatest primal spot was formidable, romantic Kalalau Valley. As on all the other Hawaiian Islands, Kalalau was part of a rugged northern valley system, the Napali coast, that could not be reached by road. In prehistoric days, it was far more accessible than in my time or after; back then all such valleys were evenly populated because their inhabitants survived by subsistence agriculture and did their traveling by trail or outrigger canoe. Just as on Molokai, the shift to a money economy emptied Kalalau, Hanakapiai, and the intervening valleys of the formidable Napali coast. Everywhere on the Napali trail you saw vestiges of the same failed agricultural experiments—sisal, coffee—growing wild by the side of the trail in what I came to think of, like something out of Spenser or Bunyan, as the Allegorical Valleys: one small gulch seemed entirely taken over by huge yucca or hemp plants, another by bird's nest ferns, and so on until you descended the rocky path into Kalalau.

A thousand rituals quickly sprang up around this journey down the Yellow Brick Road to Oz—though there never was nor will be anything cute or storybook about the ominous, imposing spires of Kalalau, Valley at the End of the World. The eleven-mile trail was rocky, eroded, and, with a sheer drop of hundreds of feet to the boiling white and turquoise surf below, in many parts not for the faint-hearted. But soon it was de rigueur for the hip, once past the more tourist-accessible Hanakapiai a mere mile and a half in, to remove all clothes (except for the indispensable boots and socks) and hike naked into the valley—an impractical custom, since burns from the backpack straps on your bare flesh could easily get infected. Kalalau in those days left a memory image of bare, radiant young flesh cavorting in a setting of unearthly beauty, but there were exceptions. Once, coming out on the trail, I encountered two emaciated men with semitransparent skin who each earnestly shook my hand with their damp ones and said, "We're fruitarians from Maine." They had come to live off the guavas, mangoes, and coconuts, and they already looked sick.

Beneath its tall green sentinels the mouth of the valley was choked with lantana and wild cherry tomatoes sprouted from seeds left by campers. Brilliant cardinals pecked in the dirt. Out of the underbrush (you smelled him before you saw him) sprang a beautiful stinking mountain goat, brown and black, with huge curving horns. Scrawny, hissing feral cats—signs of the ongoing hippie occupancy—stalked the bushes.

The Kalalau surf was often too high and treacherous to swim in, but over at the famous beach cave on the other side of the stream mouth, Kalalau's own natural Holiday Inn, you could shower under a fifty-foot waterfall, your body brilliantly outlined in white spray against the black of the volcanic rock. Farther up the valley were luxuriant *ti* plantings, old terraces and house platforms overgrown with lantana; banana and mango grew wild and patches of taro and false taro still choked the streams—all unmistakable signs of a formerly fertile, densely populated settlement.

A book, ten books, could be written about this strange valley universe that imprinted itself in the souls of so many young Americans. Here was the site of all those Full Moon Feasts. Here the "bong"—the infamous bamboo pipe for dope smoking—reigned supreme, along with a set of rituals that rivaled the Japanese tea ceremony in complexity. Here one young woman had insisted, at great expense to the County of Kauai in emergency helicopter evacuation, on having her babies. Here another young woman, a prostitute in California who was delivering porno movies for her employers, the mob, hid out after leaving the reels of film revolving in the baggage carrel at the Honolulu airport and heading straight for Kauai. Rumor had it a big black car was parked up at the Haena Point trailhead waiting for her, but she was never caught. Here lived the world-famous Bobo of Kalalau, who used to walk naked by the side of the road from Haena to Hanalei—so regular, so determined, so *relentless* in her habits that as the years went by the Kauai police opted finally, so to speak, to look the other way.

Here I once stood, at the Waimea Canyon overlook, watching helicopters haul Portatoilets across a purple-red sky as a film company shot *King Kong* in the next valley over from Kalalau, picturesquely dubbed "Valley of the Lost Tribes" by the hippies. Waiting to see the great beast himself, that strange shadow of my inner life, slung up on ropes, swinging under rotary blades in the tropical sunset, but that never happened; he was in a studio back lot all the time.

Following an impulse that would become habitual, I "came back" to Kauai in 1978 to visit Tom Riley's latest dig. What should it turn out to be but a ruin from my own still extremely recent time—Taylor Camp, now about to become part of the state beach system. Little remained of the houses themselves, but wandering in the middle of a forest of the huge, flavorless "pig" papaya—like something out of *The Island of Dr. Moreau,* a genetic experiment gone bad—I stumbled upon the remains of the famous Taylor Camp communal latrine, a throne on a raised dais in the middle of a clearing. In an ironic bow by commune members to Health Department requirements, it had once proudly occupied center stage in the settlement. Now, just eight years later, it was a ruin from an age as vanished as Hawaii's prehistory.

Earliest habitation date in the rich cultural layers in the dunes: A.D. 1200. Latest: A.D. 1973. Among the artifacts excavated from the Taylor Camp layer: guitar pick, mosquito coil, piece of rubber zori, a dime with all the mercury worn off (it could still be dated as post-1970 because it had a copper center), plastic thermos cup, ammo, round disks that came from a *Star Wars* toy gun (post-1973, actually; archaeology is full of these unexplained little glitches). Tom and his wife, Karma, wrote up an analysis of the midden that revealed, in the best manner of systems theory archaeology, a symbiotic economic relationship cemented by ritual exchange of food stamp coupons between Taylor Camp and the Ching Young Store in Hanalei.

These top few inches of hippie remains quickly gave away to a two-foot historic and prehistoric cultural stratum that dated from the time the site was known as Ke'e, not Taylor Camp. This rich layer included remains from an old poi factory, marks of the 1946 tidal wave, followed by hundreds of deceptively smooth-appearing layers of occupation straight into the ancient outcroppings of dune burials.

By the late seventies, the surviving hippies had already assimilated into the Kauai economy as small capitalists, wage earners, or dope entrepreneurs. In spite of the strain they initially imposed on the economy and patience of a close-knit society, those who stayed on, who became, finally, integrated into Local life, were not the ones who brought the Great Mahele of the Outer Islands, 1970s' style. In the original Great Mahele of 1848, King Kamehameha V had 4 million acres of land transferred from the old feudal system into private ownership by himself and the great chiefs, thereby paving the way for sale of these lands to sugar planters and other outside interests.

Directly off the Leeward side of Kauai lay visible evidence of the original Great Mahele, the island of Niihau. In 1864 Niihau had been purchased for $10,000 by a man named Francis Sinclair from one of Kamehameha V's land grants. Fifty crucial acres, however, were still owned by an old Hawaiian couple who refused to sell. In Robert Wenkham's excellent account, *Kauai and the Park Country of Hawaii,* Sinclair's friend Valdemir Knudsen, a man greatly respected by the Hawaiians, came to Niihau with one thousand silver dollars,

> traveled overland on horseback to the Papapas' grass hut on the western shore, and introduced himself. As he talked with the old couple, he carefully stacked the silver dollars in orderly rows across the lauhala mat spread over the floor. The old man kept shaking his head "no," emphasizing again and

190

again his unwillingness to sell. Knudsen continued to stack the silver coins, telling the couple of the new merchants on Kauai, where the land was gentler and greener, and where they could enjoy their remaining days without ever working again. The piles of coins, ten to a stack, grew on the mat. The old man repeated no, as his wife's eyes opened wide in wonder. She listened silently. At last Knudsen shrugged and began unstacking the coins. Suddenly, the wife uttered an ancient Hawaiian exclamation, "Schah!," reached out, and pulled the treasure into her lap. The Sinclairs at last owned all Niihau.

This kind of leverage was still being applied, for by now Outer Island real estate speculation was entering its corrupt and feverish peak. The same pattern unfolded on Kauai as on Maui, though with each stage lagging a few years behind: first intense friendly curiosity from Locals, then polarization, then—as Rent-a-Car tourism and land speculation exploded simultaneously—utter alienation. In formerly funky old Lihue you could walk through a Southern California–style shopping center with a franchised Rusty Scupper staffed with friendly young blond waiters and waitresses only to meet the deadly stink eye of the old guys in shorts and zoris who had sold their taro patches to a California dentist to build an A-frame on. So they got the new Boston Whaler or the Ford Bronco, but sooner or later they realized they didn't have their land. And what they were still able to hold onto, especially beachfront land, they could no longer afford to pay the taxes on.

No longer Subjects, tending their own lives and businesses, the old guys did not take kindly to their new role as Objects, part of the quaint tropical backdrop, someone to chat up in the Tahiti Nui bar in Hanalei so you could go home and say you spoke to a real Hawaiian while at another table a female haole real estate agent is boasting of having just closed her third multimillion-dollar deal in as many weeks.

The Taylor Camp dig proceeded. One day we helped clear off Lohiau's hula platform on the Atherton land at the Napali trailhead. Here I discovered that the great Hawaiian Renaissance and revival of the old ways in the late 1970s was not acclaimed by everyone concerned. One of the girls described to me her grand-mother's warning about not reviving prayer on the *heiau*. The gods that were worshipped in the very old days were the kind that turned on you and destroyed you, she said. Her own uncle started praying at this *heiau* and went into a trance that turned him deaf, dumb, and blind. There, right there at Ke'e, he started to walk into the water, where a shark waited for him. His family stopped him but he died anyway, possessed by the god that had eaten him up.

In the very old days this shark god had been a real shapeshifter. According to the folklorist and Hawaiian scholar Martha Beck-with, there were shark-men on land who covered up their dorsal fins with shirts and men-sharks in the sea who protected their human family members while they were swimming. Human corpses were also ceremonially interred underwater so that they could turn into sharks, an underwater transformation in which the new shark bore markings duplicating the tapa cloth the body had been wrapped in.

To my ears, these stories already sounded muted, more far-away than the tales I had heard on Molokai in 1970. It was grandparents' knowledge, it was book knowledge, it was not firsthand, the sharks at Haena had long since divorced them-selves from the Hawaiians and from the *Kumulipo* order of the universe as well.

Those two lost tribes the hippies and the ancient Hawaiians began to merge in my imagination. The hippies had left ghosts behind, too, some living and some dead. Instinctively people came to Kauai, to Kalalau, if they were hurting inside and need-ing to be healed; the Islands exerted their powerful seductive pull to psychic death and rebirth on a whole generation. But for all the bouncing spirit babies reborn into the world from the bountiful womb of Hawaii there was an equally impressive har-vest of stillborns and physical deaths.

The Walkers, for example, were a phenomenon that did not appear until the tidal wave of hippies began receding from the Islands, leaving this flotsam beached high and dry without their cover group of fearless, energetic, idealistic youth. These were the burnouts, the casualties who had to do something with their tremendous psychotic anxiety. Fueled by a complicated inner world of voices and delusions, muttering and staring intently into the distance, they paced rapidly along the highway shoulder from Kapaa to Lihue and back to Kapaa every day. You saw the same Walkers in hip country areas of Northern California like Bolinas, but I have never observed anyone striding with a higher sense of purpose than the Kauai Walkers. This circumambulation, on the same lines as painting the Golden Gate Bridge, seemed to give their lives some structure, a sense of mission, and there is no doubt it also left them a great deal more physically fit than most of their more mentally balanced peers.

Chronologically, the Mutes preceded the Walkers. They were most in evidence when the mystic psychedelic movement was in full swing. One was a woman who stayed at Valley House. Occasionally my friend Kathryn would pick her up hitchhiking and the woman, sitting in the back seat, would hit her own lips gently with her forefinger as a symbol of Keeping Silence. Once Kathryn came upon this woman in one of the clearings behind Valley House. Standing naked and motionless like the commune's own Statue of Liberty, a peacock feather sticking out of her rear end, she looked at Kathryn. Then gently hit her finger to her lips.

The other notable Mute lived in a beach cave on the way to Kalalau. Before the great hurricane of 1981 it was still possible to walk to Kalalau at low tide along the beach, where many shelter caves lined the cliff face. One day this silent man, well known to all the freaks, vanished from his cave. Twenty-four hours later a search turned up his shoes on the edge of the shore next to a big wet cave. The surf was up; waves pounded the low-hanging entrance of the cave. From the interior loud screams were clearly audible.

Because the surf was too high for them to tackle alone, the searchers hiked out and returned with two Hawaiian firemen—the lifeguards of the Islands—who dove under the overhang and came out with the hermit, who had been perched for all that time on a tiny ledge deep inside the cave. His shouts for help having somehow, obscurely, primed the pump, for some time after his dramatic rescue from drowning this Mute talked like everybody else. But the next year Kathryn came upon him in Kalalau, dumb again, somberly stacking piles of cut guava wood

193

into a kind of Lincoln-log ritual structure at the mouth of the valley. His cargo-cult attempt to impose order on the natural world was a doomed effort here, for there is simply no place on earth so powerful, so frightening, and so unorderly as Kalalau. Hawaii had healed the Mute by scaring his pants off. Then, just as capriciously, she had awed him straight back to silence.

Where are those Kalalau people now, I wonder—the ones who did not go home, go mad, grow up, or become entrepreneurs? I hear Bobo in middle age has recanted, joined AA, apologized to all concerned for the trouble she caused, and wears a dress! On a flight from San Francisco to the Islands all these years later I sit near a shockingly old Nature Woman with wizened, nut-brown features, hobbitlike in her leaf-bark and hand-stitched clothing. As I watch her miming and bobbing in her discount coach seat, I ask silently: Were you, could you have been one of those golden bodies? No, it can't be—oh, say you aren't beautiful Diane or Vikesa or Noni, say it isn't so.

In my time a man had starved himself to death on the "mucous-free diet" up on one of the ridges above Valley House. His regime consisted of papayas and oranges for two weeks, fasting for one week, then back to papayas and oranges. In the final months he caught pneumonia. The extra congestion this disease produced made him even stricter in his efforts to purge himself of the hated "mucous" until his exhausted body succumbed. By the late 1970s, the Spaulding land had a new owner, but what, I wondered, was he going to do with the burned foundations of a mansion, a jungle of high-class plantings, the remains of a city of bamboo huts, and the emaciated ghost of a dead fruitarian up on the ridge?

The two groups of tribal ghosts, Hawaiian and hippie—so it seemed to me—had passed each other on the road headed in opposite directions. On the Hawaiian side, the men-sharks in the water off Ke'e had joined the haole order *Squaliformes* and the shark-men on land had signed up for the U.S. Marines. My own race, meanwhile, had managed for once by dint of sheer earned effort, not money or coercion, to gain backdoor entry into the original club, that pitiful, urgent legion of true Hawaiian spirits.

29

The Big Island

If Kauai was the spiritual island, Hawaii, or the Big Island, became allegorically attached in my mind to Great Natural Forces: live volcanoes, giant surf, that sort of thing.

Lapakahi, Christmas 1970: a two-week holiday break cleanup dig at a dryland coastal habitation site was my introduction to the Big Island. Lapakahi, an ancient fishing village, was about a quarter of a mile south, down a short footpath, from Mahukona Beach Park in the North Kohala district. Mahukona was an abandoned harbor with an old concrete wharf where the burnt sugarcane stalks harvested from the fields of North Kohala were formerly loaded on the Spreckels barges for processing down at the plant in Kawaihae, South Kohala. Our Holo-Holo campers were set up in a grove of *kiawe* trees whose notorious two-inch thorns could penetrate the thickest zori devised by Japanese technology, and the night was periodically rent by the screams of the unwary en route to the camp toilets.

Every evening we jumped from the dock to wash off the Lapakahi dirt, and in this way my friend Joe Kennedy, one of the archaeology students, shortened his little finger a quarter inch by diving straight onto a lava rock. Underwater the little bay was like an aquarium gone mad; hundreds of thousands of vivid fish wheeled and turned, pressed their tiny mouths lightly against your body. Even from the dock you could make out huge masses of manini like slowly revolving yellow clouds—it seemed outrageous, somehow, to see these fish directly from our own medium of air, not water.

From the Mahukona wharf one Saturday morning we watched a winter storm surf hit the concrete bulwarks, sending cascades of seawater high in the air. Dancing around in the shower twenty feet back from the edge was a stupid thing to do; there was always a wave, not necessarily the seventh, twenty feet bigger than the rest. When one of these finally broke, the spray alone was powerful enough to knock me flat and drag me face down clear across the concrete. A foot or two from the sheer drop to the rocks, someone caught me by the ankle and hauled me back, shaken and bloody. Great Natural Forces do not tolerate child's play.

As further evidence of GNFs, the Big Island had lava fields, huge ones the size of cities. They were great fun to explore, providing you had a good destination. Bouncing in a four-wheel-drive jeep across the wasteland of the great Kona lava flow, mile after mile of shining frozen black cowpie, and suddenly over the rise came a flash of turquoise, a white crescent of sand, an old frame house with an outrigger beached nearby, under the coconut palms—a bit of the old days, nineteenth-century Hawaii, once the old Magoon summer house, in my time a scuba diving ranch but slated for development: Mahai'Ula.

Our host, the current Magoon, remembered traveling to Mahai'Ula as a little boy by motorized outrigger from Kailua-Kona. This Magoon's great-great-grandfather was that Chinese merchant of King Kalakaua's day considerably fictionalized by Jack London in his famous story "Chun Ah Chun": the eight Chinese-Hawaiian daughters married off and the lucky ur-Magoon, like all those other New England sailor adventurers who found themselves in the right place at the right time, soon to be the proud possessor of the *ahupua'a*—the traditional pie-shaped land unit stretching from mountains to seashore—of South Kona, much of it lava flow, much of it also green and verdant, all of it, eventually, valuable beyond imagining.

Something unbearably touching obtained in the atmosphere of Mahai'Ula. In the living room, under fins, masks, and old *Na-*

tional Geographics, squatted the huge battered mahogany din-
ing table shipped over from Honolulu that King Kalakaua himself had once played poker on. Like the strange overlapping
symmetry of the Napali valleys, this white frame house on the
beach in the middle of the lava flow opened up a layered series
of "times," lost worlds: pre-Statehood, prewar, pre-Territory,
back to the genuine old days, when all haole tourists, in accordance with the nineteenth-century Romantic worship of Nature,
made pilgrimages to Great Natural Forces. In Hawaii that meant
traveling to the Big Island, home of the live volcanoes. Witness-
ing an eruption from a prudent distance became the equivalent
of viewing the tears of Christ on the shroud of Turin—the climax
and crowning event of any supplicant's visit.

Denied the spectacle himself, Mark Twain was obliged to record in his notebooks the account of one Mrs. Henry MacFarlane,
identified as the wife of a Honolulu liquor merchant. Let her eyes
serve as his, and mine, too:

30 miles from the house—eruption began slowly at dusk—at
4 AM was shooting rocks and lava 400 feet high which wd
then descend in a grand shower of fire to the earth—crater
overflowed & molten waves & billows went boiling and surg-
ing down mountain side just for the world like a sea—stream
from 1-½ to mile & ½ wide and hundred feet deep perhaps—over cattle, houses & across streams to the sea, 63
miles distant (7 years ago) ran into sea 3 miles and boiled the
fish for 20 miles around—vessels found scores boiled fish 20
miles off—natives cooked their food there. Every evening
for 7 weeks she sat on verandah half the night gazing upon
the splendid spectacle—the wonderful pyrotechnic display—the house windows were always of a bloody hue—read
newspapers every night by no other light than was afforded
by this mighty torch 30 miles away.

Except for a quick junket to the sulfurous rim of Halemaumau,
plus sightings of the twin snow-covered peaks of Mauna Loa and
Mauna Kea from my frequent vantage point atop their neighbor
Haleakala Crater across the channel on Maui, Hawaii's most famous Great Natural Force did not impinge heavily on my own

consciousness. Evidence of the live volcanoes reached me in subtler ways: as an almost indetectable shaking of the house in Honolulu like a cat walking across the roof, followed, a few days later, by a light rain of ash, Pompeii style. And the detail of the boiled fish in Mrs. MacFarlane's description was enough to put me off my single idle fantasy, vis-à-vis volcanoes—namely, to rent scuba gear and see what flowing lava looked like underwater.

For me the real Great Natural Forces were always valleys, valleys, valleys. On the Big Island I found the same inaccessible Windward northern system as on Molokai and Kauai. This group, consisting of the valleys Pololu, Honokanenui/Honokaneiki, and Honopue, was linked by a formidable network of cobblestone donkey paths used by workers maintaining the huge fluming systems that watered the canefields of Kohala. The North Kohala Ditch Trail, as it was called, came to a definitive stop at the far rim of Honopue Valley, after which you encountered an impenetrable series of sheer gulches, then the lava flat known as Laupahoehoe sticking out into the sea, and eventually the yawning enormity of Waipio Valley, which could be reached by road (barely) from the Hilo side of the island.

Our semiofficial status by virtue of the Lapakahi dig gained us otherwise disreputable students, haole and Local, permission from the owners, complete with signed document, to hike the North Kohala Ditch Trail. Off we trotted on the contour trail cutting midway between the valley floor and the top of the thousand-foot cliffs to the head of Pololu. (At the mouth of this valley several summers later Tom Riley uncovered, then reburied, the stone fish god that had stood as a sentinel at the entrance.) Nights we spent in the ditch workers' tin-roof shacks in the upland wilderness. In the neglected yards of these loneliest of houses bumpy-skinned Mexican lemon shrubs grew; inside, yellowed Tagalog comic books lay scattered under the sagging iron bedsteads with their bare soiled mattresses.

Before we set out we were warned by a member of the Solomon family up at the Parker Ranch in Kamuela that crossing the stream mouths of the North Kohala valleys was dangerous because of the big sharks lurking along this coastline. There was a test you could make—throwing *ti* leaves in the water. If the shark was hungry enough to snap at them, it wasn't a good idea to cross.

198

If the Big Island seemed to have more sharks and more fish off its coasts than any of the other islands, it also seemed to have more pigs in its mountains as well. All over the uplands you saw their traces: big rooted-up patches of eroded earth near the trails where they fed, lots of droppings. These feral pigs were a blend of the species the early Polynesians had brought, along with chickens and dogs, and the European pigs introduced by Cook, who had noted in his log for January 1778:

> No dependence can be placed, in the hogs taken on board at these islands, for they will neither thrive nor live on board a ship. This was one great inducement to my leaving of the English breed as the hogs we got at Otaheite, that were of the Spanish breed, thrived and fed on board the Ships as well as our own, at the very time that others were pining away and dying daily.

The hardy mutants resulting from this cross-breeding escaped domestication and ran wild in the uplands, where they flourish to this day.

Pig hunting is still a regularly practiced art in all the Hawaiian islands, even on urban Oahu. Fierce, battered pig dogs help hunters track down the enormous creatures and hold them at bay. Once a rather ghastly incident was reported in the Oahu newspapers—it's wrong of me to laugh, I know—namely, a haole woman walking her little poodle on one of the ridge trails behind Honolulu encountered a pack of pig dogs struggling up from the valley below. Just the sight of the frou-frou little creature with the ribbon in its hair was enough to madden them; with no further ado, they tore it to bits. Their owners, emerging from the underbrush behind them and making a two-second inspection of the carnage, called out a hasty apology over their shoulders and quickly vanished down the side of the other valley.

The wild pigs had tusks like a fantasia of curlicues; they actually curved back, ingrown, into the jaw. A few times in burials I had uncovered separate pieces of bracelets made of these carefully matched tusks, the connecting sennit cord long since rotted away. But somehow it remains my impression that pig bones, like a lot of other land animal artifacts, were never as prized by

Hawaiians as their magical *Kumulipo* counterparts from under the sea—whale tusks or shark's teeth, for instance.

Kama'pua'a, the pig god of the very old days, was known to have rooted lecherously into the land, leaving many gulches behind. "They call me Prick-eye the great, I've plowed up all the islands," boasts Kama'pua'a in a famous hula. Once this notorious "night-digger" (as he was celebrated in the *Kumulipo*) was lured by a goddess's vagina that left its imprint as Koko Head Crater behind Hanauma Bay.

My one face-to-face with a wild pig occurred on our North Kohala Ditch Trail hike. A large gap had opened between me and the person behind on this narrow contour trail, which fronted a cliff face on one side and dropped off steeply on the other into underbrush about twenty feet below. As I looked casually over my shoulder, I saw a large black dog galloping toward me on the trail, a sight that frightened me much more at first than I felt the next instant, when I realized it was a pig.

Trapped in my heavy backpack, I had nowhere to run. Mainly, I was trying to melt seamlessly—as literary critics like to say—into the side of the cliff when the charging pig reached a human's length from me. It was then I saw his eyes, realized he was just as spooked by me as I was by him. At the last possible second he veered away and plunged headlong over the sheer drop, landing with a thunderous crash in the bushes below. More thrashing, a few squeals, then silence. Pig-Pan had come and gone.

Our trip came to an abrupt stop about fifty feet down the cliff from the end of the trail above Honopue, where it was quickly determined—first man on the rope dangling in midair, the rest of us frantically digging in above, holding onto guava roots that were ripping out of the wet soil—that we would kill ourselves trying to get down that eroded valley wall.

Here at the end of our trail I ran into a variant of the story-behind-the-story theme of the Hawaiian natural landscape and its eerie serial duplications of cliffs overlapping cliffs, waterfalls pouring into waterfalls, like an M. C. Escher print. This was a valley above a valley, that is, a landlocked valley. In the very old days, these upland valleys that did not open directly onto the sea were said to be the birthplace of the highest nobility. King Kamehameha the Great, first ruler of Hawaii, was supposed to have been born in a valley above Halawa Valley, but even in an airplane over the three rugged East End valleys of Halawa, Wailau, and Pelekunu I couldn't manage to locate this place.

Between Honopue Valley and the twin Honokanes (-nui and -iki, big and little, respectively) there was a toy version of a landlocked valley. A short distance up a culvert next to the trail you could climb up the side of a rockface, hook your head over the top, and peer into a tiny water-drenched secret valley, complete with its very own banana trees, passion fruit vines, and regulation waterfall. A chill fell over me at the terrible perfection of this hidden miniature, a kind of Nature's designer showcase. Like one of those enclosed gardens of the medieval European and Islamic imaginations, a valley behind a valley is an allegorical spot that accumulates its power simply by being what it is. The Hawaiians correctly viewed this kind of valley as a supreme birthing spot, embodying as it did the pull backward, the regressive urge. In such a wet verdant flowing place you were back in the *Kumulipo* darkness, a murky uncertain symbiosis of plants, animals, and half-formed human thoughts. This little valley was a Great Natural Force.

A sudden premonition overcame me. If I pulled myself up and over the edge, if I walked into this valley, I would disappear. What a relief, it seemed at first, to turn away from the dawning of imperfect, troubled consciousness and merge gratefully with the perfection of original night! Then came the catch: Rapturously seduced by the natural world, letting yourself be swallowed whole, you discovered that, far from being reborn, you were going to be digested, excreted, and composted instead.

I climbed back down to the trail in an uneasy frame of mind. I had stumbled again on the real secret of these jumping-off places, the Outer Islands: Getting to them was no problem. The real trick was getting out of them.

Koolau shadows

30

Sheena of Manoa

I fetched up, in the end, back in Honolulu. It was 1973 and things seemed fine. I owned a car now, I could drive, even though the Honolulu pavement seemed indecently smooth after the jolting dirt tracks of the Outer Islands. I moved from Punchbowl to Manoa Valley, directly behind the university and preferred residence for professors, 90 percent of whom, in my time, were haole. When I traded my tin-roofed and screen-windowed house on Green Street for the little studio attached to the back of the Mizukos' house on Pamoa Road—where the old Japanese *tutus* patrolled the block in their nightgowns at day's end just as the mother of my Korean landlady on Punchbowl used to do—I had the distinct feeling of having scrambled up one rung into the lower middle class. If my sense of direction was no clearer, at least my life in Hawaii now began to correspond more subtly to Mainland expectations of class and education.

Big green Manoa Valley rose above the flatlands of Moiliili, its mouth squarely blocked by the U.H. campus. Manoa had been a gracious, sleepy agricultural-residential valley before the Safeway and the bakery were expanded into a full-fledged shopping center and traffic increased by a Malthusian ratio. What became a well-traveled thoroughfare to the shopping center was, in my time, a dirt road with horses grazing in the thick grass by Manoa

Stream. As in Halawa, punctually at four every afternoon a few gentle sheets of rain swept out of the valley and stopped dead—from respect?—at the doorstep of the new Medical School Building.

Manoa was home to many rootless young haoles connected in some form or another to the university. Every day thousands of laser beams of intellectual energy bounced off the high green valley walls right back into the conflicted souls of their owners. Much of this energy ended up channeled into earthy short-term pursuits—marijuana cultivation, car repair, illicit tin-roof house building. When the first cappuccino parlors on Oahu appeared in the late seventies, they filled up overnight with a crew of regulars who must have been flown in straight from Berkeley, for where had these people been taking their dream journals before? Surely not Zippy's or the St. Louis Drive-In. And the dreams themselves were collectively vaguer and softer than Mainland dreams, colored through the semipermeable membrane of consciousness by the gentle Hawaiian environment. When middle age is reached and one day the corner is finally turned on dreams, is the regret not so urgently felt in this soft air as under the harsh spotlight of Mainland ambition?

One could, of course, follow the road laid out before one and become an academic, Hawaii style. Manoa vision: the young bachelor English professor walking down Oahu Avenue in regulation reverse-print aloha shirt, bearing an aluminum foil–covered casserole on his way to a department potluck. Even with the spectacular backdrop—lush, passionate vegetation, the Manoa cliffs, a lurid tropical sunset over Waikiki—he did not manage, casserole in hand, to look lush, lurid, or passionate himself. Not a fate I aspired to.

Haoles who grew old in the Islands, I had noticed—genteel professional Manoa haoles as well as hippie haoles and broke, desperate Outer Island haole-no-more-moneys—had a curious habit of fading, even under their beautiful tans. The moist Island air was gentle to delicate haole skin, it plumped out the tissue, softened the wrinkles, but the fact remained: many aging haole *kamaainas* looked curiously washed out, like one of their tasteful reverse-print aloha shirts run through the hot cycle too many times. Vigorous, healthy, energetic—yes. But faded. The expres-

sion on their faces didn't look right. It was hard to say why. "Look
Contented but pine for home," Mark Twain noted of Mainland
Americans in mid-nineteenth-century Hawaii. "They live within
themselves—within their shells—and are not—if I may be allowed to suggest it—not happy."

This was not your stereotypical Outcast of the Islands scenario,
the white man who has lost his "moral fiber" in the sensual,
promiscuous tropics. No, the opposite, rather: a sense of people
born in Pennsylvania, New York, Wisconsin carrying the hard
little nugget of their own haoleness inside them no matter how
many leis and muumuus they put on. Like Japanese born in
Japan, they may have lived in the Islands, adapted to the Islands,
felt at ease in the Islands like nowhere else in the world; but the
possibility remained that in the center of their souls they did not
belong in the Islands. For some—via a decision made totally
beyond the reach of consciousness, in the realm of genes, spirit,
whatever you want to call it—Hawaii was not home. Sitting on
your lanai in upper Manoa Valley watching the sun sink behind
the hotels in Waikiki, relaxed in mind and body, the satisfaction
of a profession pursued as conscientiously and honorably here as
on the Mainland, except you did it in Hawaii, surrounded by all
this beauty, just think how lucky you are, really you are very
lucky, and still that faded expression on the face, unreadable, sad.

In my time the university's English Department of about a
hundred faculty members was divided down the middle between tenured professors who taught upper-division courses and
untenured instructors with M.A.s who taught the compulsory
lower-division courses. The latter, hired during rather zany
yearly recruiting junkets on the Mainland, were given a five-year
contract once "on board," after which time they were politely
asked to move on. I had been hired on the spot during my two-
week Hawaiian visit to replace one of these recruits who had
broken contract midyear and bolted back to Terra Cognita.

The young professors: The truth was, as a group we professed
more than we instructed. A wildly mixed bag, polarized late-
sixties fashion against the older tenured faculty, but in Hawaii the
game was played out in far gentler terms than its counterpart on
the Mainland. Ken Davids had his students writing pornography
(homework: add a chapter to Terry Southern's *Candy*). The re-

KOOLAU SHADOWS

sults he got were so highly imaginative we fought among ourselves reading them, and were ever student papers so enthusias-
tically written, so eagerly read? This famous assignment caused
the worried program head to issue an ultimatum in which each
young professor had to swear not to teach fiction in freshman
composition (I had to take this oath to get my job, and felt just
as ridiculous doing it as I had in 1962 swearing not to overthrow
the United States by violence in order to get my job as a salad girl
in the U.C. Berkeley cafeteria).

Another young professor led his class in group therapy sessions—or "T-groups," as they were still called in those distant
days—and assumed the role of Daddy, counselor, and friend/
adversary during interminable after-hours rap sessions with his
mesmerized student followers. This instructor shared the funky
temporary barracks office space with me and a few other instructors; at a garage sale he held before leaving the Islands, I found
I had purchased, for five dollars, one of the institutional green
couches from our communal office. There was the young professor who enjoyed placing late-night calls to the president of the
United States, Richard M. Nixon, and others, of a more interesting nature, to his female colleagues. And there was the young
professor who slipped her unsuspecting parents a dose of acid
while they were visiting on vacation, sending them on an all-
night rampage in Waikiki.

Teaching in my time was a strange mix of excitement, bonho-
mie, slackness. Most of the hip young professors made Carlos
Casteneda, Eldridge Cleaver, and Kurt Vonnegut required reading for their students, and there was a good deal of class canceling
generally—for Vietnam protests, films, even instructors' birth-
days. The other side of the fence, however, still featured plenty
of hardliners, including one perky, invincibly smiling young
woman married to an army officer, who made her classes rise to
greet her every day as a mark of respect. The truth was, all
parties shamelessly inflicted a whole range of personal biases on
our hapless victims.

Most of my students were of Japanese descent; next came
Chinese; there were, proportionately, only a sprinkling of
Hawaiians and Filipinos. And big differences in classroom style
existed between Hawaiian Asians on one hand and Mainland

208

haoles, accustomed to shooting off their mouths at the drop of a topic, on the other. The Local kids felt, with some justification, that this cultural trait of extroversion in the face of authority gave haole students an edge with their mostly haole teachers, who tended to reward "class participation" and penalize the respectful but stony Asian silence that often fell when student opinions were sought. In the same breath that we deplored racism and ethnocentrism, we young professors were constantly devising schemes to get students to "open up" via round tables, discussion groups of four of five people, and the like, measures that met with only a modest degree of success.

Compared to our counterparts in the Political Science Department, however, we young English instructors were models of conformist deportment. Lacking such a bourgeois deal with the university as bona fide "instructors" had, the Poly Sci teaching assistants were busy jumping with both bare feet into the seventies. A handful lived clandestinely in Farrington Hall, the former university auditorium whose backstage cubicles they had converted into primitive offices and still more primitive (and illicit) living quarters. In a fit of handyman mania, Farrington's occupants had tunneled through concrete walls to create a rabbit warren of cavelike rooms with concealed entrances. To keep these living and other arrangements under wraps required continual bribing of the campus security guards with cases of Primo.

These Poly Sci guys were more physical than we were, or at least they were trying to be, what with their construction projects and car repair scams and so on. Imperceptibly Farrington Hall took on the appearance of an auto body shop. One T.A. kept a blue Triumph on the moldering auditorium stage along with a red chassis of the same model; he was always trying to sell me this car along with the extra body, like a Barbie doll whose outfit you could change at whim to match your own. Another T.A. was the proud owner of not one but two enormous tail-finned 1957 Cadillacs, a white convertible and a purple hardtop, installed proudly outside Farrington end to end, like matching brontosauruses.

The Poly Sci instructors found time in their hectic schedule of construction projects and radical politics to establish the Martin Heidegger Hiking Society, one of whose main aims in its early days seemed to be to walk, collectively, as far and as fast as possible under the influence of LSD—one of the most nerve-wracking experiences I ever had, all that unquenchable Mainland ambition and energy winged out on acid and rechanneled into purposeful striding, a kind of demonic cross between a Sunday stroll and the robotic marching of the Kauai Walkers.

To the best of my knowledge, none of the young Poly Sci professors grew up to be old professors. These days, I hear, they all lead extremely various lives as millionaire entrepreneurs, politicians, bureaucrats, what have you. Farrington Hall, fittingly, is now a parking lot. The big old cars are gone, the life is gone, only a ghost impression of scruffiness, confusion, scraps of lumber and machine parts, cigars, Karl Marx, dogs, bright aloha shirts.

Meanwhile I took a rash step and legitimized my love affair with archaeology: I applied to the Anthropology Department and was accepted as a graduate student, rearranged my teaching schedule in the English Department to serve as financial support, signed up for a full complement of courses.

I should have known better. My Hawaii was not a place for formal long-term relationships.

First day of class, Anthro 320: Culture History. Something felt vaguely familiar here and it was making me uncomfortable. Two graduate students in front of me were engrossed in discussion, peppering the air with foreign-sounding phrases—"cognitive inferences," "symboling," the "processual approach"—but the undercurrent of maniacal competition was not foreign, no sir. Now I knew where my feeling of *déjà vu* came from: I'd heard it all before, in medieval studies. Just substitute Old English metrical analysis for any of the above, and you had the same old game: the graduate school *mano a mano*.

I can't do this, I thought. I can't go sit in the stacks of the U.H. library and learn enough of this stuff so that, after a great deal of time and sterile effort, I too can engage in this clash of wills in the name of higher learning, which is the carrot most disciplines dangle above their acolytes: namely, the chance, once having crawled to the top over the bodies of peers, to reward yourself with the pleasure of kicking your graduate students just as you yourself were kicked. The comparatively austere and solitary researches of Old and Middle English, hardly a hotbed of grant funding, had also not prepared me for the backbiting, jealousy, gossip, and adolescent rivalries of professional archaeology, wherein as much time was spent sharpening the adze, vis-à-vis one's competitors, as studying it.

No one saw me close my Binford and Binford, creep quietly out of the classroom. Yes, I had to admit, in terms of the life of the mind the Islands lacked something, but whatever it was, *this wasn't it.* I hadn't come to Hawaii for this. Not me. I was here to be Sheena and Sheena I meant to stay, even as the roaches devoured my books, even as the jungle vines I swung from frayed and came apart in my hands.

31

Ghosts

The world's original captive audience, my students, absorbed the brunt of my Molokai adventure. Writing down a few ghost stories they had heard was the first order of business in the sophomore Narrative course, and this assignment presented absolutely no problem for anyone in class. Oahu, I now discovered, had its own legacy of the supernatural, and we soon assembled an impressive collection of the old standbys familiar to any Oahu teenager: the dead man hanging from the tree at Morgan's Corner, the Chinese woman with no face at the Waialae Drive-In, assorted spooks at Manoa cemetery, the latter seemingly a "terror place" of the first order—though in broad daylight nothing seemed more prosaic than the big red wooden arch with the Chinese characters and the faded, peeling notice: "Fire-Crackers Permitted by Police Dept. 8 A.M. to 5 P.M. ONLY—Manoa Chinese Cemetery Association," the hillside with its plumeria and banyan trees, the anthuriums and dried-up chrysanthemums on the graves.

Through my cousin Lorca the Buddhist, who was learning Japanese at U.H. summer school in transit to her zendo outside Tokyo, I had imbibed a healthy dose of Japanese movies—a near overdose, in fact, with all those screenfuls of red samurai blood reflected moonlike on the rapt wrinkled faces of the old ladies in

Ghosts

the front row of the Nippon Theater on Beretania Street. One day I stopped off in the manager's office and asked if I could take home some of the posters, which I had grown to admire: it was fun, for instance, picking out Western exclamation points in the blizzard of vertical calligraphy. The dumbfounded manager, who had obviously never gotten such a request before (and from a haole!), dragged out a huge pile from the back. Flipping through them, he began an enthusiastic recital of their contents. When he came to a horror film poster featuring a lurid blue-skinned she-monster (Japanese movies feature many more female demons than their Western counterparts), he remarked, "We prefer to show ghost movies in August." When I asked why, he said, "It's hot then, yeah? Ghosts have a cooling effect on our audiences."

Some of my students belonged to sects like the Dancing Goddess Cult, an ecstatic offshoot of Buddhism (they had prayed and danced to the Goddess during the 1960 earthquake, thereby saving a family's house in Hilo), the Alpha and Omega Christian Church, and other splinter evangelical groups. In one of the great Shinto holiday observances, the honoring of the dead, it is customary to make a food offering to deceased family members. In Hawaii this meant plunking down on top of the grave a plate lunch, two scoops rice, disposable chopsticks, and an open bottle of Primo. Not surprisingly, the Island cemeteries were patrolled by armies of sleek feral cats.

Compared with the Molokai stories, the tales my students brought me made up in sheer ethnic diversity what they lacked in quantity and intensity. Especially interesting was how such stories functioned as an integral part of Local elementary and high school lore. In contrast to Molokai, on Oahu the most frequent explanation given for apparitions was not "coming back" to family and friends but the more depersonalized, abstract theme of the violated graveyard: "This structure [Waialae Drive-In or whatever] was built on an old burial ground." In these stories the graveyards were always Hawaiian or Chinese, never Filipino or Japanese or Korean or haole—whether because Hawaiians first and then Chinese antedated other large groups in the Islands or because their spirits were more powerful, I never was able to determine.

213

You sensed a certain amount of cultural unease or confusion reflected in the different racial backgrounds of the various Oahu ghosts, which raised the interesting question: Do another culture's ghosts have the power to frighten you as much as your own? If my students' responses were any guide, the answer was yes. All this time live candidates for ghosthood pressed in all around me—less picturesque and interesting to me, of course, because they were not from the very old days but from Now. When I showed a book of stories *(Flying Fox in a Freedom Tree)* by the Western Samoan writer Albert Wendt to a young Samoan student, his comment about the cover picture, the silhouette of a suicide hanging from a tree, was simply: "Sure, you see that all the time down there. No jobs. They don't know what to do with themselves."

In my time young Hawaiian men hit the wall of Mainland career expectations when they left high school—sensitive, intelligent, athletes and thinkers, but alienated, very alienated. Many deserving young people never made it to my classroom at the university because they had been told by school counselors, "You aren't college material." This judgment conveniently managed to ignore the fact that so far the fine young minds had gone unchallenged. The vibrant nineteenth-century Hawaiian world with its love of reading and books had been effectively wiped out by the same American colonialism that imposed its own English language, its own culture and educational system. Going crazy over *Na 'Lii O Sekotia* with your own king in Iolani Palace, yes. Reading *The Scottish Chiefs* as a second-class citizen in a foreign country, no. The degree of psychic injury this rape of culture and language produced down through the generations cannot be underestimated.

The death of a culture, like the death of a star, lasts longer than anyone can possibly imagine. The sadness, the echoes and ambiguities, persist for hundreds of years. It's not over after the death of the first generation, or the second, or the third. It goes on and on past any decent limit of sanity for all those affected. What is left for the survivors, now members of the dominant culture whether they like it or not? They get to hold a two-century Maori-style *tangi*, a funeral wake with outbursts of joy and grief, to mourn and celebrate its passing while that fixed point, Contact, recedes ever farther into the past.

Ghosts

Even now, a century later, the reverberations can be felt—the waste of all that unchallenged and uneducated spiritual and intellectual energy on menial jobs, on drugs, the latter representing a doomed fishhook attempt (doomed because drugs provide no permanent trellis for the vine of consciousness) to reel oneself into a state of higher sensibility. In the life of a middle-class overeducated young haole the pathetic fallacy experience might be a needed compensation; in the lives of other young people, haole and Local, those transcendant inner experiences ended up the sole and not very adequate substitute for meager outer-world education and prospects.

To many Hawaiians of my time there was something secretly contemptible in the slick goal of being a "winner" at the expense of the others in the group. Yet what did your deep appreciation of the natural world, your knowledge of the waves and the water count for, in Land of Opportunity terms, by the time you were a fifty-one-year-old busboy? That so many Hawaiians in my time managed to come through this ordeal with their personalities intact showed a modern and completely private heroism that is the real tribute to the Polynesian warrior spirit.

A notable outgrowth of alienation: bank robbing in Hawaii, the world's most futile occupation. The dreadful naïveté of taking, in the heartbreaking tough-innocent words of a young Hawaiian friend of mine, "a gun and a big chance" to get for yourself what all the middle-class haoles and Japanese and Chinese had—when all your friends, enemies, and relatives were going to recognize the hidden camera photo printed in the *Advertiser* the next day and phone the authorities. And now that you were in Oahu Prison, the easiest jail in the world to break out of, what to do? Why, escape, naturally, right back to your home or girlfriend's apartment where the police picked you up the next day and the whole farce began all over again.

And even now the Polynesian men keep dying, and they die young because late adolescence is when everyone gets his first taste of the hideous struggle ahead, and possibly something in them senses instinctively whether they are up for it or not. Since for them it is going to be a struggle nobody else will give them a medal for waging, some say, "No, thank you," stepping off the battlefield before the fight begins. Signing up for the ghost battalion instead. Of my group of friends, the young surfers Kanaina

215

and his friends, two out of five were dead by age twenty-one: one of an overdose of reds, the other of a gunshot wound to the head, self-inflicted, in Punchbowl Cemetery. They did not come back.

A ghost vision in my memory, all light and shadow like the dreams of one of those middle-aged characters in an Ingmar Bergman film: on the lawn outside the old Lihue jailhouse on Kauai, yet another unlikely repository of the old ways, four young men—inmates, I suppose, though no guard is visible unless, as is likely, he is one of them—four young men mend fishnets strung between trees, and the white nets glint in the sunshine like cobwebs over the green grass, these imprisoned human souls.

32

A Modest Proposal

In yet another mark of Island upward mobility, when I moved to Manoa Valley I changed thrift stores. By this time all the hip young Locals and haoles knew about the Goodwill, but not so many knew about the store in Moiliili, just below the university, a wondrous repository of well-to-do *kamaaina* castoffs, ridiculously underpriced and vigilantly guarded by a fierce platoon of elderly female volunteers. Though hand-lettered signs posted in strategic positions around the store advised that "Taking Things from this store is Stealing from Little Children!" and "You Break It, You Bought It," never mind, my simple tastes were ready for fancier stuff, and here I got the handsewn Dora C. Derby white muslin holoku, the Indian brass bowls, the samovar, the genuine Hopi bowl, the hand-carved koa wood bookends, the only slightly fire-blackened French cooking pots and omelette pan, the souvenir King Kamehameha statue plate, and on and on. It was here I bought the thirty-odd men's neckties that, with plenty of help from a friend with a Singer, I sewed together into the fabulous (so long as not too closely scrutinized) necktie skirt I had seen in the hippie fashion magazine *Rags*.

The thrift shop regulars included a simpatico middle-aged couple, ex-nightclub performers, both of whom dyed their hair an identical muskrat brown; antique dealers; *mahu* interior decora-

217

tors; and an assortment of *akamai* (clever) Local bargain hunters, packrats of all races and ethnic backgrounds—for the big stuff in the garage annex like refrigerators, bamboo *punees* (the Island chaise lounge), TV sets, and old stereos went dirt cheap, cheaper than Goodwill.

On May 6, 1970, the day of the U.S. invasion of Cambodia, in the ghastly mix of political idealism and underlying flakiness that characterized me and many of my fellow instructors in those days, I canceled class and, at a bit of a loss for what to do— meditate on war crimes?—ended up at the thrift store. There I found a Chinese temple wall hanging dedicated to the goddess Kwan Yin that had been presented to the Nuuanu Valley temple by a group of Honolulu businessmen (so a friend translated the characters embroidered vertically down the side).

Observing this tapestry now hanging on my wall, I began to feel like that Vietnamese monk in the documentary film *Sad Song of Yellow Skin* who paced up and down inside a ground-plan of his country, laid out in the manner of a miniature golf course, as a sympathetic magic way of uniting North and South— with the rather obvious difference that I utterly lacked the monk's purpose, political idealism, and goals. In many ways I felt little better than an Oahu Walker sleepwalking through my own symbolic topography, touching the magic nodes of my Honolulu compass—though since I came back from the Outer Islands they had mysteriously begun to lose their power—paying lip service to outrages I acknowledged intellectually but, like a child, had never genuinely felt.

My stage of deepest immersion in Hawaii coincided with the fiercest and bloodiest years of the Vietnam War. Besides being a center of strategic operations, Hawaii was the prime mid-Pacific R&R (rest and recuperation) center for servicemen. Soldiers were plucked out of jungle fighting for a few disorienting days on the beach in Waikiki, then flown straight back to hell. Antiwar protests in Hawaii never gained the intensity they did on the Mainland for a number of complicated reasons, two of which were surely Hawaii's new statehood and a generation of Asian-American parents whose loyalty had been put in question during World War II. Now that their sons were of draft age, many Local people wanted to underline their patriotism and resented

A *Modest Proposal*

the demonstrations that were mainly organized by young Mainland haoles. Riding past a protest at Fort Ruger in Waikiki, I
heard the bus driver comment, to general approval among his
passengers: "Hey, we send some Local boys down, show those
kids a thing or two." But the Local boys were already gone, in
impressive numbers, straight to Vietnam.

I knew a few haole veterans, who had no desire to talk about
what they had been through, and one deserter—skinny, dark,
marmot-quick, city-street Italian. He worked as a house painter;
everybody knew him. Mainly I remember the whitish rind of
dried spittle caking his lips as the staccato burst of words tumbled
out, spilling over each other, a Burroughs or Kerouac stream of
consciousness: here was a *heavy* Methedrine habit. I don't know
if he picked it up in Vietnam or later, after he deserted during
the Waikiki antiwar demonstration while he was on R&R; his
stories of being stoned on patrol were certainly hair-raising
enough. In Honolulu you saw him here, there, all over the place:
a celebrity deserter, the least hidden hider of the whole war, a
gutsy little guy. It took the authorities at least two or three years
to catch up with him—or did they? I don't remember.

Someone at the university was writing her Ph.D. thesis about
the deserter, and it came out during a conversation that after
nine months of interviews she wasn't aware he was a speed freak.
A bit like not being aware that the pope is Catholic but what the
heck, it was only a thesis, albeit in psychology. "Subject appears
nervous and talks rapidly. Often rambles. Manic tendencies?"

Though both my young students at U.H. and I were unbelievably and willfully sheltered from the war, once in a while the
bubble popped. One day an older Hawaiian student—at my age,
about twenty-six, he had already finished his tour of duty in
Vietnam—raised his hand during a discussion of Jonathan Swift's
"A Modest Proposal."

"I know exactly what he means," Kimo said. "It's like when we
were on missions and somebody got burned up from a flame-
thrower. You'd smell the cooking flesh and it made your stomach
growl." Laughing, he looked around him, at the uncomprehend-
ing faces. "Gross, huh?"

Laughed again quietly to himself and said no more.

219

33

Paradise

Most of us young professors in my time were very young indeed; the consolidation of character that, coincident with the fusion of vertebrae in the upper spine, is supposed to occur during one's twenties still eluded us. Our unformed, fragile personalities, patched together with baling wire, unraveled all too easily under pressure and so we cast about for this or that belief or amulet—"pretechnological" was best, of course—as some kind of anchor on the drifting tides of the Pacific. I would have happily worshipped my Kwan Yin tapestry, if only I had known how.

Somebody in Honolulu, I remember, was busy laying plans for postnuclear survival in the South Seas, where he intended to sail on his well-stocked schooner and travel like a Louis Becke supercargo from island to island. Sagely calculating that dental service would not be available where he was headed, he had all his teeth pulled and replaced with a gleaming set of cavity-proof porcelain choppers.

Others like him who embraced the dream of an Earthly Paradise where life was simple and happy, vacuum sealed from moral and atmospheric toxins, where there was no divorce and no crime, quickly realized that (1) Oahu and then (2) the Outer Islands were not this Eden—though of course they had been once upon a time, before our time, "before it all got spoiled"—

and so setting their sights to the horizon once again, legions of plucky young couples steered their ketches for the Tuamotus. The more land-oriented dreamed of emigrating to Australia or New Zealand, building from scratch (as they fancied, in a weird combination of the look Westward and the look Backward) a primal hygienic life free of the moral ambiguity of urban technocracy. Paradise is there, and we are here.

As of 1973, my own personal Paradise was still located squarely in the silk scarf I had bought at the Nuuanu Street Goodwill for seventy-five cents. Some anonymous genius had screened one of Eugene Savage's Matson Line cruise menu covers of the 1940s, a pagan triptych celebrating the gods of Food and Love, onto a silk scarf: a haolefied Hawaiian woman in a long gown and a white lei bears fruits, a man with his back to us balances a set of calabashes. Behind them men and women haul nets out of the sea. Freshly caught fish spill from tumbled baskets; piles of fruit (pineapples, melons) lie heaped on a stone altar strewn with leis. This happy vision in brilliant greens, oranges, and blues was my Grecian urn. The pair, I imagined, were greeting each other in the great *Kumulipo* ceremonial encounter, man for the narrow stream, woman for the broad stream. I thought: They love each other!—failing to notice that Man and Woman were bearing burdens and that, as in real Hawaii, the landscape had a way of overwhelming individual personalities, including love affairs. Oh, no, I thought, they love each other, a perfect union in this timeless gentle world where everyone stays young and happy.

We young haoles played our Hawaiian music and wore our Hawaiian clothes, sewed our love dreams, Hawaiian pillows and curtains in bright aloha prints. We would live and love in Hawaii forever, yes. Wear muumuus and learn the ancient hula and eat kim chee and all our thoughts would be Hawaiian. Happy lovers and happy families. Where it would always be this way. Paradise.

Reality? Not so lovely. The shaven-headed woman crouched on the beach in Waimanalo with her baby boy, abandoned by his father; one morning she had got up and decided to cut her hair and before she knew what had happened she had shorn herself of all of it. She was mourning the vision of the Matson print scarf. Another time, looking down from the road over Makapuu on a young haole couple performing a "spontaneous" dance next to the ocean, he in bell bottoms, she in a peasant dress: they were trying to reach the place in the Matson print scarf. They whirled and leaped and oh, how they tried! But what was meant to be impromptu and joyous looked strained, self-conscious. It was no hula, that awkward improvised *pas de deux,* and I had danced every step of it myself: full of stiff high intentions, violent feelings, doomed.

Hearing stories about the sanctity of a baby's umbilical cord among the old Hawaiians, some friends of mine saved their own baby's when he was born. Uncertain about what, exactly, to do with this increasingly withered souvenir, the wife left it in an ashtray on the bedroom dresser where it lay forgotten until one afternoon the husband and his cronies, mistaking it for a piece of hash, threw it in a pipe and smoked it.

A twenty-four-year-old with equally vague proto-Native notions, I once asked my Korean dentist's nurse for my wisdom tooth after it had been extracted. The artifact was returned to me, scrupulously without comment, all scrubbed and dried in a little Styrofoam padded box labeled "My Lucky Tooth." One glimpse of that bumpy tusk—from *my* mouth?—was enough to make me realize that, organic or not, it would not look attractive dangling on a pendant around my neck.

All along I owned a real amulet authentic to my own culture, but typically, since it was not made of feathers or bone, I neither recognized nor valued it. This was my graduation watch. I lost it carelessly, in Halawa Valley, up by the waterfall, not during the dig but several years later, on a trip back. On *two* trips—the trip there from Oahu, and the acid trip we took in the valley. With that relentless stoned obsessive concentration I looked for it and looked for it, but the watch was gone, washed down the stream. Halawa had swallowed it up.

Not that long after my college graduation, but already I was too old to be doing this sort of thing and suddenly I was starting to lose a lot—no longer the things that were a relief to lose, but the good things too. Play lost its flavor. Waking up in the morning on Oahu, a light teaching load, unable to decide which of twelve beaches to go to—and now the graduation watch. On an acid trip. So excessively symbolic I flatly refused, for the sake of self-respect, to acknowledge the loss.

Paradise

The first task I faced, though I did not know it yet—still wrapped up as I was in the vision of the Matson print scarf—was to retrieve my soul from the landscape into which it had flown, happily, during my first split second in the Islands. I did not realize I was suffering from loss of soul. A joy at first, this condition becomes increasingly a malaise. A great sacrifice was in the works, one my conscious mind utterly rejected. Leave Hawaii? Jump out of the Matson print scarf? Unthinkable.

Yet many were doing just this—had already done it, in fact. Ken Davids had long since returned to California, John Derrick would go to Brazil, Buzz Poverman to Tucson, Jim MacDonald to Washington, D.C., Tom and Karma Riley to Urbana. Slowly the young professors were molting into their predestined Mainland identities and careers, though not without a great deal of evolutionary backsliding in the form of return visits, one-year appointments, and the like. The first week or so off the plane, I noticed, these pale, angry strangers talked quickly, their social manners were noticeably abrupt and "haole"; and they seemed, last but not least, grotesquely self-absorbed in matters relating to career. After a day or two they relaxed and took on as if they had never been away. But I sensed my old friends knew something I didn't know, they were in on some grimy but substantial Mainland secret hatched on that formidable gray continent during the years I had stayed in the bright Islands. This new something had hauled them right out of our little Hawaiian universe into an alien, charmless environment that nonetheless seemed to have properly got its hooks in them. What could this secret be?

In my own inner epic, meanwhile—which, as always in Hawaii, was faithfully reflected in outside events—King King was winning out over Sheena, had more or less taken her prisoner, in fact. The repetitiveness of this emotional drama had come to make the Islands seem a kind of prison. But where and in what circumstances did I dare to free the Leopard Queen? Was it not better to wait where I was, here in the Rainbow Isles, and simply let nature takes its course?

So the graduation watch stayed underwater and it was not till years of hard struggle later that I had the dream of walking in the Florida swamp, a nine-year-old tomboy again, and a helpful little black dog dropped the gold watch at my feet, shiny and good as new. Everything of mine thrown underwater in Hawaii I would manage to reel in again, not tarnished but transformed. But this happened only because the effort of retrieval was long and bitter, and there were many, many times I came within a hair's breadth of losing it all, my whole life, down Halawa Stream.

34

Makapuu

Meanwhile my Island life unrolled the same as always. I remained engrossed in symbolic retrieval, that is, archaeology, even after formally withdrawing from graduate school. In my first survey back on Oahu we inspected some of the many ancient dune burials that constantly washed out on the southwest Windward side of the island. The abandoned Nike missile-launching mounds at the old Bellows Air Force Base were, to my eyes, a far more impressive archaeological site than any of the ancient ones (at last, the Templo del Sol!). The beach at Bellows, known colloquially as "Sherwood Forest," was a favorite hangout for teenage Hawaiian boys and Local folk who were just plain tired of looking at haole faces all the time. In my time this place had, as the name suggests, a tough reputation. Ringed by large, very large fellows on roaring motorcycles, we uncovered a burial under the ironwood trees in the heart of Sherwood Forest, recorded the remains, quietly filled in the pit and tiptoed away, thank you very much, goodbye.

Our main target lay just below Waimanalo at Makapuu ("bulging eye" in Hawaiian), a little bay under beetling cliffs full of burial caves and the premier bodysurfing spot on Oahu after Sandy Beach. Next door to Makapuu was a kind of miniature version of the bay, prominent in Local legend as the place where the love scene in *From Here to Eternity* had been filmed. Because the state wanted to enlarge the parking lot at Makapuu, we had been commissioned to do an archaeological survey of an old lava tube due to be filled in during the improvements. Highly satisfactory to us all was the primo location of our dig—it could so easily have been a mosquito-infested guava thicket deep up some valley—and we showed up the first day in the parking lot with our fins and bathing suits at the ready for the lunchtime break.

By nine the beach was full of people. Heading for the ladies' changing room before we started, I was nearly knocked down by a little Local boy about nine or ten running for his life, followed by a haole woman, a tourist, whose handbag he had just stolen; both looked equally upset. We cleared the rubble away from the mouth of the lava tube, which had been used during modern times as a kind of natural-formation garbage can. Among the beer and Pepsi cans, and duly noted in the record, emerged an assortment of sun-dried empty wallets.

Under the modern-era midden, the layer of dirt covering the bottom of the tube quickly revealed a long prehistoric seasonal occupation. Fishermen came, probably only during the summer—this dry southern point had no reliable water supply—and lived in this cave. We found a poi pounder, the ubiquitous broken fishhooks, parrotfish beaks, even a bone tapa needle.

Our efforts in the lava tube attracted much idle attention from Makapuu beachgoers, in large part because of our magnificent sign professionally printed in large block letters: University of Hawaii Department of Anthropology Archaeological Survey. (All official signs in Hawaii were like the credits on a big-budget movie; they told you, down to the last bureaucrat, contractor, and secretary, who in city government was responsible for this glorious construction/improvement/alteration.) Ultimately this sign attracted the attention of the producers of *Hawaii Five-O*, then a popular television series. They needed the paraphernalia of an archaeological site for one of their stories, and so—mainly to get their hands on that sign—hired us all to stage a mock dig around the bend in the *From Here to Eternity* inlet, where two old storm drains let out on the beach. In these old Hawaiian burial caves, went the story line, the intrepid investigators discover a *new* body, etc.

226

Makapuu

Somehow the enterprising producers managed to "borrow" a number of prehistoric artifacts from the Bishop Museum that were then scattered like Easter eggs on the beach and sprinkled over with a thin layer of sand. I was chosen to uncover with my whisk broom—registering suitable cries of amazement—a handsome basalt adze, serial number lettered neatly down the side, and carry it up to the bearded nightclub singer in knee socks and pith helmet who had been cast, to Tom Riley's chagrin, as our professor. And he was to give it a cursory look and say "Adze. Sixteenth century," while waiting for the union actress with the speaking line to come rushing out of the storm drain with news of her grisly discovery.

All went according to schedule. We earned a half-day's salary and a catered lunch. Denied a look at the show's temperamental star (who was rumored to use mascara pencil to accentuate the cleft in his chin), we did get to witness a prime bit of Hollywoodiana: The assistant director, a decent civilized man, had violated the union taboo by carrying a piece of camera equipment across the set himself. As punishment, the director, who was not so decent and civilized, picked the assistant director up by the collar and ears—the assistant director was very short—and carried him bodily across the set. As neatly executed a piece of public humiliation as you'd expect to see in marine boot camp, silently attended by all.

Learning that this show was to open the series season, we crew members eagerly pitched in to rent a color TV set for the occasion. I remember a great deal of inchoate celebration before the distinctive *Hawaii Five-O* breaking wave came on the screen and then, bang, there I was—or think I was—"Adze. Sixteenth century," "Professor, *look!*"—then, bang, the breaking wave again and a commercial. And that was it, all in a little under six and a half seconds. Dimly our minds registered a sense of shock, for we had somehow developed the fantasy that the whole show was about us. What followed was a prosaic tale in which the only further point of interest was the green Mercedes owned by one of our older, more affluent volunteers that the producers had hired, for more money than all of us combined, to park in front of a mansion.

It was about this time, though not while we were still digging at the parking lot lava tube, that the ocean current brought into

227

the bay at Makapuu the body of one of my fellow English instructors. Surfers behind the break were first to spot it, bobbing face-down and headed for shore. The body's tied hands immediately triggered the rumor that this was a gangland victim. But, having asked for and been denied tenure in the English Department, she had driven to the ridge and fastened her own hands so that she could not save herself. Then she jumped. And floated in at Makapuu.

Here at Makapuu and all up and down the Windward coast of Oahu, the Koolau mountains looked like nothing on earth: sweeping green palis riven into thousand-foot pillars by the constant onslaught of the northeast trades, Mount Olomana with its pointed twin peaks slapped together by Gustave Doré in a romantic frenzy. In the late afternoon the shadows deepened, boldly exaggerating the lateral folds and furrows. On Waimanalo beach the wind rose off the ocean, stirring the dead brown fronds in the heart of the coco palms into a dry crackling, the sun dipped over the edge of those impossible spires, turning the seawater a buoyant light blue-violet, and walking in the shadows, in the already cool sand, I would feel it like a punch in the heart: It's *late.*

The cliffs at Makapuu, the open mouth of Kahana, those rain-misty headlands at Kaaawa, the flat plateau of Waialua, suburbs giving way to tin-roofed houses on stilts and their gaudy croton hedges, a Hawaiian girl walking her dog by the highway, all in shadow, the dark Koolau shadow, bright colors hushed, only the fringe of surf still wedding-cake white and a few fishermen in their trucks watching it, watching it. The same never-changing picture at the end of every Windward Oahu day, I dreamed the university assigned me the drowned instructor's classes, and there isn't much time left, it's late.

35

Over the Handlebars

I resigned from the university. But in the end it took a different sort of fishhook to reel me out of Paradise. What was this fishhook?

A zori, of course.

My head boiled with projects but I was still up in the air about what to do: Should I return to the Mainland? It seemed, vaguely, that was what I *ought* to do. But the prospect of going back terrified me; at the first suggestion my head immediately filled with negative paranoid fantasies about what awaited me in California (fantasies, let it be noted, that would be greatly surpassed by reality).

Two weeks after quitting the English Department I was riding my bicycle across campus. I have no memory of the wheel hitting a pothole, my body flying through the air, my head hitting the pavement. What I remember is a journey, a journey to a familiar country in which, behind my own back so to speak, I had been secretly pursuing a separate life. Unlike those out-of-body experiences other people have reported, this life, my real life, wasn't especially transcendent. An extremely intimate vision, it was more engrossing, more complicated, more *whole,* somehow, than waking life. In catapulting over the handlebars of my handsome white Schwinn, I had leaped into another world, where the true story of my life, that valley behind the valley, had been quietly unfolding.

Many interesting, eventful years passed in this magic kingdom. Governments, dynasties, rose and fell. Now and then, though, as in a badly spliced film, my cosmic adventures would be interrupted by a bizarre and incongruous image: a brown rubber zori. Flashes of the humble shower slipper came at shorter and shorter intervals until finally it managed to blot out entirely the marvelous new world in which I had happily pursued an indescribable life. Dragged reluctantly from that place, I found myself laid out on a hospital examining table. The brown rubber zori, my own, lay in a corner of the room where it had dropped from my foot.

Pincher Martin drowned with his seaboots on. Life imitates art, and a zori had mimicked those seaboots with uncanny exactness to puncture the dangerous fantasy that had spirited me away. Real as only a 39-cent shower slipper can be, my zori wanted me back in the world. I had been sinking down with the pillow in Choptahatchee Bay, but the brown zori had pulled me back up to air.

The effect was powerful and immediate. For the first time since it had awakened and matured in the gentle Hawaiian landscape, my soul was back in my body.

I found myself looking at reality more clearly than I had in years. It was like seeing the ocean floor on a "dead bottom" day, when you can look straight through the water like a piece of glass. Dead bottom, my situation was this: I was twenty-eight years old, unemployed, and my time in Hawaii was over. I had expelled myself from Paradise, I sensed, at the moment I flew over the handlebars. But what manner of new time was beginning?

First I had to tend to the accident's immediate consequences. Enough gravel had been ground into the left side of my face to leave a distinct pattern of eerie blue streaks under the skin. Looking in the mirror, I saw the horrifying truth: I had given myself Queequeg's *moku*, the ancient Polynesian tattoo. My choices were now entirely clear. Either I could take my tattoo and head straight for Kapingamarangi, or I could get rid of it and go—here I felt my lips forming the word spontaneously for the first time in five years—home. And, after a hair-raising reverse initiation at the ultra-haole Straub Medical Clinic on Young Street in which the offending *moku* was ceremonially sliced, gouged, and sanded off my face, go home is exactly what I did.

STORY AFTER THE STORY

36

Surfacing

San Francisco, 1974, I am surfacing, on Columbus Avenue, and it's overwhelming: sharp sounds, cold dry air, harsh light, pale colors, dingy streets and buildings, the absolutely overwhelming ugliness of my own race—those pasty, raddled complexions, the frizzy, weird-colored hair sticking out on all sides like troubling thoughts instead of lying sedately in neat black caps, as hair ought to. And these haoles look like bikers in their tough denim gear and boots, either bikers or Mormons—goodness, what a lot of Mormons there are on the Mainland, I think, seeing all the blue business suits. Then I remember: Men wear suits here. My feet sweat and peel in their unfamiliar armor of socks and boots. I have aged overnight; away from humid Hawaii my skin has shriveled. A sense of doom, a crushing diffuse anxiety, oozes out of me and hovers like a second fog over this hostile gray landscape. I had sunk all the way to the bottom of the Schofield Barracks reservoir only to burst up five years later choking, gasping for breath, spitting water into the thin Mainland air.

Surfacing is an experience I find strange, frightening, uncomfortable—not serene, untroubled, and merged, like my life underwater. I have decided to be Ishmael, not Pincher Martin or Arthur Gordon Pym, and I am learning that this is not the easiest fate. But what is there to be anxious about here in San Francisco,

235

a place generally regarded as beautiful? I discover I'm not alone in my unease. A feeling of palpable fear and paranoia hangs over the whole city. A block away from where I am living on Telegraph Hill a woman is beheaded by the Zebra killers, a group of black men roaming San Francisco in a van making random assassinations. Over in Berkeley Patty Hearst is kidnapped by the Symbionese Liberation Army and I listen on the radio to the grisly shootout that triggered the group's fiery end. Murder after murder; the dailies revel in them. Random: a new wrinkle. In Hawaii it wasn't hard to get raped or beaten up, but at least you always knew *why;* there was a traceable cause-and-effect sequence. In California crime has taken a quantum leap from the personal and explainable into the surreal.

I duck a block over to Stockton Avenue and start to breathe easy again. Chinatown. Here I am among Asians, the only place in the city I feel safe, strolling past the char siu ducks strung up outside the groceries, a windowful of dried toads, stores selling Hawaiian sweet bread and velvet-and-lauhala zoris just like in the Islands. But even this security is an illusion. With the advent of the Hong Kong gangs Chinatown has stopped being safe; just the other day in the Golden Dragon Restaurant six or seven innocent diners, stuck in the middle of a tong feud, were gunned down over their potstickers and mushi pork. A more profound difference emerges as well: the people bustling around me on these tiny jammed streets aren't Local, they are—to an Island eye—*exaggeratedly* Chinese. They wear Chinese clothes, for heaven's sake, and they aren't talking English. Why is this?

For the first time I come to understand the unique Hawaii experience, where all the Asian immigrants, happily tossing aside millenarian traditions of language, culture, and costume, assimilated far more thoroughly than on the Mainland. Children and grandchildren born in Hawaii were given aggressively Anglo-Saxon names—Clayton, Russell, Shepherd—with the middle name reserved as the ethnic identity tag—Yukio, C. K., Kealoha. Back in late-fifties Southern California, my own Japanese-American high school classmates had Japanese first names. They had also been born in detention camps, an environment that presented no special incentive for naming your firstborn Clayton.

Surfacing

The plain truth is, Hawaii was *nicer*. As I am finding out for myself, far more culture shock is involved in hitting the icy wall of the haole Mainland than in melting into the benign gentle womb of Hawaii. The big-city toughness doesn't make you want to open up like a little flower the way Hawaii did. It makes you want to curl up in a tight ball of friends, family, traditions, and to hell with the crazy world out there. On the corner of Stockton and Broadway a drunken black man staggers past me, muttering: "White people are so *cold,*" and it feels hard here, not soft, hard and dry, no luminous wetness. I've shifted from Technicolor to black-and-white and somehow there's no backing down.

37

To the Monkey's Skull

Time passes more quickly on the Mainland than it does in the world of the Matson print scarf. Ten years go by like nothing. My twenties reel into my thirties. I become a writer. I return to Hawaii for four years, but it is an utterly different experience from "my time." By 1981 I am back in San Francisco for good. One day I am invited to a party in Sausalito. Some unlikely California descendants of Fletcher Christian—a vague impression that they are blond and tanned, drive a white Mercedes, live in Tiburon—are celebrating "Pitcairn Island Day" on the old houseboat that serves as informal clubhouse for Sausalito boat-owners. Propped up around the main cabin are a copy of *Mutiny on the Bounty,* a lauhala hat, monkeypod bowls, and other Pacific memorabilia. A no-host bar serves mai tais.

The climax of the afternoon is an exchange of greetings by shortwave radio with some Christian fifth cousins way out on Pitcairn, about five thousand sea miles from Sausalito. A blast of static fills the room; under its roar a dim current of Island patois begins to flow. There is a short, frustrating, mostly inaudible exchange. The Tiburon Christian shouts "Goodbye!" and, trapped like a sad mouse inside the receiver, the disembodied Pacific Christian chirps "Goodbye! Goodbye!" A final crescendo of static, then silence so profound I can hear my Mainland heart beating quickly, quickly. Queequeg stirs inside me. The ghosts have spoken, from the Isle of Voices.

More years pass. I am in New Zealand, standing on the westernmost point of the North Island, the town of New Plymouth. Here at the edge of the Tasman Sea a large rock next to an oil rig has garnered a rich harvest of suicides. With the strangest feeling I realize I am standing at a bona fide Maori jumping-off place, a *leina-a-uhane,* and that night I have a dream: At this spot, in the company of a few faithful friends, I am preparing to jump in the ocean, embark on a harrowing journey from which not all of us will come back alive. The bottom level of my psyche had accepted this Polynesian image and offered it back to me as a way of explaining my life, warning of hardships and sacrifice ahead. And thanks to Queequeg's gift—this foreknowledge of what will take shape as a different reality in the outer world—I survive, I pop up again like Ishmael.

My Mainland life rolls on. One night the tumultuous romantic adventures of my time in Hawaii surface in another dream: I am back on Maui, where a signpost points: "To the Monkey's Skull."

Run, run, down the road below Hana, late afternoon light hitting the cliffs, the tin-roof shacks. In valley after valley a green tangle of morning-glory vines thickly carpets the treetops. Run to the bend, and there it is—

King Kong's skull. On a stick.

The skull of the great ape (not a monkey at all!) marks the opening of a plaster-of-Paris Walt Disney cave, with lurid backlit stalactites and phony "artifacts." You have to pay to get in. Through King Kong's large eye socket I can see quarters piled up in the cranial cavity.

Pay to see that stuff? No thanks. First, because I'm cheap. Second, because—well, because I know all about King Kong. I know about the blonde screaming in the big hairy palm, the unchained rage, tops of skyscrapers snapped off like toothpicks, the soulful eyes, the tragic death. Sure, he's sympathetic, in a scary sort of way. But I'm glad he's dead.

I walk into the little valley behind the cave: Nature, a free exhibit. It's Kipahulu. Here a series of small pools spill into each other down to the sea. Up I go, knee-wading. A movable wall of minnows, thousands of them, swirls and regroups around my legs as I step high over each miniature waterfall into the next pool. The light fades, the pools turn black. I have reached the waterfall at the back, the big one. Up here at the top a spring bubbles reddish water from a hole at the base of the cliff. Now what was the story that went with this spring and its rusty ocher flow? Something about death and violence, a princess and her pursuer?

No, it's gone, erased from memory—too old and faded, all these tales. And so, when I look down and see the blood in the water, I know it's not victim's blood, not the beast's ransom, but my own bright blood, Sheena's heart blood, the source and the beginning, this holy spot, and these are tears of joy, not grief.

38

Coming Back

Exactly eighteen years, give or take a month, after my first swim there, I return to Waimanalo. And what does the former archaeology student uncover right away, lowering her forty-one-year-old body onto the Castle's ancient rattan couch? Pillows out of Wordsworth's lake, fished up from the bottom of the Choptahatchee Bay, right here in my own two human middle-aged hands! Cushions, old homemade Matson print cushions from my time, a cultural stratigraphy of lost loves! All those years ago I watched the gently stoned seamstresses lovingly stitch up these bright new covers, by hand and on the Singer—the sweet, childlike Hawaiian patterns so deliberately chosen, Mary's and Susie's love wishes, that old dream of innocence.

Now the cushions are old, stained, faded, full of moth holes, they are waterlogged with time. They're unspeakable, in fact; why hasn't Steve thrown them out? Does the sight of this mortal ruin sadden me, however? Not a bit. On the contrary, it's a glass of champagne. The cushions with their burden of fantasy never realized buoy me up, exhilarate me. Impermanence, failure, hopes frustrated—what does all that matter, in the end? Innocence, after all, is calculation in its purest form. How fine to see those naive schemes, that cunning desire, shining nakedly as ever through the threadbare cloth!

I step outside in the early morning Windward air and I am all the way back now, in that familiar fourth dimension of heightened reality where the outlines of objects grow supernally clear and sharp. Against the Castle's mildewed stucco the candystripe plumeria buds do their mystic dance. From this sheltering bulwark of my old, lost life I tread carefully through the burr-strewn ironwood forest on pale and tender Mainland feet I scarcely identify as my own. Bright strips of water flash through the branches. Up close, I know, the turquoise will turn green.

It is a common neurotic displacement—so a prominent psychoanalyst once noted, with an audible cluck of disapproval—to project an inner ideal of harmony and integration on an environment in the real world and "run away to someplace like Hawaii" in a vain attempt to make your insides match up with the outside. To this objection there can be only one response: Long live running away from home. Long live puerile escapism. Long live youth. A real youth is easier to let go of than the ghost of lost opportunities. Middle age is wonderful, if you had a real youth. I had a real youth, and I had it in Hawaii, in my time.

So here I am again on the Beach of Voices, smack in the middle of somebody else's time. Waves crash, ghosts from the future collide with ghosts from the past, my whole life, all three floors of the Bishop Museum melt into Now, this water and this air, this place. Behind me rise the massive gray-green Koolau palis and every bump against the sky is charged with secret meaning. The names, passwords to that meaning, what are the names? I can't remember them and a voice inside me says, Just guess. But now as then I still can't guess the secret because I know nothing. I knew nothing then and I don't know anything now. Just as I am thinking this, the pathetic fallacy experience kicks in. The ocean brightens and here comes one of those complicated sunrises, all clouds, showers, columns of light, bouncing water, warm wind, pink beach, Rabbit Island unreachable as ever, even the shadow of Haleakala visible behind it, over the low rise of Molokai. I am my own ghost, and I came back.